"Sherwonit takes us around Anchorage and its fringes, and over much of Alaska, showing us creatures we rarely take time, or have the good fortune, to see, like the lynx on Turnagain Arm Trail: it is April, there are catkins and early mosquitoes, and right there, a lynx staring at him, becoming 'part of his relationship to this forest trail.' But he also takes us to Denali Park for Dall sheep, the Chilkat Valley for 'this meeting of eagles, the largest in the world at the Bald Eagle Council Grounds.' We go to Kodiak for brown bears and also discover it is 'an unexpected treat to be paddling among porpoises' off Homer. Bill shows us the fur seals at St. Paul, the wolf in the John River Valley whose howl will haunt his memories and dreams. Thought of it may haunt us too. He walks unarmed in bear country in the Brooks Range and calls to mind his totems: 'bear is one, squirrel, chickadee, wolf, spider . . . they are teacher, messenger, guide' for him and become so for us. 'I want to understand what wilderness means to me. And what sacred means,' Bill writes. And every account of animal, bird, or fish encountered includes a mini-encyclopedia of information about the creatures he sees.

"Like porcupine whom the Koyukons call 'the off the beaten path wanderer,' Bill Sherwonit's *Animal Stories* takes us on trips that 'give us greater vision and a better understanding of our world.'"

—GARY HOLTHAUS, author of *Learning Native Wisdom* and *From the Farm to the Table*

"Whether tracking beluga whales in a citizen science project or tracking robins on his front lawn, learning lessons from a charging brown bear or stopping to listen to wood frogs, Sherwonit writes with grace and ease about his encounters with Alaskan wildlife. Commuting ravens. Insouciant wolverines. And the redpoll's exuberant chorus of song. The author combines personal experience and careful research in a journey that will compel and delight."

—SHARMAN APT RUSSELL, author of *Standing in the Light: My Life as a Pantheist* and *An Obsession with Butterflies: Our Long Love Affair with a Singular Insect*

"A well-crafted, eclectic, and engaging combination of memoir, natural history, and keen insight, *Animal Stories* delivers a fine read. Bill Sherwonit's three-plus decades of experience with Alaska wildlife, and his love for them all, from grizzlies to robins, shines forth."

—NICK JANS, author of *A Wolf Called Romeo*

"Whether writing about grizzlies, dancing cranes, or mad hares, Bill Sherwonit enchants and inspires, reminding us that wildness surrounds us, even if we don't live in Alaska."

—TIM FOLGER, series editor, *The Best American Science and Nature Writing*

"In his *Animal Stories*, Bill Sherwonit reminds us that community is built and sustained not only by humans caring for one another, but by humans noticing, coming to know, and caring about their animal neighbors. From the black-capped chickadees at his feeder, to the wood frogs in an urban pond, to the wolverines he encounters on the alpine tundra, Sherwonit celebrates Alaskan wildlife in all its forms with his eyes, ears, heart, and curiosity wide open. In prose that's clear as a rain-washed sky, he observes and writes as a true citizen-naturalist and nature writer."

—EVA SAULITIS, author of *Into Great Silence: A Memoir of Discovery* and *Loss Among Vanishing Orcas*

Animal Stories

Encounters with Alaska's Wildlife

BILL SHERWONIT

ALASKA
NORTHWEST
BOOKS®

The essays in this book have appeared, often in different form, in the following newspapers, magazines, journals, and books: *Alaska; Alaska's Accessible Wilderness: A Traveler's Guide to Alaska's State Parks; American Nature Writing, 2001; Anchorage Daily News; Anchorage Press; Appalachia; Backpacker; Best American Science and Nature Writing 2007; Changing Paths: Travels and Meditations in Alaska's Arctic Wilderness; Christian Science Monitor; Crosscurrents North; Danger! True Stories of Trouble and Survival; Defenders; Living with Wildness: An Alaskan Odyssey; National Wildlife; Orion; Pilgrimage;* and *Wildlife Conservation.*

Library of Congress Cataloging-in-Publication Data

Sherwonit, Bill, 1950- author.
  [Essays. Selections]
  Animal stories : encounters with Alaska's wildlife / Bill Sherwonit.
    pages cm
  ISBN 978-1-941821-08-4 (pbk.)
  ISBN 978-1-941821-30-5 (e-book)
  ISBN 978-1-941821-35-0 (hardbound)
  1. Animals—Alaska. 2. Natural history—Alaska. I. Title.
  QL161.S526 2014
  591.9798—dc23
                    2014017708

Front cover photo © 2014 by Tom Walker
Edited by Michelle Blair
Design by Vicki Knapton

Published by Alaska Northwest Books®
An imprint of

GRAPHIC ARTS
BOOKS®

P.O. Box 56118
Portland, Oregon 97238-6118
503-254-5591
www.graphicartsbooks.com

For the animals, who enrich our human lives
And for my grandchildren, Tristan and Alyssa

CONTENTS

AUTHOR'S NOTE

I first began writing regularly about wild nature in the mid-1980s, while employed as an outdoors writer at the *Anchorage Times*. My interest deepened, and my approach shifted, when I began life as a freelance nature writer in the early 1990s. At the newspaper I'd primarily written articles, but as a freelancer I became a student of the essay form, which has allowed me greater latitude in the ways that I explore the nature of Alaska's wildlife and wildlands. I have especially embraced the personal essay, which enables me to weave my own experiences, observations, perspectives, and insights, with what I learn through research plus interviews with people who represent a wide range of experiences and expertise, for instance scientists, managers, conservationists, hunters and trappers, and Alaska's Native peoples (recognizing overlap among those groups).

Over the past two decades, I have written scores of essays about Alaska's wildlife, which have been published in assorted newspapers, magazines, literary journals, and anthologies. Some I've included in my own books, either as essays or woven into a larger, nonfiction narrative. Here I have collected thirty-four of those essays.

These animal stories have a wide reach, in a number of ways. Besides essays about Alaska's best-known and most charismatic animals—for instance grizzlies and wolves, moose and Dall sheep, bald eagles and beluga whales—I introduce readers to many of our state's largely overlooked species, from wood frogs to redpolls and shrews. Other essays describe encounters with well-known animals that people rarely meet in the wilds, for example lynx and wolverines. The stories are also geographically diverse; they stretch across the state, from the Panhandle to the Arctic, and also from Alaska's urban center, Anchorage, to its most remote backcountry. Part of the intent is to remind people that we share the landscape with other creatures wherever we are, even where we least expect it. And that even the most easily overlooked or ignored animals lead remarkable lives.

The essays also show, and examine, the complicated relationships we humans have with other animals, and consider different ways of knowing, and relating to, these critters. In sharing what I've learned in my own explorations (near and far), I intend to open up new worlds and possibilities to readers, just as my own life has been enlarged by both firsthand encounters and what I've been able to learn from research and interviews. The essays are intended to be thought-provoking as well as entertaining: to increase readers' awareness and get people thinking about their own relationships with our wild neighbors, our wild relatives, and the inherent value that these animals have, irrespective of what they give to us.

The stories are organized into four sections: 1) Meeting the Neighbors; 2) Along City and Highway Fringes; 3) Backcountry Encounters; and 4) Oddities, Surprises, and Dilemmas. The first three sections start close to home and gradually move farther afield. The fourth section is a grab bag of sorts—many of the essays in other parts of the book could have ended up here, but these eight seemed to present encounters or discoveries that seem especially provocative or unsettling.

While the stories are grouped by geography and theme, they are not in any kind of chronological order. In other words, the essays skip around in time. It will therefore help the reader to know that from 1993 through 2006 I lived with Dulcy Boehle in the foothills along Anchorage's eastern edge, an area known to locals as the Hillside. In 2002, we were joined by my then eighty-year-old mother, Torie Sherwonit, who we uprooted from her East Coast home because the infirmities of old age—chiefly manifested as advanced degenerative osteoarthritis, but also (in retrospect) the earliest stages of dementia—had made it impossible for Mom to live alone. In 2006, with my marriage to Dulcy ended, I moved to Anchorage's Turnagain area, at the west end of town. And because I refer to the Anchorage Bowl in a few essays, it's also worth knowing that the "bowl" in which most residents live is a roughly triangular piece of lowlands bounded on two sides by the waters of Cook Inlet's Turnagain and Knik Arms and on the other by the Chugach Mountains.

It will also help the reader to know that during close or extended encounters with wildlife, I sometimes assign the animal a gender. This seems especially true for mammals. In some circumstances it's easy to determine whether a critter is male or female. Yet even when the gender isn't obvious, I may intuitively identify an individual as "he" or "she." Even if wrong, the choice in those instances seems preferable to "it." The personal pronouns imply a living *being*, while "it" suggests an object, a thing. I'm among those who believe such distinctions matter, that they influence the way we relate to other species. There's plenty of evidence that we humans behave more respectfully toward other creatures when we accept the possibility that they're not simply hard-wired mechanisms or unfeeling objects, but rather sentient, aware beings with emotional lives and perhaps even what some call spirit.

Two names that appear in several essays also merit mention here. One is connected to a mountain: Denali. Like a large and growing number of Alaskans, I prefer that Athabascan name when referring to Alaska's—and the continent's—tallest peak. Though officially still recognized as Mount McKinley, Denali seems preferable for several reasons. Not only is the name more poetic, it honors the 20,320-foot peak itself (in English the name translates to "The High One") rather than a political figure who never saw the mountain; and it honors the indigenous people who named and revered the peak. The second name is that of Rick Sinnott, who served as the Alaska Department of Fish and Game's wildlife manager for the Anchorage area from 1994 until his retirement in 2010. Rick was (and remains) a frequent source of valuable and reliable information, so he is part of several stories. In those essays I will generally refer to him as the state's local wildlife manager.

One final thought. Though I've been blessed by many memorable, even astonishing, encounters with wild animals in Alaska's wilderness, several of my most extraordinary—and in some instances, life changing—experiences have occurred within Anchorage, sometimes without leaving my yard. Or house. Thus one of the great lessons that the animals have taught me, and which I am excited to share here, is the reminder that nature's wondrous wild surrounds us all the time, wherever we live, if we'll only open our senses and pay attention.

ACKNOWLEDGMENTS

First and foremost, I wish to express my appreciation to the animals who have informed, enlarged, and enriched my life, and who've stirred in me joy, wonder, mystery, humility, laughter, and occasionally also sadness, regret, shock, and even fear. In a very real sense, they've been—and continue to be—my teachers and guides.

Thanks to all those people who've shared memorable wildlife experiences with me and/or added to my understanding and appreciation of the animals who appear in these stories, with special gratitude to William Ashton, Larry Aumiller, Ellen Bielawski, Dulcy Boehle, Helene Feiner, Wayne Hall, Colleen Handel, Richard Nelson, Leonard and Irene Peyton, Torie Sherwonit, and Rick Sinnott. Thanks also to Sam Barber, Brian Barnes, Dan Bosch, Pete Buist, Marty Caress, Barbara Carlson, Mark Chihuly, Jessy Coltrane, Bob Dittrick, Angela Doroff, Howard Golden, Dave Harkness, Marilyn Houser, Allen Jobes, Pat Pourchot, Mari Reeves, Marian Snively, David Tessler, Vic Van Ballenberghe, Carolyn Van Hemert, Bill Zack, and Randy Zarnke. And of course I'm deeply thankful to my boyhood fishing partner and mentor, Herman Sherwonit, my late Uncle Peach. There are likely others I've forgotten and I apologize for any oversights.

I'm also deeply grateful to the editors who've published my essays over the years, whether in newspapers, magazines, journals, or books. Though it's always a pleasure to have work appear in a national and/or literary publication, I owe a special debt to the string of editors who've run my essays in the local weekly newspaper, the *Anchorage Press*. Besides providing a forum for several of my longer pieces, the *Press* has given me the opportunity to share my observations, musings, and perspectives with a broad spectrum of local residents, many of whom have much different backgrounds, attitudes, and beliefs than I. The opportunity to present these readers new or alternative ways of relating to and thinking about the wildlife with whom we share this northern landscape is no small thing.

I also extend thanks to Tim Frew, who invited me to share my *Animal Stories* idea and essays with the staff at Graphic Arts Books; editor Kathy Howard and publishing director Doug Pfeiffer, who enthusiastically embraced the book; copy editor Michelle Blair, for her thorough work and thoughtful questions and suggestions, which strengthened this collection of stories; Vicki Knapton, for her work on the book's cover and interior design; and Angela Zbornik for her marketing expertise and support.

One final note of appreciation: two canine companions have enlivened many of my local outings in recent years and at times made me aware of wildlife I would have missed except for their keen senses (while offering a dog's perspective). The first of those was Coya, who's included in a few of this book's essays and who died in 2012; the second is my current companion, another mixed-collie rescue dog, Denali. They too have enriched my life.

PART I

MEETING THE NEIGHBORS

THE SONGS OF ROBINS
STRETCH ACROSS TIME AND SPACE

The afterglow of a late-evening sunset filtered through the upstairs windows of my home on Anchorage's Hillside. To the northwest, a crimson band of sky hung over a mountain known locally as The Sleeping Lady, as if ready to enfold her in soft, red robes for the night. I'd spent much of that late spring day in the yard, raking my unruly lawn, cleaning up debris from winter storms, and working in my strawberry patch. Now, freshly showered and relaxed, I sat in the dwindling light and listened to one of the world's great singers.

Perched in a nearby spruce, a male robin serenaded me with a sweetly familiar melody, his warbled song touching some deeply buried memory, from a time and place far, far away. Though fascinated by animals, I didn't pay much heed to birds while growing up in Connecticut during the 1950s and '60s; my interest was instead drawn to more exotic species, for instance snakes, frogs, and turtles. Still, a few species got my attention, none more so than the robin.

I still vividly picture robins running across Dad's well-manicured lawn, then suddenly stopping, dropping their heads to the ground and lifting up a worm or caterpillar. I remember their rusty red breasts, dark gray backs, and sharp yellow bills much more than their songs from those long-ago days. But the voices of robins must have been among the most recognizable wild sounds to echo through my Trumbull neighborhood in spring and summer, along with the chirps of crickets, the croaking of bullfrogs, and the shouts of friends playing softball in the open lot beside my family's yard.

I don't recall robins inhabiting the places I lived en route to my adopted home, Alaska: Maine, Arizona, California. Yet the map in my field guide to North American birds clearly shows we shared those landscapes. It must be that my attention was focused on other things during my twenties and thirties. First there was college and grad school, followed by a short-lived career in geology, and then a shift to journalism; plus sports, romantic relationships, and my first tentative steps along the long and winding path of personal and spiritual growth.

I've always loved nature, but it was only after I settled in Anchorage in 1982 that I began to seriously pay renewed attention to "the natural world" as I once did in my Connecticut youth. Though I wouldn't fully welcome birds into my life for another decade or so, early on I noticed an unexpected thing about my new home: robins.

Like most people, I'd built images of Alaska that included polar bears, wolves, Eskimos, great mountains, and glaciers. But robins? They didn't seem to fit somehow. They seemed too . . . I don't know, too eastern, maybe. Or maybe too commonplace. I'd imagined them to be creatures of milder, tamer environs.

Then again, I never imagined myself becoming a resident of America's "last frontier" until I came here.

In an odd way, robins deepened the link between my original and adopted homelands. While providing a natural connection between Connecticut and Alaska, they also stirred sharp memories of my boyhood. As some other familiar critters have done—for instance chickadees, rainbow trout, frogs, and dragonflies—robins increased my desire to better understand my boyhood bond with nature and, at the same time, learn more about the wild community of my new home.

If watching a robin in Anchorage seemed strange, imagine how I felt upon spotting one deep in the Arctic wilderness, miles and miles from any well-kept lawns, or gardens, or trees. Traveling alone, without anyone to verify the sighting, I thought I might be hallucinating. Until I saw another. And another. Since then I have learned that robins seasonally occupy nearly all of Alaska, from the Panhandle's old-growth forests to the North Slope's tundra plains.

Here in Anchorage, robins are among the first migratory songbirds to arrive each spring (a growing number are also overwintering, another surprise). Come April, I anticipate their fluid, high-pitched song, along with the trill of the varied thrush and loud whistled notes of the tiny ruby-crowned kinglet.

Once arrived and settled into their spring and early summer routines, robins seem to sing all day long and deep into the night. Often their voices are what I hear first in the morning and last before sleep. At the end of a long, dark winter—or a long, busy spring day—few, if any, sounds are more delightful.

Another connection has deepened my appreciation of robins. After eight decades of East Coast living, my mother came north to Alaska in 2002 to spend her last years with me. In her eighties and suffering from advanced degenerative arthritis, Mom couldn't get outdoors like she used to. Even sitting on the front deck became a project. And, like many older folks, she'd lost the ability to hear high-frequency sounds.

Even when I opened the windows and sliding glass doors, Mom usually couldn't hear the chirps, buzzes, warbles, and whistles of our backyard birds. For someone who had welcomed songbirds to her house for many years, that was a hard, frustrating thing. Yet the robin's song was loud enough, and apparently deep enough, that it sometimes registered. On one outing along Anchorage's Coastal Trail—Mom in her wheelchair and I pushing—I asked if she could hear the bird's whistled notes. "I think so," she replied. Then, listening intently, she turned her head toward me when the bird whistled again. "Is that it, over there?" she asked, pointing.

"Yep, you've got it."

We both smiled at that.

Then, early in the evening of that spring yard-work day, a robin began singing right outside the sitting room window. Before I could say anything, Mom turned in her chair. "That's the robin, isn't it?"

Hours later, Mom was in bed, her door closed. But the robin continued to sing, a little softer as the sky darkened. He was still singing when I headed to bed, sending forth a calm, assuring sort of lullaby with its own touch of wild magic that stretched across the continent, across the years.

THE HIDDEN LIVES OF
HARES AND SHREWS

With breakfast finished and the daily sports section skimmed from cover to cover (a favorite morning ritual), I rose from the dining room table and piled newspaper, coffee cup, crumpled napkin, and plastic yogurt container on the kitchen counter. Then, drawn more by instinct than deliberate thought, I stepped to the dining room's north-facing window and peered outside. The window was a favorite observation post, a looking glass through which I could study the nature of my Hillside backyard, a semi-wild mix of lawn and spruce-birch forest.

On that September morning, my attention was drawn to a smallish, rounded, brown form, huddled in the grass and nibbling on clover: a snowshoe hare. A favorite food of lynx, great-horned owls, northern goshawks, foxes, and coyotes—all of which prowl Anchorage's wooded areas—hares survive by stealth and camouflage. Completely white in winter, except for large brown eyes, they are nearly invisible on snow. In summer, their grayish-brown fur excellently blends with the forest's mottled, shadowed floor.

A hare's natural disguise doesn't work so well on monochromatic green though, which is likely why I would see them most frequently from May through September, come to dine on lawn grass and clover.

To be honest, I didn't normally pay much attention to the neighborhood's hares. Their habits don't make for easy or interesting study: in the open, they tend to remain still, depending (for better or worse) on the effectiveness of their camouflage; in the forest, they're almost impossible to track. And though secretive in

17

nature, they're common creatures of the woods. Seeing a hare is nothing like catching a glimpse of a bear or lynx, or even a moose or hawk. Their furtive qualities also make them less engaging than other common forest residents, for instance the excitable chickadees and squirrels that visited my backyard, looking for meals.

That day, however, the hare held my interest. The animal's fur was what initially grabbed my attention. The year's first heavy snows were still a month or more away, yet the shift to winter white had already begun.

I grabbed binoculars and took a closer look. Hares always retain some white on their undersides, where it's easily hidden in summer. But this one's long back feet were solidly white from toes to ankles and above, as though it had slipped on large white slippers. Small patches of white also marked the hare's face: around the mouth, under the chin, on the cheek. Atop its head, the hare's ears were already mostly white, with brown-and-black tips.

Maybe it was the sharp contrast in color between white ears and brown body, but I more easily noticed how the hare almost constantly moved its ears, often independently of one another, like thinly oval, furred, mini-satellite dishes.

Nose twitching steadily, the hare was busily munching clover when a magpie called in its loud, raspy voice. The hare sat tight, motionless except for its rotating ears. One ear forward, another turned ninety degrees to the right or left. Both ears forward. Both ears turned to the sides, and then flicked backward.

The hare's transitional coat stirred a series of questions. When had the transformation begun and when would it be complete? How long does the color shift take? Does it vary from year to year, from individual to individual? And why did I almost never see hares in winter? Is the white disguise that good?

A week later, while working at the computer, I glanced out the sliding glass door, and noticed two hares in the backyard. One I recognized by its pattern of white patches; the other remained more fully brown. While I watched, the two engaged in behavior I'd never before witnessed. As one hare sat still, the other jumped high into the air, again and again. Leaping, it punched the air with its back legs, quick, sharp jabs. What was going on?

The jumping and kicking had a frolicking nature and I imagined it to be a spirited attempt at play. But I was also reminded how little I really knew about hares; or for that matter, my other wild neighbors.

Curious now about both the hare's behavior and changing coat, I did some reading, tracked down a couple of wildlife researchers. This is some of what I learned: the hare's jumping and kicking is not play but ritualized aggression, a show of dominance that apparently communicates something to the effect of "Get outta here. This is my turf."

Things get especially wild in spring and early summer, the time of mating. Male hares chase and scrap and generally lose all good sense—namely their normal instincts for secrecy—in their frenzied desire to breed with females in heat. In losing their heads, sex-crazed hares often also lose their lives, either to predators or to cars, while madly dashing across streets. Females stay in estrus for only a few hours at a time, so the zaniness is short-lived. But it's intense enough to lead to the notion of "Mad March Hare Syndrome."

As for the color shift: that usually lasts about a month, though the duration and timing varies from hare to hare. Scientists believe the change is driven mostly by daylight, but temperature also likely plays a role. And the transition is indeed patchy, rather than smooth.

One other bit of natural history helps to explain their annual "disappearance" in winter: *Lepus americanus* is a mostly nocturnal creature. Given the length of Anchorage's winter nights—more than fifteen hours of darkness from late October through mid-February, with a peak of eighteen and a half hours on the winter solstice—hares have abundant time to feed and move about unseen. Combine that with their superior camouflage and my own greater tendency to remain indoors during the cold, dark months, and it figures I'd be less likely to notice hares in winter's white. Come spring and summer, daylight hours lengthen, I spend more time in the yard, and hares go crazy with passion. So our paths figure to more regularly cross.

September gave way to October and several days passed without any sign of the hares. It had already snowed once on the Hillside, but here, at one thousand feet, the snow melted within a few hours. A fully or mostly white hare should have been easy to spot on the gray and brown late-autumn landscape. Had they already gone into nocturnal hiding? Vanished for the season?

Curious to know how white the hares' coats had become, I continued to check for them daily, but usually only for moments at a time. One morning while I watched, a cow moose passed just outside the sliding glass doors. We gazed at each other a few moments, and then she sauntered off into the woods. Here, then gone, so quickly.

The episodes with both hares and moose got me thinking (again) about how much goes on in my yard and neighborhood that I never see or sense. I'm given glimpses now and then. But those only hint of the "hidden" world that I too rarely notice. Even with my passion for wildlife, for nature, I easily become cocooned within the walls of my house, consumed by work, or distracted by computer, television, and newspaper. I urged myself, once more, to make room in my busy schedule; to watch, listen, pay attention, get "out there" more often. And have patience. These wild neighbors, after all, have added immeasurably to my quality of life here on the Hillside. Whether bears or moose or hares, they are all worth knowing better.

By winter's end, large piles of snow mixed with seed debris would normally cover the ground beneath my Hillside home's back decks, the remnants of a season's worth of bird feeding, shell sweeping, and snow clearing. One year, though, the snow piles melted away by early February, leaving only the debris: a mix of opened and unopened shells, sunflower seed bits, bird poop, and mold.

It seemed a good idea to get rid of the mess, rather than wait for spring. Without the snow to complicate matters, I raked and shoveled and hauled away several bucketfuls of the slimy, putrid stuff; some thirty gallons in all. A job that typically took me several hours (usually spread over a week's time) lasted only forty-five minutes.

More shells piled up in the following weeks, intermixed with the few inches of snow that fell in March. So I still had a bit of April raking and hauling to do. But Anchorage's peculiar winter, with its record-setting warmth and dearth of snow, made my annual seed cleanup so much easier. And by mid-February I'd largely eliminated a possible temptation for any early rising bears.

The melted snow piles did perhaps rob me of a late-winter spectacle, however. The previous year, in winter's last days, I noticed that some new neighbors had moved into the yard. Well, not exactly new. But ones I hadn't paid much attention to before.

One bright morning, while standing on our upper deck and listening to birdsong, I happened to glance at the snow piles below. And I noticed something unusual: flashes of gray. As I kept watching, those dashing bits of fur took shape. Shrews were darting in and out of the snow. This discovery both surprised and pleased me.

Shrews, as you may already know, are the smallest of the Earth's mammals, weighing no more than a few ounces. Because they're such tiny creatures, and they stay under cover while rushing about the world, we humans rarely see shrews. And few people, besides researchers, tend to seek them out. Most Anchorage residents, I'd guess, don't even know—or care—that we share our local landscape with these voracious insectivores. Yet they're all around us, living secret lives.

Over the years, I'd seen an occasional shrew in the yard. But no more than a handful in all. Yet here below me, at least a half-dozen were poking their noses out of tunnels they'd dug through the snow. I watched for a while, entranced by this discovery. Why hadn't I ever noticed them before? Surely this wasn't the first winter that a colony of shrews had moved into the seedy snow mounds beside the house.

Wanting a closer look, I headed downstairs and out the door, then sat a few feet away. Perhaps because they'd heard or otherwise sensed my approach, the shrews stayed hidden for awhile. Awaiting their reappearance, I noticed more and more holes in the snow. The piles were honeycombed with dozens of minute entranceways and passages. Clearly they'd settled in some time ago.

In my stillness, I began to hear a faint scratching. Then a miniature head popped out, its pointed, twitching pink nose bright against the gray fur. A new entryway had been completed. Soon another head appeared, in a different opening. And another and another.

It was hard keeping track of their numbers, as the shrews almost immediately pulled their heads back in, after poking them out. A few darted completely out of their burrows, trailing thin gray tails nearly as long as their tiny bodies. But none ventured more than a few inches, before rushing back inside. During their brief but frequent forays into the light, they'd worn narrow runways across the snow's surface.

I knew that a handful of different shrews live in the Anchorage area; these were almost certainly common or masked shrews (*Sorex cinereus*). The most widespread of their kind, they inhabit much of North America. Though I didn't catch any (or try to), I estimated the shrews measured between two and four inches, from the tip of their noses to the tip of their tails. Their bodies constantly twitched and quivered, giving them a skittish, nervous appearance.

I tried to imagine the network of tunnels, passages, and chambers they'd built beneath the snow. And I considered what had lured the shrews to this spot.

Was it something about the piles themselves? Or the abundance of seeds? The shrews seemed to be grabbing bits of seeds when they scampered from their holes, but I couldn't be sure. Though shrews are insect feeders, maybe they were taking advantage of the seeds to more easily survive the winter, much like insect-eating songbirds turn to seeds during Alaska's coldest, harshest season.

I kept watch on the shrews until mid-April, when the piles began to melt away and the tunnels collapsed or flooded. They disappeared long before the snow did, escaped back into their hidden world.

A year later, with winter all but past, I still hadn't seen a single shrew. While I did some final raking and hauling of seeds in April, I couldn't help but ponder how my secretive neighbors fared during that warm and mostly snowless Alaskan winter.

LIVING WITH MOOSE THROUGH THE SEASONS AND ACROSS THE YEARS

LATE WINTER: MOOSE AND WOLVES

The ravens were what tipped me off. Their presence and behavior suggested that something out of the ordinary had happened in the woods bordering the Turnagain Arm Trail. As I rounded a bend, three of the large black birds left their perches and flapped, cawing, across the trail. There they settled high in other trees. Though I didn't see their exact positions when they lifted off, it seemed at least one of the ravens had been on or near the ground.

Both the number of birds and their positions were unusual. While I often see or hear ravens while hiking this trail, they're usually flying above the canopy, headed up or down Turnagain Arm. I've seldom seen gatherings of perched ravens in the hundreds of times I've walked here.

This woodland path at the southern end of the Anchorage Bowl is one of my favorites, a place I visit regularly throughout the year. In spring and fall, when the forest is busy with change, I may hike the trail three or four times a week; but in summer (when I'm often exploring other parts of Alaska) or winter (when the forest is largely dormant), weeks may pass between my walks.

By mid-March, with the days lengthening and warming and hinting of accelerated changes, I'd begun coming here more frequently again. Still, more than a week had passed since my last, uneventful visit.

The ravens and I watched each other a minute or so, then two of them departed. The one that lingered followed me with its intense, shining eyes as I resumed my walk and passed beneath its cottonwood perch. When I'd gone another fifty feet or so, the raven flew back across the trail to where I'd first spotted the birds, now joined by a loudly yakking magpie. Something was making the raven reluctant to leave.

My first thought: it's got to be food. Maybe there's a carcass up there in the woods. Putting binoculars to eyes, I scanned the forest but couldn't see any sign of blood or body. I then thought about going to check, but the idea of post-holing through wet, soft snow in low-cut walking shoes held me back. I mentally marked the spot and resumed my walk, telling myself I'd return and check it out but not really being sure I would.

I did come back the following day. No ravens were present. But the late-March air was cooler, the snowpack not so punchy, and I wore high-topped backpacking boots for my off-trail foray. Slogging and weaving among spruce, birch, and cottonwood trees, I looked left and right and ahead, searching for signs. The last week or so had been warm during the day and cold at night; any tracks would have been softened and blurred by the freeze–thaw cycle. Still I could make out some moose and canine prints in the snow. Then I started seeing small, scattered patches of moose hair. But there was no blood, no bones, no evidence of a kill.

I was just about ready to give up. But before leaving, I took one last look around. And there, seventy or eighty feet uphill from me, was a bright splash of red. My binoculars confirmed the sighting: a large patch of blood darkened the snow.

Moving slowly and cautiously, I decided to clap my hands, make some noise. The calendar suggested it was still too early for bears to be out of hibernation, but you never know for sure. The closer I got, the more tracks I saw: bird, canine, moose, and at least one set of boot prints.

Finally I reached the kill site. A large circle of snow had been stamped down. And within that circle was a skull, jawbones, patches of hair, yellow- and red-stained snow, and a large pile of what looked like peat moss. That was the rumen, undigested remains from the moose's belly.

Beyond the first circle of death was a second. Here were the remains of the ribs and backbone and legs and the moose's emptied hide. I was amazed by how thoroughly the moose had been scavenged. The skull and ribs and other bones had been completely cleaned of meat. Even one of the legs was bare bone down to the hoof. I'd walked this trail just over a week ago and saw no evidence of the kill then, no sign of scavengers. How fast would a moose carcass be cleaned of its meat?

I'm not an expert on "reading" moose remains, but the size of the skull and hooves and hide suggested an adult. Given the season (late winter) and the absence of any bear sign, I assumed the animal died from starvation and was then scavenged by all manner of critters: coyotes, ravens, magpies, certainly. And what about foxes, weasels, lynx, squirrels, rodents?

I briefly considered the possibility that wolves were involved, but dismissed that notion since I'd never noticed signs of wolves along this trail.

Back home I e-mailed Rick Sinnott, the local wildlife manager, briefly describing what I found and asking if he'd heard anything about a moose kill along the Turnagain Arm Trail. Rick e-mailed me back: Larry Aumiller had found a moose carcass during a recent walk. And Aumiller, the longtime manager of Alaska's famed McNeil bear sanctuary, thought the moose might have been killed by wolves. Sinnott then added, "Larry's pretty good at this stuff and I think he uses that trail a lot, so I believe it."

The mention of wolves surprised me. But I've known Larry for many years; and, like Rick, I trust his knowledge and instincts. I arranged a meeting to learn more.

Over coffee drinks at a south Anchorage cafe, Larry recounted his discovery.

Unlike me, he'd been hiking the trail after a recent snowfall that left three or four inches of powder over a hardened crust: perfect tracking conditions. The first thing he noticed was a large splotch of blood on the trail, plus a bunch of tracks. Looking more closely, he then saw a trail of blood and moose hair heading off into the forest, accompanied by at least two sets of wolf tracks.

There may have been more than two wolves, Larry told me, but at least two sets were distinctly different in size. And the trail of blood and tracks suggested that the wolves had been hounding the moose, harassing and injuring it, until finally going for the kill. The carcass itself was about 150 feet downhill and had already been largely cleaned of meat. From the size of the skull, it appeared to be a yearling.

"Wait a minute," I interrupted. "Did you say downhill?"

"Yeah, it was downhill from the trail, not real easy to see until you were right on top of it."

"So where exactly was this?" I asked.

"You know the Christmas tree [a spruce that someone decorated with ornaments during the holiday season]? A little ways beyond that."

I couldn't believe it. Larry had found a different carcass, about a half mile as the raven flies from the one I discovered. From all appearances, both had died within the last couple weeks. Wolves had killed at least one of the animals, perhaps both, yet they'd nearly gone undetected. Only Larry's attentiveness and curiosity had led to their discovery. I wondered if anyone else had noticed the blood or tracks and whether the wolves howled during their hunt. If so, did people who live higher in these hills hear the howling?

I knew that wolves roam the eastern edges of Anchorage. I'd heard stories from homeowners who'd seen them and had myself noticed their tracks while walking Chugach State Park's Middle Fork Loop Trail. Yet for some reason I'd never imagined them here, in these woods, along this path. Perhaps I've assumed that they wouldn't come this close to the highway, which is just a few hundred yards away, or less, along most of this trail's nine and a half miles; or that they'd never approach a trail so frequently traveled by people.

But as Larry noted, human use of the Turnagain Arm Trail is concentrated within a few hours each day for much of the year, particularly in winter. There's plenty of time for wolves to pass here while avoiding people. Plus there's good cover and a good number of moose. So actually, this might be ideal terrain for wolves on the hunt. What seems unusual might, in fact, be quite ordinary.

I'm reminded, again, how much is happening in these woods—and in larger Anchorage—that we human residents will never know or guess, even when we think we're getting to know the place well. That's part of the appeal of hiking here: the surprises and the mystery, which nicely balance the familiarity of a place well known. Both aspects make it special.

I returned to the moose carcass a few days later. The skull was gone, the hide had been moved around, bones had been nibbled, more tracks marked the snow. Soon the snow would melt and the evidence of the kill would gradually disappear. Pregnant cows would give birth to calves, wolves would move through the forest like shadows, and I would keep returning—to exercise and refresh my spirit and see what else I might learn about these woods, so familiar yet full of the unexpected.

SPRING: A GIFT OF NEWBORN MOOSE

Back home late in the evening after a walk in local woodlands, I was retrieving gear from the back of my car when a small, gangly creature the color of chestnuts stepped around the corner of my house.

The moose calf stopped, aimed its dark brown eyes at me, and gazed intently.

Surprise and exhilaration surged through me even as two thoughts streaked through my mind. *Wow, this is great!* followed immediately by *Where's the calf's mom?*

Cow moose are notoriously protective of their newborns, and will aggressively charge, and sometimes pummel, any perceived threat. This calf's tiny size and tentative, awkward movements suggested it was no more than a couple of days old. I might have been the first person it had ever seen, which could explain why it showed no fear.

Taking a few cautious steps to the right, I spotted the cow, calmly browsing on greens where my semi-wild lawn gave way to forest. I ducked back behind the house, then rushed upstairs to tell Mom the good news.

"We've got a calf in the yard," I announced.

"A calf?" she asked. "You mean a moose calf? Where?"

"On the side of the house. I'm going to see if I can spot it from up here."

Slowed by her eighty-three years and aching arthritic joints, Mom no longer moved around so well and I hoped we could see the moose without her having to negotiate the stairs.

I finally spotted them, a cow and *two* calves, outside my bedroom window.

"Mom, come over here. Hurry, before they're gone."

Of course she couldn't hurry. Pushing her walker, she made her way slowly down the hallway.

Worried that the moose would move out of view, I again urged her to move faster.

"I'm coming, I'm coming. I can only go so fast, you know that."

It turned out there was no reason to rush. The three moose were grazing in the middle of the front yard. As usual, I was struck by how calves in the first months of their lives so closely resemble foals—minus the long tails, of course.

Mom finally joined me at the window. "Oh, they're so little," she whispered, practically cooing. "And their mother is so big! They're so cute. No, more than that; they're precious."

Mother and babies did indeed present a sharp contrast. The dark brown cow stood nearly six feet tall at the shoulders and weighed close to half a ton. Her cinnamon-colored calves likely weighed thirty to thirty-five pounds.

After a pause, Mom worried, "They won't go out in the road, will they? I don't want them to get hurt."

The family wandered out of sight and I ran to another room, then out onto the back deck. I traced their movements as the moose roamed through the yard. I felt confident that this cow was the same one we'd seen regularly in our Hillside neighborhood, who'd brought other calves into our yard in past years. Did she instinctively know that our yard was "safe"? Unlike many of our neighbors, we had no dogs or kids to bother the calves, even if unintentionally. We'd always been content to watch quietly from the house, recognizing the gift that these animals are and hoping they would stay a while longer.

The moose we watched were part of a largely unhunted population that inhabits the Anchorage Bowl and the adjacent Chugach Mountains. Local wildlife biologists have estimated that two hundred to three hundred moose reside in the bowl year-round, with winter numbers rising to as many as fifteen hundred animals when they're driven out of the mountains by deepening snow and lured into the city by Anchorage's relative abundance of food, much of it in the form of fruit-bearing ornamental trees and shrubs. That robust population has, not surprisingly, caused moose–human conflicts. Most residents seem to like having moose around, but some are angered by the animals' taste for ornamental plants and garden vegetables and want their numbers thinned.

Others, particularly parents with young children, worry about the threat that moose present. Cows with calves can be every bit as dangerous as bears. And in extreme cold or deep-snow winters, stressed-out moose may attack with little provocation. Life-threatening injuries are rare, but twice in the 1990s Anchorage residents were stomped to death by agitated moose. One fatal attack was caught on video and made national news. It also added fuel to a local debate. Should moose hunting be allowed along the city's perimeter?

Another local dilemma is moose–car collisions. Each winter, drivers strike one hundred to two hundred moose on Anchorage roads. Only rarely are people seriously harmed. Most often the damage is to the vehicles, sometimes wrecked beyond repair, and to the moose, which usually die immediately or are so seriously injured they must be euthanized. Hoping that some good might come from such tragedies, the state allows local charities to use the moose meat. Yet accidents, too, have been cited as reasons to have a local hunt. Better for moose to be killed with bullets or arrows, the reasoning goes, than to suffer after being smashed by cars or trucks.

An experimental Hillside archery hunt in the 1980s didn't go well: residents sighted moose with arrows protruding from their bodies; some bulls were killed and butchered in people's front yards. As memories and outrage over that fiasco faded, state wildlife managers began to envision a much smaller and more carefully monitored hunt. Eventually a new and lower profile cow-moose hunt would be approved in Chugach State Park above Anchorage's Hillside, with only a few animals to be killed.

Sitting in my home, reveling in the presence of calves and cow, I found it hard to support moose hunts in these foothills. I understand the concern of wildlife managers and those who feel endangered or besieged. But I'm not convinced that controlled hunts along Anchorage's perimeters will ever solve the problems of moose–vehicle collisions and occasional attacks. Sinnott, the local wildlife manager, agreed the hunt would do little or nothing to resolve the city's moose–human conflicts, but argued that it gave residents an opportunity to locally hunt an admittedly overabundant population.

Anchorage residents face a number of such difficult wildlife-management decisions. We want to share the landscape with wild creatures, yet conflicts inevitably arise. We have "problems" with the moose that have run-ins with cars; the beavers that inhabit local waterways and sometimes flood neighborhoods or attack dogs in lakes; the wolves that occasionally enter yards and kill pets or livestock and more rarely intimidate walkers and runners; and the bears that develop a taste for human garbage, dog food, and birdseed.

In recent weeks the newspaper had run several letters, sent by people complaining that Anchorage's moose and bears and other wildlife inconvenience or endanger their lives. Cities are for people, these letter writers argued. Why should we humans have to compromise our lives for animals? Other Anchorage residents responded that it's we who are encroaching on their habitat and lives, as our city continues to expand. Why live in Alaska if you don't want to share a neighborhood or yard with wild animals? I'm among those who welcome and embrace the city's wildlife. Their presence in our daily lives is a big part of what makes Alaska's urban center a unique place to live, along with the nearby Chugach Mountains and the city's many parks and trails.

The moose returned to the front yard and I called Mom to the sitting room window, while I watched from the deck. The cow continued browsing on springtime's fresh greens, while her calves pranced and danced around the yard on spindly legs, then stopped briefly to nuzzle each other and their mother, before returning to their play. How else to explain such prancing around, except as playfulness?

A steady rain began to wet the landscape, but the moose hardly seemed to notice. I joined my own mother in front of the TV to watch a favorite show, and then checked back outside. I again called Mom to the window; the calves had begun to nurse in the middle of our yard. Could there be a stronger sign of the safety that they felt?

Finishing its late-night meal, one calf moved to the front of the cow, who licked her youngster gently. The ritual was repeated when the second calf finished nursing. Then the cow leaned forward, knelt, bent her long legs beneath her, and settled on the lawn. The two calves folded their legs too and soon their heads dropped to the grass as they napped.

I returned my attention indoors, but checked outside several more times before heading to bed shortly after midnight. Each time I looked, the cow was awake, alert. I imagined she must have dozed now and then, but like any attentive parent she likely got little sleep in those days and weeks following the birth of her twins.

Before going to my own bedroom, I checked on Mom.

"Are they still out there?" she asked.

"Yep, they're still in the front yard."

"I can't believe they've stayed around. Boy, are we lucky. Well, sweet dreams. May God and His angels watch over you."

"You too, Mom."

Three years had passed since my then eighty-year-old mother moved to Anchorage. The transition presented Mom with many challenges, but life in Anchorage also had its joys. And among the greatest are the encounters with our wild neighbors: the songbirds that swarmed to our feeders in winter, the squirrels that scampered up to our top deck, the geese and gulls that flew past when we visited the Coastal Trail, the moose that found refuge in our yard.

I peeked out the window one last time. In gathering darkness, the cow kept steady watch over her calves.

EARLY SUMMER: MOOSE CHARGE

The hour was late, nearly 11:00 P.M., but plenty of early summer daylight remained when four friends and I headed back to the trailhead after hiking a woodland path at the southern edge of Anchorage. The five of us were spread out, in single file, and we walked quickly while sharing stories and laughter. In other words, we weren't paying close attention to the trail ahead or the surrounding woods.

I was talking with Brad, in the lead and several steps ahead of me, when a cow moose suddenly appeared, charging down the trail no more than thirty feet away.

Where this moose came from, I still have no idea. Maybe she was standing around the corner, just out of sight. Or perhaps she was hidden behind the dense alder-willow thickets that border parts of this trail. But at the time it seemed she simply materialized out of the late-evening air, coming toward us at a full gallop. Head down, ears flattened, hackles, raised and legs kicking high, the cow was huge and dangerous, a picture of maternal fury.

I had no time to think, only react, and my survival instincts took over. A spruce tree stood to my right, just off the trail. The spruce wasn't especially large, but it was the nearest possible cover and big enough that the moose couldn't easily run over it or through it. I lunged behind the tree, ducking my head. But the animal's attention was focused on Brad, not me. He'd been turned toward me while talking and he swiveled his head forward a split second after I spotted the moose, but before she smashed into his body. Later I'd ask myself if I could have—should have—shouted a warning or done something else to help him. But it all happened so frightfully fast, in a blur of bodies and emotions.

The cow slammed into Brad's upper body with a full frontal attack of nose, forehead, and legs, knocking him over. Then, as quickly as she struck, the moose wheeled away and disappeared into the forest. It was all over in five or ten seconds.

We quickly gathered around Brad, who was laid out on the ground, stunned and disoriented but somehow not seriously injured, as far as we could tell. He wasn't bleeding or moaning or yelling. I recall a jumble of voices, as we shared our amazement at the suddenness and severity of the attack and asked Brad, "Are you OK?"

"I think so," he said, looking around, his eyes enlarged. "What the hell happened?"

"You got flattened by a moose," someone replied. "Didn't you see it coming?"

"A moose? Really? I didn't see a thing. Where'd it go?"

Brad then spit but coughed up no blood, we were happy to see. He started to stand but we urged him to stay put, afraid he might be in shock and harmed more than he realized. He was lucky, in a way, that he didn't see the moose coming, didn't have the chance to tense up. His relaxed body gave way to the blow without resistance. He was lucky, too, that the moose only knocked him down, didn't trample him with her deadly hooves. While moose attacks are rare, all of us in the group had heard the stories about the two people stomped to death by agitated moose right here in Anchorage.

Cows with newborn calves are notoriously dangerous animals and we suspected that this moose was simply protecting her young. Wildlife biologists estimate that up to two hundred calves are born in the Anchorage Bowl from late May through early June. Knowing it was the season of birthing, we should have been more careful, paid closer attention to our surroundings.

While the rest of us encircled Brad, James cautiously walked up the trail forty or fifty feet to see if the cow was still hanging around. Looking to the right, through thick alder he glimpsed a cinnamon-colored shape that suggested a calf and quickly backed away. Almost certainly the mom cut her attack short to return and safeguard her calf.

After ten minutes or so, Brad assured us he was all right and said he wanted to go. There was no longer any sign of the moose so we resumed our hike, more cautious now. Brad walked to the parking lot under his own power, which both amazed and relieved me.

The next morning Brad sent us an e-mail: as the adrenaline rush and initial shock wore off, his upper body had become so achy he could hardly sleep, even with pain medication. Weeks later, bothered by back and neck pains, Brad would get checked by a doctor, and diagnosed with symptoms of whiplash—no surprise to those of us who saw him leveled. What's astonishing is that he wasn't more seriously hurt by one ferociously protective mom.

MIDSUMMER: CITY OF MOOSE

Anchorage is a self-proclaimed "City of Lights" but as I've already suggested, Alaska's urban center could easily be called the "City of Moose." In fact I'd wager that for much of the year there's no better locale in Alaska to see North America's largest member of the deer family. Many that inhabit the city prefer the parks, greenbelts, and wooded lots of west Anchorage, including the Turnagain area, where I settled in 2006 after more than a dozen years on the Hillside.

One cow, usually accompanied by a calf or two, I could count on seeing at least a couple times a week on walks to the nearby Coastal Trail. Occasionally a bull would pass through the neighborhood, munching as he went. And I've watched a pair of yearlings graze in a neighbor's garden, relishing its peas and other greens.

I've always felt confident that I could track down an urban moose or two on short notice, if asked to show off the local wildlife by visiting family or friends. That confidence was put to the test when my mother's two sisters visited us several years after I hauled Mom to Alaska from the East Coast. As their visit wound down, the three sisters agreed they'd had a grand reunion. But neither of my aunts had seen much of the local wildlife.

On their last night in Anchorage, younger sister Evie joined her son Jim (who accompanied his mother north) on a drive to the Chugach foothills. Jim had watched moose there several times during the visit and wanted to share the experience with his mom. Not much of an adventurer, Emily seemed happy enough to spend her last night at our house, packing and spending a quiet evening with Mom.

My girlfriend, Helene, had different ideas. "Hey," she said, "why don't we drive Emily and your mom around and find our own moose."

And so we did. The four of us piled into my aging Toyota and, at Helene's suggestion, we headed toward Kincaid Park, a forested haven for Anchorage moose. Driving slowly, we scanned the wooded landscape for moose. Fifteen minutes passed, then thirty, then forty-five.

"There's always moose here," Helene moaned. "Where are they tonight?"

"So it goes," I said philosophically, though just as disappointed. "There are other places we can try."

Circling back out of Kincaid, I was just about ready to give up when Helene shouted, "Look, over there! Two moose on the left."

Sure enough, a cow and yearling grazed among a small grove of birches, maybe fifty yards from Raspberry Road. Doing a U-turn, I pulled over to the shoulder. While Mom watched from the car, Emily joined Helene and me along the road's shoulder. Moments later, a second yearling appeared.

"I told you," Helene exulted. "I knew we'd find moose here."

In her own understated way, Emily too seemed excited. "Wow, there they are. That's great."

Within minutes, several other cars pulled over and a dozen murmuring people lined the road, many armed with binoculars, cameras, and video recorders. Clearly we weren't the only moose hunters out that night. I suppose evening expeditions like ours go on throughout the summer.

Pleased but not fully satisfied, I proposed that we continue our moose search, hoping for a clearer, closer look at the critters. We next headed for a birch-spruce forest near Anchorage's international airport. Leaving pavement for a dusty, gravel road, we slowed to a crawl. Within a few minutes, I noticed a young bull in a meadow behind some birches. The moose was partly hidden by trees, so I pulled over and we waited for a better look. To our surprise and glee, the bull's browsing led him in our direction.

"Omygosh," Helene cried out. "He's coming right at us."

In the backseat, both Mom and Emily cooed their appreciation.

Approaching to within twenty-five feet, the yearling bull raised his head and picked leaves from the top of a willow.

"I didn't realize how big they are," Emily gasped. "He's gigantic."

"And he's a young one," I told her.

The bull began walking up the road. I drove slowly ahead, and then turned the car around for a better view. As I did, Helene spotted a second, larger moose browsing among the birches. This one was a mature cow, likely the young bull's mom. The engine off, we watched silently for several minutes more. Both moose continued to gorge on greens, unconcerned by our presence. Noticing another car's approach, we decided it was time to leave and let others take our place if they so wished.

"That was great," Helene said grinning. Turning toward the backseat she added, "It really doesn't get much better than this."

And then it did.

Nearly 10:00 P.M. with the light dimming, we agreed it was time to return home. Still, we didn't stop looking. About five minutes from home I noticed two shadowy forms, right beside heavily traveled Northern Lights Boulevard.

"More moose," I shouted. "And this time there's a little one."

Little indeed. A tiny, chestnut-colored calf the size of a small pony stood beside its mother in an open, grassy area. We pulled over to the shoulder and, our windows wide open, slowly rolled toward the pair.

"Oh, it's so *cute*," Mom whispered.

"It's beautiful," Emily agreed. "And so small."

Because cow moose are protective of their young, I watched for any signs of upset. But this one showed no evidence of being the least bit agitated. She lifted her head slightly and looked our way, then calmly resumed her grazing.

Not wishing to distress the two, we lingered beside them less than a minute. In deepening darkness we finished our tour of Anchorage's west side. Back home we awaited Evie and Jim's return, Mom and Emily eager to trade Anchorage wild-life stories with their sister, Helene and I more impressed than ever by the city's abundance of people-tolerant moose.

LATE SUMMER: MOOSE IN THE BERRY PATCH

I now more fully understand the angst of northern homeowners whose ornamental trees and flowering gardens have become meals for moose, for I caught one raiding my prized strawberry patch.

The first hints that something was amiss appeared when I found a couple of the plants uprooted, ripening berries still attached. I considered what—or who—might have pulled the plants. A rambunctious dog? A marauding teen? A rogue rabbit? (Nearby neighbors had "rescued" a few domesticated rabbits and later turned them loose; they then became regular visitors to my yard, but from what I could tell they preferred clover and dandelion leaves to berries. Hooray for that good fortune.)

Because the plants had been pulled but not eaten, and the patch as a whole was largely undisturbed, it didn't even cross my mind that a passing ungulate might be the culprit. Besides, in all the years I had lived on Anchorage's Hillside, no moose had ever shown a taste for our patch of feral strawberries. In fact the only animal I'd ever seen foraging in our small, unkempt berry garden was a robin, which simply took bites from several ripened fruits. Berry-burrowing bugs and occasional slugs were bigger problems than bird or furry beast.

To be completely honest about this, for several years my "patch" was hardly big enough to attract much attention from anything larger than a beetle (or the occasional bumblebee, when the berries' flowers were blooming). But for the past half decade, I'd let the berries run wild and the fruits greatly expanded their range. Covering some forty square feet, my personal—and by most standards, still tiny—strawberry fields annually produced one to two gallons of small, pinkish fruits that were juicy and lip-smacking sweet. Still, they never attracted much attention, beyond the occasional robin. Until the midsummer morning I'm about to recall.

Walking along the upstairs hallway to check on my still-sleeping mother, I happened to glance toward the downstairs hallway and front door. Just outside the door's window, partially obscured by blinds, was a large, brown, hairy form.

What the heck is a moose doing on our front porch? I asked myself. Then I rushed downstairs and looked out the window. To both my surprise and dismay, a cow moose was standing with one foot in the berry patch, head down and mouth chomping away. Just beyond her, a calf lay sprawled among the strawberry plants, seemingly at peace with the world even as my own peaceful morning was being shattered.

"Oh, no!" I moaned. What was I going to do? Hoping to scare the moose off without having to confront them, I banged on the door. The cow lifted her head and looked toward the house, but that was all. Clearly, more drastic measures were needed. I began to unlock the door, but had enough presence of mind to remember the house alarm was triggered. I didn't want to set it off and perhaps frighten the beast, so I punched the keyboard combination. Then, very carefully, I opened the door several inches, stuck my head outside (ready, at a moment's notice, to retreat and slam the door shut, if necessary) and talked to the moose in a calm but stern voice. "Hey, what do you think you're doing, eating my strawberries? Get out of there. Go on. Get out."

Her huge, oblong head no more than five feet from my face, the cow moose looked at me with an expression that seemed both inquisitive and bewildered; the sort of look a person might have while thinking, *Who's this guy and what's his problem?*

Happily, she seemed neither flustered nor agitated. On the one hand, this was good news. I didn't want a riled-up moose on my doorstep. On the other hand, she didn't appear ready to give up her newfound snack.

Emboldened by the cow's easygoing manner, I opened the door wider and took a small step forward. Then, once more, I softly urged them to leave my small but precious strawberry patch, while both mom and calf watched intently. I too felt calm; but I was ready to bolt inside at the slightest sign of aggression.

The calf stood. And the cow, God bless her, took a tentative step backwards, as if not quite sure how to respond. It was then that I noticed the second calf, lying twenty feet away on the lawn. Neither of the twins seemed anxious. Like their mom, they seemed more curious than alarmed by the unfolding encounter.

Ever so slowly, the cow backed out of the berry patch. Followed by calf number one she began to cross the front deck, head still turned toward me. Every now and then she would roll her tongue across her lips. I know it's a tricky and potentially foolhardy thing to read or interpret an animal's behavior or intentions, but I got the strongest sense that the cow was savoring those strawberry plants, with their dark green leaves and ripening berries. She really didn't want to leave such a tasty meal, when so much remained on the earthy plate of my garden.

"Gowan, gowan," I continued to urge the moose family. "I really don't want you eating my strawberries, so leave them alone, OK?"

Strangely enough I didn't feel foolish, talking to the moose this way. And whether it was the tone of my voice, my body language, or something else I can't imagine, the mom and her calves seemed responsive to my pleas. Very slowly, almost reluctantly, they continued their retreat across the yard. The cow looked huge; her legs likely reached up to my chest and she must have weighed close to one thousand pounds. The gangly calves reminded me of young colts; several weeks old, their heads were probably as high as my shoulders.

Within a few minutes, they reached the far end of my front lawn. There the cow began gulping down alder and birch leaves. The calves, too, picked at the bushes. But from time to time, one or more would look back at me.

By now I was out on the deck, arms crossed and gaze steady in their direction. Almost since I first opened the door, part of me wanted to go into the house and awaken Mom, tell her about this amazing spectacle. But I didn't want to abandon my post. I felt sure that if I went inside, the cow would return to the berry patch. And I wouldn't be able to so easily shoo her away a second time.

So I stayed and watched while the moose ate wild greens. At a casual browsing pace, they gradually moved downhill from the front yard to the back, still occasionally glancing in my direction. Not once did they seem agitated by my presence. From the lawn they slipped into the thick forest that borders the back yard, still eating as they moved. Nearly a half hour had passed from my first sighting to their disappearance among birch and spruce trees.

I walked over to the patch to inspect the damage. Several plants had been cleanly clipped; a few had been pulled from the ground and others trampled. But overall, the losses were light.

Anticipating the moose family's eventual return, I thought about how I might protect my strawberries until harvesting enough for at least one scrumptious pie. Yet any frustration over their raid and concern about possible future ones was softened by the absolute delight of this unexpected encounter. Moose and berries: I never would have guessed. Given our shared taste for feral strawberries, how could I begrudge the cow her nibbling of the plants?

I'm happy to report the moose family left our berries alone the rest of the summer, presumably after finding more attractive and nutritious fare. And I never found evidence of the patch being raided in succeeding years. Why then and then only? I have no idea.

Even now I can't help but chuckle at the memory of the cow moose licking her lips and reluctantly leaving the berry patch behind, much like a kid retreating from an unhappy neighbor's apple orchard, the taste still sweet in her mouth.

AUTUMN: HERDS OF MOOSE, CROWDS OF PEOPLE

If Anchorage is among the best places in Alaska to find moose in summer, spring, and winter, the city's wild neighbor, Chugach State Park, is arguably the best place anywhere to watch *Alces alces* during the annual autumnal rut. It's better than even the more celebrated Denali National Park, where every fall swarms of visitors driving the park road create "moose jams" whenever battling bulls are spotted.

Bulls, cows, and calves begin to converge in late August or early September (calves tagging along with their amorous moms). At the peak of rutting—sometime in October—dozens of moose congregate in a well-defined corridor within the Chugach Front Range: the thicketed subalpine habitat and spruce woodlands that border the South Fork of Campbell Creek, upstream of its confluence with the Middle Fork. Happily for wildlife watchers, this rutting area is only a short walk from the Glen Alps parking lot, the most popular entry point into Anchorage's "backyard wilderness."

I first stumbled upon this impressive gathering in the late 1980s. Back then, only a small number of locals appeared to know about it, most of them serious wildlife photographers. Some days you might see more moose than people. But by the early 2000s, what once seemed like a fantastic secret had been revealed to the masses. By the start of the century's second decade, the number of moose viewers had grown to the point that on a sunny autumn Saturday or Sunday, hundreds of people walked the Powerline and Middle Fork Loop Trails, most of them armed with binoculars, spotting scopes, and big-lens cameras. Many were tourists who learned, one way or another, about this world-class wildlife spectacle just beyond Alaska's urban center.

Curiously, at the same time that growing crowds were coming to watch these "Hillside moose," a handful of longtime observers—primarily wildlife photographers—began to lament the animals' decline. Eberhard Brunner says that he once regularly counted more than a hundred moose within the Middle and South

Forks valleys during this autumnal-early winter gathering, but in both 2012 and 2013 he saw less than half that total. Others estimate that the rut and post-rut numbers here have dropped between 50 and 90 percent in recent years. I haven't noticed such a drastic decline, but neither have I counted anything close to one hundred moose. Nor have wildlife managers documented such a dramatic drop. But Brunner argues that he puts more faith in people who regularly visit the front range looking for moose than biologists who go there rarely.

For most people, of course, seeing thirty or forty or even ten moose in one place is an amazing thing.

It's not only the large numbers of moose that pull people here, though that is surely a major draw. I once counted two dozen moose from a single spot, spread across a mile or so of valley bottom. And in the course of a walk I've tallied more than thirty. But an acquaintance confided that in 2012 she and her husband saw more than forty moose, a mix of cows and bulls, while standing quietly and still along the Powerline Trail.

The other thing that makes this annual gathering so unusual is the animals' tolerance of gawking humans. It's not a strategy that I would recommend, but I have seen photographers and videographers standing in an open meadow and surrounded by a dozen or more moose, with large bulls passing within twenty feet, maybe less. These are animals that may stand seven feet tall at the shoulders, weigh twelve hundred to fifteen hundred pounds, and carry antlers that measure sixty to seventy inches across (and sometimes more).

Anyone who's watched rutting bulls battle, or witnessed an agitated adult moose of either sex in a full-blown charge, knows that these animals could, if they become upset, easily gore or trample a person to death. Besides the risk of serious injury, Brunner and other photographers speculate that such aggressive human behavior, plus the increased presence of dogs, might help account for the drop in moose numbers they've observed. Maybe the moose are less tolerant of us and our pets than they seem.

Though I haven't heard of any injuries suffered during the Chugach rut, I wouldn't be surprised if it happens someday, given the chances that people take.

Neither would researcher Vic Van Ballenberghe. During his many years of studying moose at Denali National Park, he was deeply impressed by the single-minded determination of rutting bulls, sometimes expressed with explosive violence.

At Denali, the place Van Ballenberghe knows best, the ritual begins "like clockwork" in late August, when bulls begin to lose the velvet from their antlers. This is also when they dig rutting pits: shallow, elongated depressions into which they urinate. Both bulls and cows may wallow in such pits or splash the urine-mud mixture onto their antlers, head, neck, and shoulders.

Around September 1, Denali's dominant bulls stop feeding and begin their search for cows. At midmonth, bulls start to actively herd cows into breeding groups and they also become more vocal. Their grunts—described by biologists as "croaks"—are made while traveling alone, during courtship, or in response to rival bulls. Breeding at Denali normally begins the last week of September and reaches a peak about October 1. The rut then gradually winds down and ends by October 10.

The breeding groups of cows are sometimes called "harems," but they are more of a loose aggregation. "The bulls don't really have control over the cows," Van Ballenberghe explains. "A cow can leave a bull if she's serious about it." The largest assembly he has seen numbered thirty-four moose: twenty-two cows and twelve bulls. Besides the dominant bull, other males—called "satellite bulls"—hang out along the margins and sometimes breed with cows on the periphery.

It's nearly impossible for a bull to stay in charge of things throughout the rut. During the peak, the dominant bull may be challenged several times daily and the fighting eventually takes a toll. "It's sort of like being in a bar," Van Ballenberghe once told me with a grin. "Sooner or later, somebody's going to come along who's tougher."

Confrontations normally begin with displays and threats and eventually escalate into sparring and, sometimes, fierce fights. Injuries are part of the ritual. About one-third of the dominant bulls are harmed, Van Ballenberghe says, some fatally. Few bulls live beyond age ten or eleven, while the average life span of cows is fifteen to sixteen years and some live to be twenty or older.

When the rut ends, the moose split up. Younger bulls remain with the cows, while the more dominant bulls go off by themselves in loose groups of up to ten animals.

The timing may be slightly different and not as well defined, but the pattern remains the same in Chugach State Park: moose coming together briefly in large numbers to engage in mating rituals and, for some bulls, to do battle. And, where access is easy, people following the moose in growing crowds, caught up in the season's excitement.

RETURN TO WINTER: THE CIRCLE OF LIFE AND DEATH

Hiking through the mountains above Anchorage one October, I noticed a large, brown lump in the snow, about seventy-five feet off the trail. My curiosity piqued, I moved closer. And the lump became a moose. Lying sprawled in a snow-covered meadow, beneath a solitary spruce tree, its still body was growing cold in the 20°F chill. Its stomach was already taut with gases and small ice crystals circled its mouth.

It wasn't a big moose: three hundred pounds, give or take. And there were no "bumps" signaling the start of antler growth. My best guess was a female calf, one of this year's offspring.

In its dying moments the calf had collapsed onto its left side, legs outstretched and head tilted so that its right eye gazed, in an unfocused way, up into a pale blue sky. That wide-open eye, still a clear, dark pool of chocolate-brown tissue, was what tugged on me most, pulled me in close. Not a hunter of wild game, I had never been this close to a dead moose before. I waved my hand across its face, some part of me expecting the eye to blink or the moose to flinch. Nothing moved.

Eyes, it's been said, are windows to the soul. For moose as well as humans? To someone raised a Lutheran and later schooled in the sciences, such a notion might be quickly dismissed as ridiculous, if not blasphemous. But growing older, I find myself heartened by the ancient—and in some parts of our modern, western culture, resurrected—belief that everything has a spirit, a soul: moose, ravens, spiders, spruce trees, snow, clouds, rocks, mountains, Earth, stars. I find it arrogant that we civilized, industrialized and modernized, technology addicted humans are so certain that we know better than more primitive and intuitive peoples, while assuming that either we alone are soulful beings or that there is no soul at all.

As I considered these notions in the presence of the moose, a shift occurred: *it* became *she*.

This particular eye offered no revelations, except to tell me that the calf's physical life had very recently ended. Eyeballs are a delicacy to ravens, usually among the first scavengers to find and pick at a carcass. Ravens on their daily winter commute between Anchorage and the Chugach Mountains—morning flights into town and evening trips back to the hills, as though playfully mimicking the area's human residents—would soon spot a lifeless moose stretched out in the snow and rush in to begin their feast.

The image of an eye being pecked has always seemed gruesome to me. I've seen the same behavior with gulls feeding on dead or dying salmon: the eyes are gobbled first.

Still considering the notion of eyes as windows to the soul, I whimsically pondered whether the scavengers' choice might have something to do with their wish to not be observed by the dead animal's spirit while picking at a carcass. Biologists offer a simpler, more organic explanation: eyes, being soft tissue, are easy pickings to scavengers. Plus they're among the more nutritious body parts. It makes good sense for opportunistic feeders to go immediately for soft, nourishing spots like the eyes, for the same reason that larger scavengers, like bears, go for the guts: easy entry, easy feasting.

Circling the body, then kneeling beside it, I found no signs of predation or injury. Beside the calf's head was one discolored patch of snow, pinkish-yellow and silver-dollar-sized. The fluid could have come from nose or mouth. But there were no apparent wounds, no blood on the fur. And no tracks that hinted of other animals, no tufts of hair pulled loose, no sign of a struggle. Starvation and exhaustion were other possibilities—but so early in winter? The weather had been mild in recent days and less than two feet of snow covered the ground. Down in Anchorage, internal injuries might have been suspected, from a run-in with a car or truck. Here the nearest road is more than a mile away and it seemed unlikely that a crash victim would head for the hills to die. Besides, I could see no outward evidence of trauma.

What, then? Perhaps some illness, though local biologists say there's little in the way of moose diseases here. Maybe an injury that my untrained eye didn't notice. Or some genetic weakness. Goaded by uncertainty, I thought about the calf's final days and hours. What brought her to this place? Was she alone? Sick? Abandoned? Did she simply collapse, too weak to regain her feet? Backtracking along the moose's trail, I found no evidence of other falls or stumbles, no sign of other animals. But there may have been much written in the snow, in the calf's posture or her body, that I failed to notice. The more I looked for evidence, the more I realized how little I know about moose specifically and wildlife in general. Again I asked myself: *What am I missing here?*

More questions floated past, moving beyond science and simple observation. Did the calf's mother know she was dying? And when did the cow leave her offspring? Do moose in any way grieve? And why does all this seem to matter so?

Had the moose calf touched some fear I have of dying alone, abandoned? I seemed unable to find any good answers, only more questions. Some days it's that way.

Kneeling beside the moose, I stroked her fur and touched her face, back, hooves, and ears. And I stared again into the fathomless depths of that dark, unblinking eye. Seeking some connection, not certain what I'd found. I didn't stay long, maybe fifteen minutes. But before returning to the trail and my afternoon hike, I offered a prayer—a simple bow of respect—to the moose, the circle of life and death, and the magnificent mystery of it all.

WATCHING BELUGAS

The afternoon was a beauty, with abundant sunshine, an ocean of blue skies, crisp air, and just a wisp of a breeze. But as beautiful as it was, the day had an ordinary feel as I accompanied my collie mix, Coya, along Anchorage's Coastal Trail, a popular pathway that borders the city's western edge.

Then, out of the corner of my eye, I noticed a large splash, or something like it, in the dark waters of Cook Inlet.

Over the years, I'd made it a habit to bring binoculars on my daily walks with Coya, for moments such as this. Raising lenses to eyes, I spotted another splash of white. Now magnified, the splash became a beluga whale. Moments later I saw another whale. And another. And still more. Some of the whales were brilliantly white against the inlet's dark waters, others were gray.

I can't say I was shocked to see belugas only a few miles from downtown Anchorage. An isolated and genetically distinct population of the smallish, northern white whales has long been known to inhabit these waters. Anecdotal accounts suggest that a few thousand belugas resided in Cook Inlet less than a century ago and as recently as 1979 the National Marine Fisheries Service (NMFS) estimated the inlet's population at thirteen hundred whales. Their numbers have dropped dramatically since then. That decline was initially blamed on overharvest by subsistence whalers. But beluga numbers continued to fall even after the hunt ended, suggesting other unknown factors to be at play. What those are remain unclear.

Nowadays a few hundred closely monitored belugas inhabit Cook Inlet year-round and their seasonal movements sometimes bring them within a mile or less of Alaska's urban center. Still, in more than a quarter century of living here, I'd seen belugas from the city's edge only a handful of times. So if not stunned, I was surely elated by the encounter.

The sighting carried added meaning because the previous year I had joined a brand-new citizen-science effort. Called the Anchorage Coastal Beluga Survey, it was intended to help federal mangers track the whales. The survey was the brain-child of Barbara Carlson, a longtime resident and driving force behind Friends of the Anchorage Coastal Wildlife Refuge. Consisting of tidal flats, marshes, and boggy forest, this state preserve stretches sixteen miles along the city's coastline and is seasonally inhabited by more than 120 species of birds plus assorted fish and mammals, including the belugas that sometimes pass through refuge waters at high tide (and whose bodies occasionally wash up on shore).

Carlson's concerns about the belugas' health inspired the citizen-survey pro-gram, whose goal was to gather data on the distribution, behavior, and relative abundance of belugas along Anchorage's coast. By the fall of 2008, she was ready to launch the volunteer effort, with help from several partners: Defenders of Wild-life, independent researcher Dr. Tamara McGuire, and the National Oceanic and Atmospheric Administration (NOAA), along with that agency's research arm, the NMFS. Some two dozen people responded to the call. After a start-up orienta-tion, volunteers were divided among three different sites considered ideal for spot-ting belugas.

The timing of this citizen-science effort couldn't have been better. After years of studies and controversy, NOAA/NMFS had finally listed Cook Inlet's beluga whale population as an endangered species. That listing required NOAA to iden-tify critical habitat throughout Cook Inlet that merits special protection. To do that, researchers would have to learn more about the whales' seasonal habits and distribution. And that's where the citizen survey came into play.

The first year's survey got a late start and lasted only a week, before wintry weather ended the effort. I was among the very first volunteers to look for the belugas as they moved through the upper inlet—and also among the first to record a sighting.

The memory of that October day is still vivid. Three of us stood atop a grassy, sand-dune bluff, along the edges of Anchorage's Kincaid Park. Only the slightest of breezes moved across the land and adjacent seascape, which made us doubly happy; first, because the air temperature hovered just above freezing; second, because the inlet was only slightly rippled, which made our job so much easier.

Five minutes into our two-hour shift, team leader Erika McDonald looked up from her data sheets and shouted, "I think I might see a whale."

Aiming my binoculars in the direction Erika pointed, I quickly confirmed the sighting. "Yep. No question it's a beluga." Not only was the whale white, it lacked a dorsal fin, one of the species' defining features. And a brief glimpse of its mostly submerged head revealed a characteristically bulbous shape.

With Pixie Siebe on the team's spotting scope and me squinting through binoculars, we began to count individuals, note the presence of calves, and determine the whales' color—calves and some adults are gray, not white—the latter not an easy task with the sun gleaming on the inlet's calm waters.

Rotating through each of the positions (spotting scope, binoculars, data recording), we followed the whales for an hour as they moved steadily along the coast, until gone from sight. In the end, we three agreed that we saw at least thirteen individuals, including two calves.

Months later, on my walk with Coya, conditions were even better for beluga watching. Not only was the inlet calm, but the sun's position in the sky fully revealed the varied shading of individual whales, from bone white to medium gray and a darker, muddy gray that almost matched the sediment-rich water. As a rule, mature belugas tend to be white, while juveniles and calves are gray. But researchers have found that the rule doesn't always hold; while a white whale is sure to be an adult, the bodies of some mature whales are, for uncertain reasons, gray.

My own body pumped with adrenaline as I tracked the whales. They moved steadily up the inlet, the tops of their bodies surfacing only a moment before disappearing again.

As I had learned the previous fall, counting belugas is a tricky thing, requiring patience. I counted and recounted their numbers as the whales approached, then passed my section of coastal flats, and gradually moved away. After fifteen minutes of steady, focused observation, I was confident I had seen at least nine whales, five of them white, three medium gray, and one much darker gray. The latter was also substantially smaller, suggesting a calf or yearling.

The whales appeared to be swimming in a line and there was something about their pace, their steady direction of movement, that suggested they were headed for some destination. Perhaps a place to hunt salmon? Voracious fish eaters, they're known to follow the schools of salmon that return to Cook Inlet streams each year, including runs to a couple of Anchorage creeks. Were they bound for Ship Creek, which empties near the city's port, after passing through downtown Anchorage? Or were they headed farther up the inlet to more remote rivers?

Returning my attention to land, I watched other trail-goers to gauge their response to the whales' passage. During the short time I was stopped, none of the other bicyclists, runners and dog walkers paused, except for a pair of runners to whom I shouted, "Hey, there's a pod of belugas out in the inlet."

Even they stopped only briefly to admire the whales' presence, and then returned to their running. All those people moving quickly past reminded me that I also spend way too much of my life rushing here and there, missing lots along the way. That's one reason I love my dog walks, done at a more leisurely pace.

Finally I turned to Coya, who showed her own great patience while I watched the whales. Resuming our walk, I realized I would never forget the belugas' passage, nor the passing of people moving fast along the trail, missing one heck of a spectacle on what had become one spectacular afternoon.

POINT WORONZOF'S
SPECTACLE OF SWALLOWS

On a cool and overcast morning in early summer, two gray-haired and bearded men stood several feet off Anchorage's Coastal Trail, joined in what appeared to be a lively discussion. Their bodies brushed against the orange plastic fencing that's supposed to keep people away from the undercut and actively eroding bluff edges that mark Point Woronzof's perimeter. Now and then one of the men lifted his binoculars or pointed offshore, the other nodding his agreement or understanding. Though they could have been there for many reasons, I guessed them to be birders.

I too had ventured off the paved trail, lured close to the bluff's edge by scores of swooping and diving swallows—swallows that, I assumed, had drawn the nearby men.

I had first noticed Point Woronzof's wealth of swallows several years earlier, but didn't think much about it then. As time passed, I would occasionally question why they seemed to congregate along this particular stretch of bluffs each June and July, a long stone's throw from Anchorage's international airport and beneath the busy flight path of passenger and cargo jets. But I wasn't yet curious enough to find out more about their lives.

Then, while on a winter beach walk, I happened to look up at this same expanse of bluffs. What I saw both startled me and solved the swallow riddle. Hundreds of small holes pockmarked the steep slope's upper layers, clear evidence of a nesting colony.

Still, I didn't know what kind of swallows. Or why they had chosen these noisy bluffs for their summer home.

Though I'd become a fairly competent bird-watcher in my middle-aged years, with a special fondness for passerines, distinguishing one type of swallow from another has always proved a challenge, especially at a distance. And I'd never looked closely enough at Point Woronzof's bunch to identify the species.

I had simply assumed the birds to be either tree swallows or violet-green swallows, the kinds most commonly seen in and around Anchorage. A little research would have revealed that neither trees nor violet-greens colonize steep sediment banks like those that form Anchorage's coastal bluffs.

After fifteen minutes or so of watching the swallows that summer afternoon, I headed back to the trail. Passing the two men, I nodded hello and commented, "Pretty amazing, isn't it?"

"Sure is," one of the men drawled.

A few steps down the trail, I glanced back. Heads upraised, the men were intently focused on a jet that roared its approach. As the airliner passed over, their heads swiveled, following it to touchdown. Only slowly did their bodies and gazes return toward Cook Inlet. And in those moments I realized that while we shared the bluff, we inhabited different worlds.

I was surprised, even shocked by my error, but I shouldn't have been. Nearly every time I walk, bike, or drive to Point Woronzof, I see people parked in cars or standing along the bluffs, many outfitted with binoculars or cameras, mesmerized by jumbo jets. I've always found it strange that people would choose to spend their free time watching jets come and go—though there's certainly no better place to do so, that I'm aware. But who's a bird-watcher to be talking about peculiar habits in an age when technology dominates?

Perturbed by this technology worship and suddenly annoyed by my own ignorance of swallows, I left the bluffs determined to know more about the birds.

Other summer diversions and adventures intervened, so weeks passed before I returned my attention to the swallows. Joined by Coya, my collie mix and faithful hiking companion, I drove to the Point Woronzof parking lot and descended to the beach.

A five-minute walk brought us to the cavity-ridden bluffs, which by my rough estimate are one hundred feet high, give or take. While my water-loving dog went swimming in Cook Inlet, I pulled out binoculars for a closer look, plus notebook and pen to record my observations.

The birds were essentially two-toned: brown on top and mostly white on the bottom, with a distinctive brown breast band, which vaguely resembled a collar. That, I later learned, clearly identified them as bank swallows.

Besides being the least showy of Alaska's five common species of swallows, *Riparia riparia* is also the smallest, though only by a smidgen. You'd have to hold them side-by-side to know that a bank swallow is a half inch shorter than either a tree or violet-green.

Like others of their kind, bank swallows are superb fliers, able to abruptly change direction to grab the insects they so love to eat. Among their favorite foods are mosquitoes and other soft-bodied insects, like flies and wasps and moths.

Over the years, Point Woronzof's bank swallows have excavated hundreds, if not thousands, of holes in the bluffs, along a stretch of several hundred feet. The abundance of holes is misleading though, because swallows dig new ones every year. Males begin the excavation by pecking the start of a hole, then show off their work to potential mates. Once a female has decided she's found the right guy, both partners will finish the job, first with their beaks and then their feet.

Were I skilled or foolish enough to climb the bluff and peer inside a cavity, I would likely find it to be a few inches across—easy for the swallows to enter, not so easy for unwanted intruders—two or three feet long, and angled slightly upward (to help keep it dry). At the far end of the tunnel there'd be a slightly larger nest chamber, lined with grass or other soft plant debris.

Nearly all of the nest cavities are within five or six feet of the top, in what appears to be silt or clay-rich layers.

Up to ten feet thick in places, the nesting layers are firmer and more stable than the cliff's predominant sands and gravels, which are actively being worn away by wind, water, and gravity. During the quiet interludes between jet arrivals or departures, it's possible to hear the steady clatter of falling rocks when standing below the bluffs. And a continuous sloughing of sand feeds the small, funnel-shaped deposits that are building at their bottom.

From the beach, I could more easily see why the municipality tries to keep people away from the edge of the cliffs. One section of chain-link fence hung over the side, a victim of the bluff's erosion. Here and there, the top layer of crumbly soil was undercut by several feet, ready to collapse. Elsewhere dense thickets of alder and elderberry and cow parsnip grew right up to the cliff face.

All of this, along with the bluff's steep face (nearly vertical to overhanging where the nests are built), adds security to the colony because it diminishes the danger of predation from egg or nestling hunters, which in Anchorage might range from magpies, ravens, and gulls to coyotes, foxes, and weasels.

Once fledged, swallows face other dangers. Several raptors that inhabit the Anchorage area are accomplished passerine hunters. Earlier in the year, I spotted a merlin—a small, songbird-hunting falcon—in the woods not far from here.

If I were patient enough and had enough time, I could map or otherwise document the active nest holes and accurately determine the size of this colony. But I'm more of a casual naturalist than scientist, so I've been content to simply watch the comings and goings of parents and from such observations have concluded that scores of swallows converge here each summer.

In the thirty to forty-five minutes that I watched the swallows and studied their colony from below that June afternoon, a handful of jets and commuter planes flew past. I instinctively ducked from the rumble and roar that the biggest and loudest of the aircraft hurled to Earth with their landings.

Long after my beach walk with Coya, I continue to be amazed that these swallows go about their lives while bombarded with the comings and goings of jets, hour after hour, day after day. It seems something of a miracle that they can coexist.

I returned in early July to check on the swallows. From atop the bluff, I observed some entering their nests, which meant their young—and those of neighboring parents—hadn't yet emerged. Swallows, like other colony nesting birds, practice synchronous birthing: females lay their eggs at about the same time, which of course means that eggs will hatch and nestlings will become fledglings across a small window of time. It's a way to limit predation on the group as a whole.

For bank swallows, the nestling stage lasts about three weeks. Once they exit as fledglings, swallows almost immediately begin to hunt on their own, though parents will accompany their young for a few days. Once the fledglings are independent, the entire flock—which oddly is called a "foreclosure"—will aban-don its cliff-side colony.

The flock will continue to hang around the city while adults replace old feathers with new in the annual rite of molting. Then they'll leave Anchorage, bound for wintering grounds somewhere in South America.

While I watched, bunches of swallows swooped and dived and streaked along the bluff edge, past the alder and red-berried elder thickets, across grassy meadows, and out over the inlet, voices faintly buzzing as they chased meals for themselves and their young. Their presence could hardly be ignored. Yet the walk-ers and cyclists who passed by barely seemed to notice. I reminded myself that I hadn't either, not so long ago.

Leaving my bluff-top post, I headed down to the Point Woronzof parking lot and pond. Several times over the past few years I had watched groups of swal-lows glide low across the pond, now and then touching its surface with a splash. I've wondered what, exactly, the splashing is about. Is it bird-bathing on the fly? Attempts to pick insects off the water? Fledgling training?

Now I know. Pat Pourchot, one of Anchorage's most accomplished birders, has informed me that the sharp-eyed swallows are scooping up newly hatched insects as they're emerging from the pond. "Easier pickings on the water than on the wing, probably," he explains.

The pond itself is something of a marvel, though few people who come here seem to know or care. Each year, dozens of wood frogs convene in this small water hole to sing and mate and lay gelatinous masses containing thousands of eggs, then head off to spend the rest of the summer in moist woodlands. Besides the frogs and their tadpole offspring, all sorts of bugs—many of them fearsome and voracious in their microcosmic world—inhabit the pond's waters and muddy bottom, some des-tined to help feed the nearby swallow colony.

Pourchot confirms some of what I've guessed about Point Woronzof's swal-lows and fills in more details. Bank swallows have been nesting here for at least several decades and likely much longer. Certainly they've seasonally resided here longer than jets have been landing at Anchorage International, which helps explain their fidelity to the spot.

Pourchot adds that this is the largest, and maybe the only, bank swallow colony in Anchorage. "It is the sure-bet place we always go for 'Big Days' [when birders observe as many species as possible in a twenty-four-hour period] to see bank swallows, although swallows range widely to feed and they can often be seen at lakes around town."

Apparently the bluff's advantages—good nest-building material, good hunting, and protection from predators—outweigh any disturbances from thundering airliners and cargo jets. Still, the juxtaposition of swallow colony and airport strikes me as an amazing thing, one of our city's more unlikely sets of neighbors for a couple of months each year.

Mid-July. Swallows continued to enter their holes in the ground, but it wouldn't be long—a few days, perhaps—before their young were ready to take flight.

As usual, people stood atop the bluffs, watching the jets. Only minutes apart, one huge aircraft after another dropped low over the inlet, over the bluffs, and onto the runway. Wingtip vortices swirled along the ground, whipped the trees and bushes.

I watched the swallows to see how they responded to the noise and turbulence. Before a jet's approach, dozens of them circled in front of and above the bluffs, hunting insects. With food in beak, they darted toward the cavities they'd dug and quickly ducked inside.

As the rumble of a cargo jet grew louder, the swallows suddenly dispersed. By the time it arrived, they'd disappeared.

Moments after the jet landed, the bank swallows were back, circling, darting, catching bugs, feeding nestlings that would soon take wing and join Point Woronzof's remarkable midsummer air show. By the end of the month, both parents and offspring would be ready for the long flight south.

SQUIRRELLY BEHAVIOR

IN THE YARD

Sitting at my office desk, I gazed absent-mindedly out the window into the back yard. My wandering thoughts were soon pulled into sharp focus by the sight of spruce cones falling to the ground. Well, not falling exactly; being hurled. The red squirrels with whom I share my Anchorage yard were once again busily preparing for winter.

Among the most common residents of Alaska's forests (and northern cousins of the gray squirrels that inhabit most of the United States), red squirrels remain active year-round. And they depend heavily on spruce cones to survive winter's scarcity. In Anchorage, squirrels begin collecting cones in August and they continue to build their caches through September and even into October, assuming supplies last.

In more remote areas, the success of a squirrel's autumnal cone harvest will largely determine whether or not it survives Alaska's longest, harshest season, but starvation isn't a problem on Anchorage's Hillside. Here, squirrels can supplement their cone diet with the peanuts and sunflower seeds put outdoors by people like me.

Still, the cone harvest remains an instinctive ritual. Watching the squirrels' frenzied movements in backyard spruces, I sensed a life-and-death urgency, as if there were no time to waste.

The squirrel I watched that September morning was a study in agility and hustle. After sprinting high up a tree trunk, it scampered out to the far reaches of a flimsy, swaying branch and stretched its body as far as it would reach. Then with quick, precise bites, the squirrel snipped several cones and, one after another, it flipped them with mouth or paws to the ground below. The cones carved a smooth arc through the crisp autumn air and landed with a soft thud on the lawn or adjacent forest floor.

Sometimes reaching far overhead, other times hanging upside down, held in place by the strong grip of back feet on branch, the squirrel was a superb contortionist, the envy of any gymnast.

Finished with one clump, it rushed to another. And another. The spruce trees in my yard alone had produced tens of thousands of cones; their tops were heavy with huge clusters of bright, scaly, greenish-brown fruits. There were more cones, by far, than I'd ever seen in my nine years here. Enough for several winters, it seemed. With so much to choose from, what was the rush? Which raised another question: did the squirrel somehow know that this was a year of plenty? Perhaps its hoarding instinct had been sent into frenzied overdrive by the unusual abundance.

Watching the squirrel, I was reminded of my own fall harvest: picking blueberries. Though I've picked and gobbled these small wild fruits for as long as I can remember, only in recent years had such casual picking become a more formal, and valued, seasonal ritual. Now, I annually head into the backcountry in late summer and early fall expressly to collect wild berries.

My motivations are different from the squirrels'. Certainly the berries feed my body; but more than that, the deliberate act of harvesting them feeds my spirit.

In Alaska, where summers seem too short and autumns are even shorter, berry picking is one way to celebrate the changing seasons, instead of fighting the downhill slide into winter's cold and darkness. It's also a way of becoming better acquainted—and more physically connected—with my home landscape. By collecting and consuming the berries that grow in my wild "back yard," I more fully participate in the seasonal cycles. I digest and absorb the fruits of my homeland.

The same year I watched the squirrels' frenetic harvest, I picked about two and a half gallons of blueberries on a handful of trips into the mountains. That's a minuscule haul by most harvesting standards and hardly worth mentioning when compared to the bulk of foods that I annually purchase at the grocery store. Yet it was enough to make a few meals of blueberry pancakes and several pies, which I would share with family and friends—another valued part of the ritual.

While the squirrel's harvest is directly tied to its survival, mine becomes a symbolic act, a personal reminder that *all* my food comes from the Earth, not from supermarkets and food-packaging producers.

Later in the day, I left my home office and walked through the yard, checking on the squirrel's work. Beneath one tree, I counted nearly five hundred cones scattered on the lawn. Beneath another spruce, I found several hundred more. I also discovered a "midden," where the squirrel had begun storing the cones it dropped to the ground.

While my harvest had already ended, squirrels would continue theirs for several more weeks. Snipping, tossing, and caching cones, rushing up and down one spruce and then another, they were daily reminders that winter was fast approaching. They also reminded me to celebrate, and give thanks for, the abundance in my own life.

ON THE TRAIL

Surprised by the sound of footsteps crunching gravel, a red squirrel rushed out of the forest understory and skittered several feet up the deeply furrowed bark of a cottonwood tree. The squirrel then stopped, swung its head, and looked toward the approaching hiker.

The hiker—me, of course—had in turn been alerted by the squirrel's anxious dash from bushes to tree, which produced a loud, leafy rustling. So I stopped too, and directed my gaze toward the squirrel, whose stretched-out, tree-hugging body was some thirty feet off the trail.

Normally I would have simply nodded my greetings and perhaps said "Hello, Mr. Squirrel," then continued my woodland walk. But on that fall afternoon, I noticed that the squirrel held a large, reddish clump in its mouth. Wanting to know more, I put binoculars to eyes, focused on the animal, and learned something new: the red squirrel's diet includes devil's club berries. He had plucked a spiny stem rich with the bright red fruits.

Though considered bitterly inedible by humans, devil's club berries are known to be a favorite food of black bears. I've also seen songbirds nibbling the berries in winter, when food choices are limited. But I had never imagined them to be part of a squirrel's diet.

I'm not sure why this surprised me so. From both research and my own observations, I know that red squirrels, like bears and humans and ravens, are opportunistic omnivores. They'll eat all sorts of forest foods, from seeds and berries and fungi and leaf buds to insects and bird eggs and even the occasional songbird nestling. Still, I tend to link our local squirrels with two basic food groups: spruce cones and birdseed.

Following the previous year's spruce-cone bust, that summer had produced a healthy crop. For several weeks neighborhood squirrels had been snipping cones from needled spruce limbs and hurling them to the ground for later retrieval.

Then there's the fondness for birdseed. Once I scattered black-oil sunflower seeds along the upper-deck railing of my Hillside home each fall, it was a toss-up as to which critters would find the seed first: black-capped chickadees and red-breasted nuthatches, or squirrels. Eventually I began to put peanuts on the ground, hoping they would satisfy the squirrels' appetite. I should have known better. Even with the peanut offering, the upper-deck feeders would inevitably be visited by one or more squirrels during the months ahead.

Truth be told, I really didn't mind an occasional raid. It was only when they became marauding regulars that I, in turn, became territorially assertive and chased them off. Squirrels, I like to think, understand such combative behavior, since they also aggressively defend their small homelands from one another, driving off trespassing sneaks.

Because they're small and common and sometimes an annoyance, red squirrels are usually overlooked or ignored by people (except for bird-feeding types defending their turf and some hunters), even those who consider themselves wildlife lovers. Rarely, if ever, do you see folks *oohing* or *aahing* at a squirrel, as they do at bears, moose, Dall sheep, or even a beaver or porcupine.

I too sometimes take squirrels for granted. And occasionally I curse them. But they're among my favorite forest critters and I listen for their chatter on my hikes, just as I keep my ears alert for birdsong. The simple fact is this: our forests would seem much emptier without squirrels and songbirds. In deepest winter, when sometimes even squirrels and chickadees are quiet, local woodlands are indeed lonelier places to someone who appreciates their company and voices.

When I'm walking through the woods, the presence of a nearby squirrel is almost always enough to get me to stop. Their energy and antics lift my spirits, bring a smile to my face, occasionally even make me goofy. Sometimes we simply watch each other a while; other times we may engage in nonsensical conversations.

I know it's silly, if not downright odd, but occasionally I chitter and chatter back to the squirrel. It's my way of being playful, though I'm not sure the squirrels agree. As often as not, they respond with what seems like agitated scolding.

In gaining my attention, squirrels reveal bits and pieces of their lives. Once, for example, I discovered that a squirrel inhabiting a campground area had somehow lugged a full roll of toilet paper high into a spruce tree. The roll was partially shredded, its new owner apparently using the paper for nest material.

I have also seen a squirrel sitting atop a drooping rose bush, eating rose hips, and another carrying a mushroom up a tree. I'm especially intrigued by their taste for fungi. How do they know which mushrooms are poisonous? Do they ever become intoxicated by nibbling *Amanitas*? As a companion once commented, "Some of them seem like they're on psychedelics."

My walks along the Turnagain Arm Trail have certainly produced their share of squirrelly surprises. Once while passing a stand of cottonwoods, I witnessed a most amazing sight: on one large limb, a squirrel squatted beside a pile of white fluff. Hunched over, tail laid flat along the branch, it was eating the seeds from green, cob-like cottonwood pods, much like a person would eat corn-on-the-cob, discarding the pod's cottony fibers as it dined. Scanning the tree, I spotted a half dozen more cotton piles scattered along its branches, some as large as cantaloupe melons.

Only a couple of months after that June sighting, I happened upon the squirrel carrying devil's club berries. I wish I could have seen the squirrel in action. I know they're nimble creatures, but how easily could one can balance itself on that large-leafed spiny plant while snipping the berry cluster from its swaying top? And aren't they bothered by the plant's thorny stalks and leaves?

For a while after I took up bird feeding, I didn't consider red squirrels to be much more than thieving little rodents. But the more I've learned, the more impressed I've become with the ways of *Tamiasciurus hudsonicus*, from their climbing and jumping talents to their dietary tastes and food-harvesting methods. I hope the squirrels have sensed my appreciation and delight, even when I've chased them from my feeders, growling in my human way while they squeak their upset.

Maybe some day I'll even go so far as to spice up my offerings to squirrels, adding a spike of devil's club berries, perhaps even rose hips and mushrooms, to the pile of peanuts I leave for my chattering, rascally neighbors.

LEAVING THE NEST

Stepping out the front door on my way to get the Sunday newspaper, I glanced to my left, toward a birch tree at the edge of the lawn. Nailed to the tree was a wooden nest box, about eight feet above the ground. And within the box was a brood of seven boreal chickadees, northern songbirds that inhabit much of Southcentral and Interior Alaska. Born sometime in early June, they had grown large enough, by the end of the month, to tightly pack the artificial cavity.

I noticed a fluttering of wings just inside the small, round entryway and at first I guessed it to be one of the parents, feeding insects to the nestlings. But as the small, brownish-gray bird emerged, it dropped awkwardly toward the ground. Taken by surprise, I worried that one of the youngsters had somehow fallen out of the nest while still unable to fly. I reached inside the door and grabbed my binoculars for a better look. Bringing the box into focus, I saw a couple more heads and beaks jostling at the entrance. Then a second bird exited the box. Flapping furiously, it flew to an alder bush beside the birch. Landing clumsily and unable to get its balance, this one too dropped and fluttered out of sight, into a dense thicket of alder and red-berried elder.

It quickly became clear what was happening. The chickadee nestlings had become fledglings. Blessed by serendipity, I'd been granted the rare opportunity to watch young birds leaving their nest.

After I realized my good fortune, two questions immediately arose: How many birds were left? And, should I awaken Dulcy? If it had been early morning, I might have hesitated to disturb my late-rising wife, who cherishes her weekend sleep-ins. But she too was thrilled by the nearby presence of nesting songbirds; the previous week we had excitedly peeked in the box together, to check on the nestlings. Besides, it was already 10:00 A.M.

I rushed upstairs, nudged her gently, and lifted the pillow she had draped over her head. "Dulcy," I whispered, "The chickadees are fledging. You'll have to hurry if you want to watch."

Bleary eyed, Dulcy rolled out of bed, grabbed her eyeglasses, and joined me on the porch. We stayed there, at a respectful distance, so we wouldn't disturb the birds in their ritual. A minute or so later, a third chickadee fluttered out of the nest and landed nicely on an alder branch. Watching through the binoculars, Dulcy murmured her pleasure, a soft echo of my own.

Now and then we heard faint nasal chirping, as heads and beaks and necks poked out of the hole then pulled back in. I imagined the box's interior to be a raucous place as the birds pushed and shoved each other in their clamor to get out.

A fourth chickadee popped out of the hole. Beating its wings hard, it floated through the air as if in slow motion, then cleanly set down on an alder that was more tree than bush, some fifteen feet above the ground and thirty feet from its launch point. A beautiful take-off, first flight, and landing.

The fifth fledgling, like the earlier ones, tumbled and fluttered into the bushes below. There was a lull then, as the remaining birds seemed hesitant to take the leap. First one, then another, poked head and upper body outside, only to pull back in. As if to encourage the reluctant fliers, one of the adult chickadees zoomed in and perched on the entrance's lip. It briefly peered inside, then left, and the other parent repeated the routine. They remained nearby, moving among the trees and bushes, keeping watch on their young.

Again a fledgling cautiously emerged, bit by bit. First beak, then head, then neck and shoulders. The chickadee looked this way and that, turned its head upward, looked toward the ground, stayed put.

"They remind me of the first time I jumped in a swimming pool; I stood on the edge for the longest time," Dulcy observed. "That would be me, the insecure one, waiting right to the end. Needing assurance."

Turning to me she added, "I bet you'd be the first, or one of the first ones out, given your competitive nature."

"I don't think so," I smiled in reply with a shake of my head. I too could identify with the birds' apparent hesitancy. I know the push and pull of conflicting impulses: a desire for safety and comfort mixed with the urge to explore and grow. With change and growth comes risk. Often, when perched on a threshold, it seems a leap of faith is required.

The fledgling was now mostly out of the nest box. At the last moment, it hooked its claws onto the entryway's ledge. Hanging against the box, the bird flapped its wings hard but refused to let go. "I think it wants to go back in," Dulcy whispered.

That wasn't going to happen. One of the parents flew in and gave the struggling bird a soft nudge. It dropped away—a falling, flapping body.

Only one nestling remained. The last chickadee poked out its head, paused a couple of moments, then launched itself into the air, a grand first flight to the alder tree where at least three of its siblings already perched. Where the others were, it was impossible to say.

I checked my watch. Only twenty minutes had passed since the first fledgling tumbled out. "It still amazes me," I told Dulcy, "that I happened to walk out the door just as it was starting and then looked over at just the right moment. The chances of that happening are so small; it would have been so easy to miss. We were really lucky."

Dulcy reminded me of something I've come to believe, but sometimes still forget: "There are no accidents, remember? This was a gift to you."

To us both.

Dulcy stayed a few more minutes then returned inside the house. I went in too, but only briefly to grab journal and pen, and then headed back outdoors. For the next hour or so, in between bursts of note taking, I tried to track the boreal chickadees' movements. It wasn't easy to do. Occasionally they chirped softly, but mostly they remained quiet and still, except for fluttering feathers.

Hidden by leaves, the chickadees were nearly impossible to spot, except when they took short flights from branch to branch, tree to tree. Soon I lost track of all but a couple of the newly fledged birds. The parents remained busy, hunting moths and flies and other foods for their offspring, and keeping tabs on their family's movements.

By midday the birds had left our yard, crossed the road, and disappeared into a neighbor's woods. I wished I could follow them, gain more glimpses into their lives. Returning to the house, I glanced at the now-empty nest box and my faint longing became a smile. *All seven*, I thought. *We got to watch all seven of them go out into the world.*

RAVENS IN WINTER

After sharing the local landscape with ravens for many years, I decided one winter that it was time to become better acquainted with the largest of North America's songbirds, to spend some time at one of their local hangouts. Not that they welcomed me with open wings. Just the opposite, in fact. Ravens—at least those that inhabit Anchorage—seem to know when they're being watched, even when that watching occurs from the inside of a Toyota station wagon. Maybe the binoculars were a giveaway. Or my scribbling in a journal.

My database is admittedly small and my evidence anecdotal; in other words, I'm relying on highly unscientific methods. Nonetheless, I've come to believe that ravens don't seem comfortable with this being-watched stuff. I think they prefer to be the watchers. When they sense that one of the city's featherless, bipedal critters is getting too close, or showing unusual interest in their doings, they exit, cawing.

So I guess it would be more accurate to say I pursued the company of ravens, with mixed results. My effort wasn't nearly as formal as an earlier one conducted by state wildlife manager Rick Sinnott, who closely studied the city's "raven society" for a few years back in the 1990s.

I like Rick a lot, but I think his pursuit of the birds made local ravens even more paranoid about humans than they might normally be. That's because he went around town baiting the big black birds with Cheetos, french fries, and dog food, then captured them with a cannon-fired net.

Rick actually missed many more ravens than he caught, but that was part of the challenge. By study's end, he did manage to nab and band sixty-two ravens.

Hoping to learn where they roost at night, he also strapped fifty-four of them with small radio transmitters. Alas, Rick never did get a good picture of their nighttime habits, but his efforts likely taught the ravens a thing or two. Like never trust a human (of course given their long history with our species, they must have known that anyway).

Just about everyone who's carefully studied ravens for any length of time agrees that these are smart birds, with pretty darn good memories. Since ravens can live forty years or more, almost certainly there's a bunch still hanging around Anchorage who recall—in whatever way that ravens remember—being tricked by a wily biped. Imagine: out-tricking the trickster. There's got to be some bad karma in that.

Based on his observations, Sinnott estimated that as many as two thousand ravens inhabit Anchorage during winter's daylight hours. Most head for the hills as sunset approaches to spend their nights in the wild. Then, come daylight, they commute back to the big city, to dine on all sorts of urban foods. They seem to have a particular taste for human leftovers. People being people—that is, sloppy— there's plenty to munch on, as long as you're the sort who doesn't mind dumpster diving or picking partly eaten burgers and fries and the like from iced-up fast-food restaurant parking lots. Ravens don't mind it at all. In fact they seem to embrace that sort of behavior.

From my home on the Hillside, and on walks in Chugach State Park, I often savored the flyovers of ravens on their daily commutes. I even had the occasional pleasure of their company in my backyard. Sometimes they were drawn into the yard by the frenzy of smaller songbirds at my feeders. I suspect they wanted to know what the fuss was all about. Or perhaps they were simply hoping for an easy meal.

But to really spend quality time with Anchorage's ravens, I knew I had to go shopping. Or at least visit the city's shopping and eating centers, where edibles get tossed and dumped. Even though I lived on the edge of town, a few fine raven hangouts were located within ten minutes' drive of my South Anchorage home: the Fred Meyer complex on Abbott Road; the Carrs business park area on Huffman Road; or the Dimond Center (which I usually try to avoid when I can, given the noise and traffic congestion). Though I ultimately made Fred Meyer the focus of my raven study, I did drive-throughs of the other spots as well.

Now you must remember that these are preliminary findings. My investigation is still a work in progress (though I'm unsure when, if ever, I'll resume that work, given that I'm not nearly as fond of parking lots as ravens). But I'm ready to share a little of what I've learned so far, which really isn't all that much.

The most obvious thing I noticed during my brief time spent hanging out with ravens is this: Even where the prospects of food are best, ravens do a lot more sitting and watching than eating. A lot more flying and aerial playing, too. Or maybe my timing was off. I tended to do my field studies in the middle of the day, when the rest of my life permitted an hour or two of raven watching. Maybe I simply caught them in between morning and late-afternoon gorgings when they're less interested in food. Which raises the question: are ravens *ever* disinterested in food?

There's a reason I suspect this might be true: once while cruising the Fred Meyer parking lot I noticed a mess of fries and sandwich leftovers that someone had dumped on the asphalt outside the Carl Junior's fast-food joint. Not far away, a raven perched atop a light tower seemed to be eyeing the easy pickings. I figured it was only a matter of time before the bird would dive in for the goodies, so I parked beside the bait. Then I waited and waited and waited, until a customer drove in and parked his SUV right over the food. End of that stakeout.

Was the raven simply not hungry? Or did he know I was waiting for him to fly in? Did he suspect something was amiss?

In any case, only twice in three outings did I see a raven eat what I'd call a good-sized meal. One raven dug into the snow to come up with something that looked like a roll or sandwich. The bird then immediately flew off and disappeared, presumably so it could consume its prize without being harassed by other ravens. The second time, a raven consumed the remains of a McDonald's sandwich. I spotted the bird perched on a dumpster, but moments after I parked and grabbed my binoculars, it flew to the top of a semitrailer truck. There it pecked away at its McMeal for a good five minutes. After eating and wiping its beak clean, the bird departed. Going in for a closer look, I found the sandwich wrapping on the ground. All that remained was some sauce and a strand or two of cheese.

I also saw several ravens pecking at ice and snow and then swallowing, but I'm not sure what they were consuming. Crumbs? Salt? Dirt? Ice?

A snow dump at the western end of the Fred Meyer parking lot, not far from Great Clips, proved to be an especially popular hangout. One or two ravens, and sometimes more, perched upon the pile for at least part of my three stakeouts. Usually they hopped or fluttered around or waddled about in their Chaplinesque way, stopping now and then to peck into the pile. Occasionally their pecks were followed by gulps, as if they had found something tasty, or at least edible, amid all that dirty snow and ice.

Once as I drove into the parking lot, eight or nine ravens were clumped tightly atop the mound. From a distance they seemed to be having an animated discussion, maybe even an argument. When I approached in my car, all but two of the birds dispersed, some cawing loudly, and I assumed they didn't want me listening to a raven dispute. But maybe it was just a bunch of birds sharing neighborhood gossip.

That group was the biggest I saw during my formal forays into raven land. The most birds I counted at any one time was twelve; most of those were looping and diving and chasing each other as if playing some form of avian tag.

This is one of the things I love most about ravens and probably the biggest reason I chose to spend time in the close company of these amazing birds: they really seem to enjoy themselves, whether frolicking in the air, tossing ice from snow piles, or talking in loud soliloquies while perched atop light towers, apparently unconcerned whether anyone might be paying attention.

Accuse me of anthropomorphizing if you wish, but I think I'm right about their playful nature. And I'm not alone; some scientists, too, and Native elders, see the play in ravens. Even if we're wrong, there is this fact: whatever its meaning or motivation, the behavior of ravens helps me take my own self less seriously. Can there be a better reason for hanging out in parking lots?

REDPOLL SERENADE:
CELEBRATING THE END OF WINTER

One of my great and simple pleasures in the waning weeks of winter is the morning walk to retrieve the daily newspaper. Not that there's anything unusually inviting in the paper. What makes these March forays through the front yard to the edge of the street especially delightful are the common redpolls that have taken up temporary residency in my Turnagain neighborhood. Quiet for much of the winter (except when alarmed or engaged in food disputes at the feeders), these small, red-capped finches are suddenly garrulous creatures.

With morning temperatures gradually warming—though of course in fits and starts—and daylight hours growing rapidly here in Southcentral Alaska, the redpolls aren't as compelled to immediately fill their bellies with the breakfast offerings of sunflower seeds that my neighbors and I put out in our yards. Instead of a dawn dash to feeders, many seem to slowly awaken to the day, while filling the air with trills and cheeps.

I first noticed this sweet seasonal redpoll chorus when I lived on the Hillside. After moving, I was happy to learn that their cheering voices also brighten the day's beginning here in West Anchorage. No doubt many other parts of our city are similarly blessed, where people put out seeds for birds.

One recent winter was an especially good one to enjoy the redpolls' serenade, because legions of them had descended upon Anchorage, the most in several years (at least at my end of town). Among the tiniest and hardiest of songbirds to inhabit the north, they vaguely resemble sparrows, but are distinguished by their red-feathered head patches and small black "bibs." At this time of year, male red-polls also have handsomely bright pinkish-red breasts, a signal of their breeding season's approach.

On the best of those late-winter mornings, my neighborhood vibrated with the avian chatter of hundreds of redpolls. It's not that I simply heard them; it's as if my body was wrapped in their voices as I walked slowly along the sidewalk, savoring their chorale tunes. The first time I experienced this, many years earlier, it seemed that I'd been transported to a tropical forest filled with the voices of birds. How pleasingly peculiar that my own northern yard could be so alive and bursting with song, in winter no less.

Actually, I'm not sure that what the redpolls are doing technically qualifies as song. The principle sound they produce is more of a guttural trill that reminds me of a purring cat or bear cub. (Yes, cubs actually purr, a behavior that I discovered first-hand many years ago; but that, of course, is a whole nother story.)

Interspersed among the gentle trills are high-pitched cheeps. Both, to me, are the voices of contentment. This may simply be my own projection, of course, but the birds' behavior suggests otherwise. Perched on birches, spruces, and cottonwoods, the redpolls showed no anxiety when I approached and greeted them with my own whispered hellos or soft whistles. Some sat quietly, while others spread and fluttered their wings much like a human might stretch and shake his limbs upon waking. Still others casually preened their feathered bodies, while a few engaged in swift chases through the yard. One following the other, the redpoll pairs weaved among the branches and streaked along the snow-covered lawn. The start of seasonal romances, perhaps?

Sometimes when the day was mild and the air was still and alive with birdsong, I simply stood in the yard a while, eyes closed and mouth spread in a grin. And I let the redpolls' soft murmurings caress and enliven my own still-waking body. There was no mistaking the happiness that filled my being, the lifting of my spirit.

Might the redpolls be welcoming the arrival of another day or the north's accelerating rush into spring? Maybe both. From late February into March is when I usually notice a change in the quality of sunlight that falls upon Anchorage. I know the change is actually a gradual one, and that our days have been lengthening by five and a half minutes, more or less, each and every day for weeks. It seems only a moment or two ago that we had less than six hours of daylight; now we'll soon zoom past twelve hours, eventually to reach more than nineteen. And with that rapid lengthening comes a brightening, as the sun moves steadily higher in our subarctic sky.

The sun is high enough, and on clear days bright enough, that I can feel its warmth on my body, something that didn't seem true on the sunniest day in December or even January. Some threshold has been passed that both my skin and spirit notice. After a tough few weeks in deepest winter, when my psyche occasionally seemed lost in deep blackness, I sometimes discover myself whistling, or even singing aloud. Others, too, seem in a lighter mood. The people I meet on daily walks are more likely to smile in greeting.

I've come to cherish these late-winter days, when the season's deepest cold and darkness have departed, but before the months of around-the-clock lightness have arrived, bringing with them a kind of manic rush. Don't misunderstand: I love Alaska's all-too-short spring and summer seasons. But they bring an energy that doesn't easily lend itself to simply being, simply luxuriating in the day. All too often, summer is a time to do, do, do, as we Alaskans try to squeeze in as much adventure and play as possible, before the long darkness returns.

Maybe that's what I've sensed from the redpolls, too, on those late winter mornings. Soon they'll be building nests, then raising and feeding large, hungry families. And there will be little, if any, time for simply sitting and trilling and welcoming the glorious light of day.

OF BEARS AND BIRDSEED

Spring had arrived late on Anchorage's Hillside. Even in early May, piles of dirty snow remained in my yard. Some of the biggest and dirtiest heaps were those on the shaded north side of the house. Besides the various bits of twigs, spruce needles, and dirt that clung to its surface, that backyard snow was sprinkled with sunflower seed debris: the remains of winter's songbird feasting.

From September through mid-April, I had fed daily meals of sunflower seeds to chickadees and nuthatches, grosbeaks and redpolls. More than five hundred pounds in all. Over the months, bunches of shells, bits of seed, and some unknown quantity of bird poop were tossed, dropped, knocked, and swept from my decks and railings to the ground below, then buried by successive snowfalls. As the snow melted, that debris thickened into a messy black mass of shells, seed fragments, fecal matter, and mold.

I was tempted to let the snow melt at its own slow pace, to more easily rake and bag the seed debris. But I couldn't wait. For weeks I'd regularly skimmed the waste from those snow piles beside my house. In a word I'll tell you why: bears.

By late April or early May, many of the bears that inhabit the Anchorage area have awakened from winter's sleep and abandoned their dens. After several months of hibernation, they're intent on filling empty bellies. Especially in this lean season, they'll eagerly consume all kinds of food, including—and perhaps especially—the savory stuff that we humans leave around our neighborhoods and yards.

When I moved to the Hillside in 1993, human trash and dog food were considered the primary bear attractants. No one talked about birdseed being a problem. Rick Sinnott once told me that people never reported bears getting into their bird feeders when he became the Anchorage area's wildlife manager in 1994 and began handling local residents' "nuisance bear" complaints. That began to change in the late 1990s, when local bears somehow learned that birdseed is both tasty and nutritious. By the early 2000s, birdseed was running neck-and-neck with human garbage and dog food as bears' favorite urban treats.

This of course made Sinnott's job even more complicated. Each spring, he and others would do their best to spread the word citywide: stop feeding birds in early April. And clean up your mess. Either a lot of people weren't getting the message or they were ignoring it. Or maybe they were just being lazy. Year after year, bears were getting into dozens of Anchorage bird feeders.

Like many folks who live here, I like the fact that black and grizzly bears wander through Anchorage, occasionally even through my yard. I think it says something positive about our community—and our tolerance for wildlife—that bears still roam our town, without threat of extermination. I want to do what I can to help keep it that way and usually consider myself part of the solution, not the problem.

Still, I too get careless or lazy sometimes. I make mistakes. In 1999 I messed up big time. That year, too, was a late spring, with cooler-than-normal temperatures in April and May and a slowly vanishing snowpack. As the snow melted, the seedy morass atop it piled up. I kept holding off, figuring I could wait until all the snow was gone, simplifying the cleanup. Still, as April turned to May, I worried. Already there'd been several bear sightings in town.

On May 7, I decided to wait no longer. Carrying a rake and shovel, I went out the front door, across the deck, turned to go down the steps to the backyard— and then stopped in my tracks. Thirty feet away, a large black bear lay sprawled in the seeds. He looked big enough to be an adult male, which is what I guessed him to be. Caught up in his feasting, with his head turned away from me, the bear hadn't noticed my approach and he continued to dine as I watched. Every few seconds he would dip his head and grab a mouthful of seeds. It must have seemed like bruin heaven.

At first I wasn't sure what to do. Then, because he was a black bear (known to be generally timid of humans) and I stood close enough to the front door if retreat proved necessary, I clapped my hands and shouted: "HEY, GET OUTTA HERE!"

The startled bear lifted off the ground several inches, landed on his feet and turned toward me, all in one motion. After a moment's hesitation, he bolted for the woods behind the house, stopping only once, briefly, to look back. As this was happening, I noticed a couple other things about the bear. First, he wore an ear tag; that meant he was one of the Anchorage bears being studied by biologists. Second, he looked fat, not skinny as you might expect a bear to be after several months of fasting. Maybe my yard was just one stop on his bird-feeder rounds.

I spent the next few hours cleaning up my seed dump, raking and hauling the debris away. The bear returned once more that evening. He approached slowly through the forest, drawn back to what must have seemed like a good deal. Again I shouted. Again he retreated, but this time more reluctantly, it seemed. I don't know that I got the bear started on sunflower seeds, but I certainly contributed to his habit. I still feel bad about my goof-up.

Lingering guilt about that earlier episode helped motivate me to get an early start on my birdseed cleanup when, several years later, we experienced another late spring and lingering snow. There was no way I could get to all the seeds as long as large piles of snow remained. But I was out there regularly, raking and bagging and hauling debris before it built up into a slimy, stinking mess that might prove irresistible to a bear. In keeping pace with the gradual meltdown, I was removing temptation from beside my house and that's what mattered.

Many years later, this hankering that Anchorage bears have for sunflower seeds remains a big concern. It draws bears onto porches and decks, brings them closer to pets and kids. And it's only gotten worse, as moms have passed their feeding habits along to cubs. We can't blame the bears for craving an easy-to-get, high-calorie meal. But we humans can become more disciplined. We can take down our bird feeders earlier, clean up our messes more promptly. It's the least we can do, if we truly want to share the local landscape with bears. Though each spring and summer we talk about Anchorage's "bear problem," the problem really begins with people's behavior.

LISTENING TO OWLS

Shortly after 10:00 P.M. on a Wednesday night in late winter, I put on a bathrobe, gloves, and boots, and prepared to haul our green plastic trashcan to the edge of the driveway for Thursday's early morning pickup. First, though, I grabbed a broom and headed out the front door to clear three inches of fresh snow from the porch. I'd just begun sweeping the soft, fluffy powder when a voice called out from the darkness.

Hoo. Hooo-hoo. Hoo. Hoo.

I lifted my head in surprise, my heartbeat quickening at this familiar yet uncommon call. Uncommon, at least, in my neighborhood. I've been told that dozens of great horns are scattered throughout the city, most often heard—and sometimes seen—in large, wooded areas like Kincaid and Hillside Parks. Yet in seven and a half years on Anchorage's Hillside, only once before had I heard a great horned owl while standing in my yard. Not that I spent lots of winter nights outdoors during those years. Except for occasional hot tubbing, snow clearing, or aurora gazing, my forays into the yard were usually brief: to and from the car for meetings, classes, basketball. To and from the road, hauling trash.

The owl hooted again. And again. It seemed to be calling from the wooded lot beside our next-door neighbors, the Nelsons. Then, off in the distance, a faint response. *Hoo. Hooo-hoo. Hoo. Hoo.* It could have been a competitor responding. But when later told of the back-and-forth hooting, local birder Bob Dittrick said it's more likely that two mates were "talking" to each other on this night. Great horned owls hoot year-round, he added, but they're most vocal from late winter through early summer, during courtship, nesting, and fledging of young.

Ears still tuned to the hooting, I finished sweeping, then grabbed the trashcan and carried it to the road. Along the way, I crossed hare tracks freshly imprinted into the day's snow. I followed the tracks, hoping to glimpse their maker, but lost them where they crossed the newly plowed road. Snowshoe hares, like great horned owls, are mostly nocturnal animals. They're also one of the owl's favorite foods, along with various rodents and birds. Trying to imagine the hare's response when it first heard an owl's call that night, I supposed it instinctively froze in place, depending on a snowy white coat to avoid detection. Perhaps the camouflaged hare was watching me while listening for owl, long ears rotating this way and that

I felt lucky. If not for my garbage-hauling duties, I wouldn't have noticed either the owls or the hare. They reminded me that nightly dramas are played right outside my door, normally overlooked. Heck, not even given a fleeting thought.

A few flakes of snow drifted groundward. The twenty-degree air was still, the night unusually quiet. The fresh snow that covered the ground and draped trees helped to muffle noises. No other sound but hooting until a jet briefly passed through the night sky, mechanical roar muted, on its approach to Anchorage's airport. Then, once more, deep silence except for the owls' periodic calls.

Returned to the porch, I simply stood and listened, relishing the owls' *hoo, hooo-hoo hoo* . . . I considered waking Dulcy, who had gone to bed early, exhausted by her work with the local school district. No, I decided, she needed her sleep. I instead hoped that an owl would return over the weekend. And, come morning, I would ask my wife if she'd prefer to be roused whenever I heard an owl calling, as she'd requested when the northern lights are especially magical.

There was no doubt that the owls were working some magic on me. The hooting had an eerie, haunting quality, but that wasn't entirely it. Their calls, like the wails of loons and the howls of wolves, spoke of wildness and mystery. The lives of owls are secrets, rarely revealed. That night I briefly glimpsed a sliver of two owls' lives through the darkness. Their repeated hoots sent messages to my brain and created images: I pictured a great horned owl perched in a nearby spruce, head swiveling, claws gripping branch, eyes wide open, calling into the night. And somewhere in the distance, a mate listening to its message and responding.

I was reminded of another winter night, six years earlier. Could so much time have already passed? Camped with two friends in the Alaska Range foothills, I'd heard the rapid *hoo-hoo-hoo-hoo* of a boreal owl. The rapture of that night's campfire, subzero cold, forest stillness, ink-black sky, wildly flashing stars, and owl calls had been forever imprinted on my brain and heart.

The hooting also reminded me how much I loved my life here in Alaska, here on Anchorage's Hillside. To be part of a world that includes the voices of owls is a gift indeed. I wondered if the Nelsons or any others in the neighborhood were standing outside their houses, temporarily pulled away from familial responsibilities or the technological distractions of TVs, CDs, videos, computers.

The calls stopped. I waited a few minutes to be sure, and then turned toward the door. Still under the owls' spell, I knew that six years from now, even twenty, I would remember this take-out-the-garbage night. I would remember the fresh snow, tracks of hare, and hushed stillness of the air. I would remember standing alone on the front porch, no rush to go inside, listening, listening. I would remember my heart beating wildly and my mind growing calm, serenaded by owls.

PART II

ALONG CITY AND HIGHWAY FRINGES

A GATHERING OF SWANS

I first noticed the swans in late October. A handful of them swam and fed in Potter Marsh, a wetlands at the southern fringe of Anchorage. Big and snowy white, they stood out boldly among the marsh's late-fall grays and browns.

The presence of swans was not in itself unusual. They stop here each fall while migrating south from Alaska. Most autumns the swans stay only a short while, then move on to wintering grounds in British Columbia and the Pacific Northwest. This year they lingered. Day by day, their numbers built: a dozen, two dozen, three. By the end of October, more than forty had gathered in the marsh, transforming an ordinary event into something astonishing. The marsh's southern end was filled with swans, its otherwise drab appearance at this time of year made stunningly beautiful.

As the swan population grew, the news quickly spread among local birders, through word of mouth and the local Audubon group's "bird hotline." Soon even those who normally pay little attention to birds began to take notice. People driving the Seward Highway where it borders the marsh would slow down and gawk. Some pulled over, rolled down their windows, got out of their cars and pickups. More and more people headed down to the marsh with cameras and binoculars. Whole families stood along the highway shoulder, pointing and smiling.

How strange it all seemed, this autumnal convergence of swans and people. No stranger than the weather, though. By month's end we Anchorage residents were celebrating the warmest snow-free October on record, which here reached back to 1916. Not since 1987, fifteen years earlier, had we gone the entire month without any measureable snowfall.

Temperatures continued to range from the midthirties to high forties as we moved into November. Normally covered by ice and snow, Potter Marsh remained a haven for the swans as well as mallards and a few less common ducks: gadwall, northern pintail, American widgeon.

I joined the throngs at marsh's edge the first weekend of November, armed with notebook, binoculars, and bird book. It was a raw day, drizzly and windy, so most swan-watchers stayed in their vehicles. But a few of us ventured outside. I counted thirty swans, including nine pairs of adults. They were joined by a dozen adolescent birds, still wearing the pale gray plumage of youth. Trumpeter and tundra swans are difficult to tell apart, but after studying my bird guide, I was confident the ones nearest shore were trumpeters: they had a distinctive pink line where the upper and lower parts of the beak join.

The largest of North American waterfowl, with wing spans up to eight feet across, the swans were both elegant and comic to behold. Their grand size, strikingly white plumage, and long, graceful necks gave the birds a regal splendor. Yet any sense of elegance was washed away when they went bottoms up to feed on aquatic plants rooted in the marsh muds. Rear ends pointed to the gray ceiling overhead, they were feathered buoys bobbing in muddied waters. And their hoarse honking calls, though vaguely trumpetlike, also stirred memories of clowns squeezing horns.

A mother and her young, giggling daughter joined me along the highway's shoulder. The woman told me about another lake, miles to the south, packed with swans and lined by dozens of cars and vans and trucks, their drivers and passengers watching intently. "Can you believe all this?" she asked. "It's the craziest thing."

It was clear she meant not only the weather and swans, but the number of people who'd been drawn out of their houses by the prolonged fall. Some chose to go for scenic drives, others for hikes or even bike rides. Local trails bustled with joggers, cyclists, and walkers, getting outdoors before snow and ice and freezing cold claimed the landscape.

Those who paid close attention might have noticed other small November miracles: a swirling cloud of midges dancing in the mild air; a late-blooming wild rose adding a bright splash of pink to an otherwise somber forest, months after most of its kind have shed their petals; moose browsing on still-green lawns in downtown Anchorage neighborhoods.

Returning home in late afternoon, I asked my mother if she would like to visit Potter Marsh, see the swans. At age eighty, her body hobbled by arthritis, she didn't leave the house much anymore, but this was too good an opportunity to pass up. Who knew when, or if, she would get this chance again?

Bundled up, Mom settled into the front passenger seat and sat quietly, patiently, as we drove from our Hillside neighborhood down to Anchorage's flats. By this time it was nearly dusk. With thick overcast and the day rapidly darkening, I hoped the light would hold a few minutes more.

As we approached the marsh, the swans stood out brightly amidst the gloom. They almost glowed in the fading light. "There they are, off to the right," I said, pointing. "Can you see them?"

Mom leaned forward and squinted her eyes. After a few moments of silence, she replied, "Yes; yes I see them now. There's lots of them, aren't there?"

We pulled over to the highway's shoulder and I reached across the car, unrolled her window. Then I focused my binoculars and handed them over. At first Mom had trouble finding the swans, but finally she got them in sight. "Oh, they're such pretty birds. And big. I didn't realize how big they are, compared to ducks," she commented. "Look at their necks; they're so long and slender."

We chuckled as they dunked for food, smiled at their trumpeting. It was a treat for us both, sharing those moments. Decades earlier, we had watched swans in zoos and game farms. But this was the first time we'd been together in the company of wild swans.

After ten minutes or so, I rolled up the window, started the car, and rejoined the highway traffic. "They are just so lovely," Mom murmured, her eyes still drawn to the marsh where magnificent pale birds floated into the November night, autumnal apparitions.

CALLED TO A PRIMEVAL PRESENCE: ANCHORAGE'S SANDHILL CRANES

For the first several minutes of our walk through spruce-birch forest, Wayne Hall and I talked and joked and laughed in spirited fashion, without worrying how far our voices carried through the woodlands. We sloshed along the soggy, puddled trail in our rubber boots and spoke of migrating birds, long daylight hours, nesting dippers, and the earliest signs of a slowly greening world, all part of Anchorage's move from winter into spring. Now and then we stopped and listened to some of the season's early singers: varied thrush, ruby-crowned kinglet, dark-eyed junco. Bright music for the ears and soul.

During one of our stops, Wayne told me we were getting close. It was time to move more deliberately, more quietly. Following his lead, I walked slowly and lowered my voice. Before long, an opening showed through the trees. Still a hundred feet or more from the wetland's margins, we heard the sounds of waterbirds: the quack of a mallard and the winnowed *hoohoohoohoo* of a Wilson's snipe, circling and diving high in the sky above us.

Once at the marsh's edge, Wayne reached for his binoculars and began to scan the swampy meadow and neighboring pond. My attention was drawn to ripples in the water close to shore. Looking through my own binoculars, I saw the head of a wood frog. Moments later, we heard the species' distinctive hiccupy call.

It was the first time I'd seen or heard Southcentral Alaska's only amphibian that spring, so in my mind our small expedition was already a success. But we hadn't come here looking for frogs, or snipe, or migrant songbirds, as happy as we were to encounter them after a long Alaskan winter. Earlier in the day, Wayne and his wife, Marilyn Houser, had heard the loud, bugled calls of sandhill cranes while walking through this same wooded area in northeast Anchorage. Leashed to their dogs, they'd chosen not to follow the calls. But Wayne was determined to find the birds, or at least try, and he had invited me to join the search. So here we were, a few hours later, looking and listening for cranes, the tallest of Alaska's birds and among those with the largest wingspans, measuring six to seven feet wide (behind only eagles and swans).

I happened to spot the first one. The crane was walking slowly on the far side of the meadow, its body hunched slightly in the hunt for food. Though sandhill cranes are sometimes confused with great blue herons where their ranges overlap, there was no mistaking this bird. Sandhills are among Alaska's most iconic animals and the only one of the world's fifteen crane species to inhabit this part of the world. The crane stood several feet high, tall black legs supporting its mottled gray- and tan-feathered body (while the bodies of adult birds are naturally gray, they often stain their bodies brown while preening their feathers with iron-rich mud and water). A long sinuous neck rose to a mostly gray head and a face marked by distinctive white cheeks, red forehead, and a long, dark, daggerlike bill.

Soon after my sighting, Wayne saw a second crane. Then a third. All three had patchy gray and brown bodies, their plumage blending nicely with the landscape's still-drab grasses and bushes.

None of the cranes seemed to notice our presence. Or if they did, they weren't alarmed enough to either call or fly off. That of course was a good thing. We had no desire to disturb these birds, only to share their company for a while, observe their behavior, and gain insights into their lives.

Wanting a closer look, Wayne led me off the trail and into a dense stand of spruce trees. We took up positions at the base of a gentle knoll, along the perimeter of a pond that was larger than a football field. In the shadow of the trees, Wayne set up two tripods. One held his spotting scope, the other his digital camera, which took both video and still images. I scribbled in my journal and noted, among other things, the several birds—and one amphibian—we had observed so far. I also sketched a cloud with partly hidden sun and wrote the date, *5/1* (the year being 2011). And I began to describe our time in the company of the cranes.

Wayne and I barely moved or talked for the next hour and a half, our conversation limited to brief whispered exchanges. It was an uncommon pleasure, to be with someone whose patient watching and quiet, still presence matched—or exceeded—my own.

Two of the cranes stalked the pond's edges near the center of the meadow, one hundred to two hundred feet from where we stood. The third slowly moved our way, step by purposeful step. It paused frequently to look or listen and occasionally crouched lower, head and neck extended, then jabbed its long, charcoal-gray bill into the water, lifted its head and swallowed something. But what? Cranes are omnivorous, with a diet that ranges from insects, worms, snails, and rodents to seeds, roots, and grains. It was impossible to tell what these cranes were eating until the nearest one speared a frog and lifted it from the water.

With the frog grasped firmly between its lower and upper mandibles, the crane shook its head and neck, rearranged the prey in its beak—briefly we saw the frog's white belly and splayed legs—then tilted its head and swallowed.

Only occasionally was the crane rewarded with a frog when it stabbed the water, and I guessed that the large, wading bird was also eating other foods. But Wayne and I agreed that the wetland's frogs were likely the primary targets of these migrating cranes and what lured them to this spot. Which raised the question: how did the cranes discover this particular hunting ground? And was this a feeding stopover for other cranes bound for northern nesting grounds?

Cranes are normally wary birds that keep their distance from people. Both Wayne and I had observed them erupt in harsh, warning cries when humans ventured too close, sometimes inadvertently, and we were amazed by this one's steady approach and calm demeanor. Now and then the bird looked right in our direction and it seemed impossible that the crane was unaware of us.

Eventually the bird came within thirty feet or less, close enough that I got a full "head shot" when looking through the spotting scope. I studied the bird's golden eyes, the bright red patch of bald, featherless skin on its forehead (one of the species' most distinctive features), the downy feathers of its white cheeks and gray upper neck, the slits of its nostrils, a small blade of grass hanging from the beak, a fly crawling across its feathers. Then, moving lower, I examined the larger feathers that grew on the crane's wings and others that formed a "bustle" over the bird's short tail (that bushy feature named because of its resemblance to the frames used beneath dresses by women in the nineteenth century) and took in its gangling, scaly black legs.

Watching through his camera, Wayne was quietly jubilant. It was by far the closest he had ever been to a crane. With one memorable exception, it was also the closest I had been. We thought it was likely a juvenile bird, the offspring of the more distant pair. And we kept expecting it to suddenly panic at our presence, but the crane remained calm, quiet, and focused in its search for food.

Out in the meadow, the two other cranes seemed less interested in eating than keeping watch, vigorously preening their feathers and occasionally socializing. One of the adults seemed especially alert, though I assumed both remained vigilant to dangers.

None of the cranes seemed to pay much heed when a couple of mallards zoomed in and made a splashy landing. But twice their attention was drawn to the sky. On one occasion they arched their necks and turned their heads upward while remaining silent. Moments later, a juvenile bald eagle swooped low over the meadow and then disappeared behind the bordering trees. It seemed likely the eagle was more interested in the ducks than the cranes; even the juvenile was a large bird, about as big as its parents that we could tell.

Only once did the cranes make a ruckus. Their heads again turned upward, they shouted among themselves in high-pitched roarking cries when another pair of cranes silently crossed the sky, high overhead. Were the meadow cranes warning the others not to intrude on their spot? Or were they trying to get the pair's attention, inviting them to join the feast? Whatever the intended message, the high-flying cranes continued on their path and showed no desire to investigate the wetland.

Later, when watching Wayne's video, Marilyn would notice that the bare red patch on the grounded cranes' heads expanded when the other two flew over, further evidence of their excited state. Researchers have determined that the blood flow to the bare skin increases when cranes are aroused; at the same time, facial muscles contract. The combined effect is that the cranes flash more red, as the bare-skin patch is "pulled" over their heads.

Once, briefly, a member of the adult pair danced. The crane opened with a bow, then it hopped and spread its wings. I'd seen such behavior before, but never for long and always from afar. However short-lived and distant they are, the displays stir both curiosity and merriment, with dance steps that range from graceful to comical, as judged by us humans.

Whether deemed stirring or humorous, there's no question that our species finds crane dancing to be among the most unusual and captivating of avian displays. It has been celebrated and sometimes copied in cultures around the world and across time, with evidence that ancient people who inhabited what is now Turkey made crane costumes some 8,500 years ago. Nerissa Russell, one of the researchers to make that discovery (and the coauthor of a subsequent article that appeared in *Antiquity: A Quarterly Review of World Archaeology)*, has noted that "cranes of various species are found all over the world, with the exception of South America and Antarctica, and so are human crane dancers. They were at ancient Chinese funerals and Okinawan harvest festivals. The Ainu of Japan, the BatWa of Southern Africa and the Ostiaks of Siberia did costumed crane dances. Plutarch writes that Theseus and his companions, after they slew the Minotaur and landed in Delos, performed a crane dance."

Two Alaskans who've spent considerable time documenting and celebrating sandhill crane dancing are Christy Yuncker Happ and George Happ, who live in Goldstream Valley near Fairbanks. Marilyn brought the Happs to my attention when she shared their *Sandhill Crane Display Dictionary* pocket guide.

I'd never suspected that crane behavior was so complex. The Happs note that to better understand—or translate—what cranes' body language is saying, a person needs to consider all sorts of variables, from the size of the red forehead patch (is it extended?) to body and neck posture, wing position, the way a crane is moving (is it walking slowly or rapidly or even running?), and whether the feathers are "fluffed or sleeked." Two pages of the pocket naturalist guide are devoted to social body language, another to preening and related behavior, one to attack and defense, and four pages to dancing. Among the identified dance displays are such moves as the run-flap, ground stab, straight-leg high step, curtsey, tuck-bob, and the more complex tour jeté (jump-turn), minuet, and salute. Every move is both described and illustrated and its function is explained.

The pocket guide in turn led me to the Happs' website (either www.AlaskaSandhillCrane.com or www.christyyuncker.com will get you there), which includes a short discussion of why cranes dance. More than simply a breeding display, "it establishes social relationships, announces territorial claims, cements decades-long pair bonding, and hastens the education of the young. It looks like fun and, sometimes, it may be play." The website also includes a "Crane Signal Dictionary" and, perhaps best of all, a series of beguiling images that show various dance moves, including those done by fuzzy, chestnut-colored colts, the name given to cranes during the first summer of their lives.

It makes sense that dance is a key element of a young crane's schooling, given the activity's importance to the species. Yet I'd never seriously considered that possibility until browsing the Happs' website, which explains, "Dance training is a mainstay of a colt's education—promoting physical coordination and fostering sociality . . . Dance moves and steps are practiced and refined as colts mature." Initially, a colt will "make tentative crouches and hops. With practice and more maturity, the colt masters 'the strut,' the 'forward wing display,' and the 'one wing spin.'" By the end of the summer, colts can perform more complicated sequences, such as the tour jeté, which involves three jumps during a complete rotation of the body.

Each spring, nearly a quarter-million sandhill cranes fly through Alaska's skies, part of the largest—and widest ranging—crane migration in the world. Most of them pass through two migration "funnels." Some twenty thousand cranes that spend their winters in California's Central Valley follow the Pacific Flyway north to funnel number one, the Copper River Delta near Cordova, then disperse to breeding grounds in Bristol Bay, the Alaska Peninsula, and the Cook Inlet-Susitna Valley region.

With the help of satellite transmitters they placed on twenty-two birds between 2000 and 2002, state biologists Michael Petrula and Tom Rothe determined that Anchorage-area and other Pacific Flyway Population (PFP) cranes begin their 2,200-mile journey north in early March and follow an inland route through northern California, Oregon, Washington, and British Columbia before veering to the coast in the Panhandle region. The Stikine River Delta is the first of five Alaska "stopping areas" where the cranes rest and refuel before reaching their breeding grounds in early May, about two months after they left central California. The cranes spend most of that time at staging-area stopovers, flying an average of only thirteen days between start and finish.

The PFP birds largely retrace their route when returning to central California in the fall though their travel time is much shorter, twenty-seven days on average, reflecting shorter stays at stopping areas.

A much larger population of Alaska-bound cranes, about two hundred thousand in number, begins its spring migration in the American southwest, Texas, and Mexico. Members of this midcontinent population travel the Central Flyway across the Great Plains and Canada, eventually to be funneled through Alaska's Tanana Valley near Delta Junction. An estimated fifty thousand cranes will eventually cross the Bering Strait into northeast Siberia. The rest spend their spring and summer in Alaska's Interior, the Yukon-Kuskokwim Delta, and areas scattered through the state's western and northern regions. It's been said that two-thirds of Alaska's breeding cranes nest and raise their young on the Y-K Delta's tundra wetlands.

One of North America's great wildlife spectacles occurs during the cranes' spring migration. A seventy-five-mile-long stretch of Nebraska's Platte River is a crucial staging area, visited by an estimated 80 percent of all sandhill cranes, or more than a half-million birds. Considered the cranes' most crucial stopover on their journey to northern breeding grounds, the Platte region has been designated an Important Bird Area of global significance.

Though I've never been to the Platte River or witnessed the mass departure of cranes ready to travel, the Alaska Department of Fish and Game's Wildlife Notebook Series offers a hint of what it's like: "When taking off, huge flocks of cranes ascend in great circling columns, riding thermal currents of rising air, then form into 'V' formations."

Even better is Hank Lentfer's description in his memoir *Faith of Cranes*. In describing the flocks that annually pass near his home in Southeast Alaska, Lentfer writes, "They might stay for a day, a week, waiting for fair winds and rising thermals. When the time is right, a single crane crouches and leaps to the air, followed by another, and another, and then a thousand more. They flap and glide in a growing spiral, calling as if lifted by their own sound. Lying on my back alongside our garden, I stare into a whirlpool of wings. At the thermal's top, the cranes spill out in a long, fluid skein, the current of a collective compass."

Once on their way, cranes may fly miles above the Earth, high enough to pass over 20,320-foot Denali and other Alaska Range peaks. Propelled by their large wings and helped along by winds, they can reach speeds of twenty-five to thirty-five miles per hour and travel two hundred to three hundred miles on an average day; up to five hundred miles with a strong tail wind.

All of the birds that migrate to breeding grounds in Alaska (along with Siberia and northern Canada) are considered lesser sandhill cranes, a subspecies known by the scientific name *Grus canadensis canadensis*. They are distinguished from the greater sandhill cranes (*Grus canadensis tabida*) that mate and rear their young in southern Canada and the Lower 48 states. (As many as four other subspecies have been identified, primarily nonmigratory birds with much smaller numbers and a limited geographic range.)

As their name suggests, lessers are considerably smaller than their greater relatives; on average they stand three to three and a half feet high and weigh six to seven pounds, versus four to four and a half feet and ten to fourteen pounds.

Even more than their dance steps, sandhill cranes are famous for their loud, distinctive voices, which have a haunting, primeval quality. Guidebooks most commonly describe their call as a rattling, bugled, or trumpetlike sound, while the International Crane Foundation's website compares it to a "Loud, rattling kar-r-r-o-o-o, with multiple variations." In his books *Guide to the Birds of Alaska* and *Alaska's Birds*, biologist and author Bob Armstrong comments that they "sound somewhat like a cross between a French horn and a squeaky barn door." I suppose that's as good a description as any.

In my own mind, the voices of cranes have a guttural "roarking" nature and that's the word I've settled upon. However they're described, the calls are usually what bring cranes to our attention; like most other birds, they're generally heard before they're seen. And because they've evolved a long and looping windpipe that amplifies their voices, sandhills can be heard from great distances, sometimes miles away.

The first time cranes grabbed my attention, great flocks of them passed over the Alaska Range while I hiked across tundra in Denali National Park. It's unlikely I would have noticed the Vs and strings of high-flying birds except for their loud, roarking calls, which pulled my awareness from the ground into the distant heavens even as they stirred thoughts of more ancient times and creatures.

Since that long-ago day, I've often noticed that when cranes fly past, shouting their primal screams and flapping their huge wings, people invariably stop what they're doing and turn toward the sky. They seem to pull us humans out of our routines, out of ourselves and into the larger world, in a way that few other birds are capable of doing. I've come to believe that's partly—and maybe largely—because their roarking voices, large skulking bodies, and great flapping wings reflect cranes' primordial roots.

It strikes me as no coincidence that cranes are among the most ancient of birds, whose evolutionary roots have been traced back millions of years. A ten-million-year-old fossil discovered in Nebraska is close enough to modern sandhill cranes that some scientists consider it the same species. Others, not quite so sure, have called it a close ancestor, with "true" sandhill cranes coming into existence only two and a half million years ago.

If the older date is correct, the same species that shares the Earth with us today once inhabited a world that Lentfer, in *Faith of Cranes*, describes as "more like the African savanna than the farm country of the Midwest," a world of rhinos, three-toed horses, hippos, and long-necked camels. All have been found at an excavation site where once "a roiling cloud of volcanic ash . . . fell fast, like an avalanche of black snow, suffocating the animals of the Great Plains beneath ten feet of abrasive powder. . . . Of all the bizarre critters rising from that ash, only the graceful skeleton of the sandhill crane looks familiar to our modern eyes."

Whether ten or two and a half million years, sandhills have been around far longer than most of us can imagine, more than ten times longer than our own species. And across that unfathomable time, these long-lived birds (sometimes reaching twenty or older) have evolved calls that not only fascinate us modern humans with their other-worldly nature, but, like their visual displays, are considerably more complex than the casual bird-watcher would ever suspect.

On its website (www.savingcranes.org), the International Crane Foundation lists three types of calls that sandhills make. Contact calls are soft, low-pitched calls that help cranes stay in touch with each other when they move out of sight. Unison calls are produced by male–female pairs standing side by side or facing each other; performed "in a synchronized duet," they help to reinforce pair bonding and may also be used to threaten predators or other cranes. Guard calls, meanwhile, are "single, loud vocalizations used to warn other cranes of danger or to threaten other cranes."

One might naturally ask what sorts of threats prompt a crane to blast out a warning call. Besides other cranes that they perceive as competitors, sandhills are wary of large raptors, for instance bald eagles and peregrine falcons, and certain corvids, particularly ravens. Wolves, coyotes, and dogs running loose also make them nervous, as do bears and lynx and free-roaming domestic and feral cats. And people, of course. We humans have long hunted cranes, for subsistence and for sport.

Given adults' large size and ability to fly from danger, predators pose a much greater threat to their young (a notable exception being humans, during hunting season), so cranes are especially alert during the nesting and rearing season.

Alaska's cranes usually begin building their nests in May, an apparently simple chore that produces either a small mound made of gathered plants or a shallow depression in the ground that's lined with grass and feathers. The female usually lays two eggs and her mate then helps her incubate them. Nestlings are born in about thirty days and almost immediately are able to walk. Though fed by their parents, the downy colts soon learn to hunt insects and other foods on their own. If they survive life's rigors and dangers, they'll be ready to fly within two and a half months. The young birds remain with their parents for both the fall and following spring migrations, nine to ten months in all.

Though the vast majority of cranes that fly through Anchorage's skies breed and raise their young elsewhere, a small number do nest here, primarily—if not exclusively—within the Anchorage Coastal Wildlife Refuge (ACWR), which stretches sixteen miles along the city's western perimeter, from Point Woronzof to just south of Potter Marsh.

As I began to discover in the early 2000s, the state-managed refuge is hardly pristine; traces of human development and debris are scattered across it. Yet as a whole it remains a largely wild and intact place of mudflats and sedge flats, of ponds and tidal guts, inhabited by all sorts of birds and mammals and myriad smaller creatures that swim, fly, and crawl. And cranes are among its most charismatic—and vulnerable—breeding species.

Part of what makes them vulnerable is their innate wariness; cranes are easily disturbed (sometimes even from distances of several hundred yards) and chased off nests. And because their young can't fly for two months or more after hatching, they're especially susceptible to predators and human harassment.

For several years in the 1990s and early 2000s, local wildlife manager Rick Sinnott conducted almost-annual crane nest hunts in the refuge. One year I pestered Rick enough that he invited me to join him and sidekick Jessy Coltrane (who has since replaced her now-retired boss and mentor) on their survey.

The day I met them, Rick and Jessy had already spent three hours tromping through the marshy sedge flats that cover much of the refuge's southeastern edges. Their combined effort had produced two nests and four eggs. That, Rick told me, was about normal. In the half-dozen years he'd conducted these counts, he'd never found more than five nests in a season or three in one day. Given the hit-and-miss nature of the survey and the number of crane pairs he'd observed, he guessed that eight to ten couples breed within the refuge.

Before putting me to work, Rick offered brief instructions: "The nests really aren't much more than matted mounds of grass. Some look distinctly nest-like, with a shallow bowl, but others don't look like much more than matted grass. To our eyes, they seem to be pretty much randomly placed, except that they're most commonly beside pools of water. So finding them is mostly luck. Most of the ones we do find are near past nest sites [which have been given GPS coordinates], or sometimes we happen to spook a crane off the nest. If you find one, just give a holler."

The three of us split up, fifty to one hundred yards apart, and continued the sweep. The afternoon was sunny but breezy, with temperatures in the fifties, so mosquitoes weren't yet the nuisances they would be later in the summer. The muck beneath and between the sedges tugged at my boots and the inside of my upper pants' legs became soaked with the muddy water we splashed through. I noticed lots of orb-weaving spiders, water striders, and iridescent green beetles. Savannah sparrows sang and flew around us, while from a distance came the voices of Canada geese, mew gulls, and various ducks. A northern harrier engaged in its own hunt passed by, gliding low over the sedges. And a handful of cranes showed themselves, either flapping and roarking overhead or skulking across the flats. But bird nests of any sort were few and far between. We found two duck nests, belonging to pintail and mallard pairs, and another built by snipes. That was all, for the next four hours.

Perhaps feeling bad that he didn't invite me for the entire outing, Rick later offered to show me a nest with eggs that he and Jessy had found in the flats, not far from the Coastal Trail. It would be easy enough to take me back there.

How could I refuse?

We met at 8:00 A.M. on a drizzly but calm Saturday. Rick expected us to locate the nest quickly and without the need of any technological guidance, so he left his GPS device at home. That proved to be a mistake. Two days earlier the female crane had jumped off her nest when the two biologists approached. But on this morning, though the male watched us from a distance, his mate hunkered down and refused to budge.

After a few minutes of fruitless searching, Rick went to a large bleached log that he remembered from the earlier hunt. The nest should be within one hundred feet of this spot, he assured me. But when we circled and recircled the log at different distances, we still couldn't find any sign of the female or nest.

Shrugging, I kidded Rick. "I guess this just shows how well they camouflage their nests."

"Yeah," he grumpily replied. "They're darn good at it."

We continued to inscribe arcs through the sedge flats for nearly a half hour. At first the male crane circled us, his head lowered and body hunched in a defensive position. But eventually he retreated to a pool of water and probed its muddy bottom for food, apparently concluding we didn't present a danger.

"I can't believe this," Rick muttered. "I know we're close. She's probably covering the eggs, with her body and wings spread flat across the ground. We could be within twenty feet and not know it."

Once more I wiped the misted lenses of my binoculars and scanned the flats. Again I saw nothing unusual. But while putting the glasses back down, I noticed a rounded, reddish-brown and gray lump off to my right. At first it looked like a rusty rock. Then, as if by magic, the lump became the head and body of a crane. Suddenly I could recognize the bird's long, pointed beak, her red crown, yellow eye, and outstretched wings.

"I see her," I yelled to Rick. "Over there."

Eyes squinting, brow furrowed, he looked hard at where I pointed. Then, "OK, I see her. Good job."

Slowly we converged on the nest. The crane in turn rose on her long legs, ran several yards, and turned toward us in what must have been intended as a threatening pose: body hunched, wings spread, mouth open wide. Though feeling guilty that we'd pushed her off the eggs—and bothered the cranes by our prolonged presence—I walked up to the nest and knelt beside a slightly matted mass of brown sedges with a small depression, hardly distinct from the surrounding vegetation. Inside that vague and shallow bowl were two eggs, slightly larger than goose eggs. Mostly a muddy tan, they were a darker, rusty brown at their larger, rounded end.

"It's to make them less obvious, help them blend in," Rick explained.

We remained at the nest only a few moments before departing. Mouth still open, the female scampered ahead of us, body crouched and open wings dragging along the ground. The male followed at a distance.

"She's trying to lead us away," Rick commented. "It's the old broken-wing routine."

Neither of the parents had "spoken" the entire time, though Rick confirmed that they sometimes squawk harshly when upset by such nest hunting. A couple of hundred feet beyond the nest the female crane began to circle off to the right and back to her eggs. The parents converged while we continued our retreat. Soon their eggs would hatch to reveal large, downy chicks. Within a day or two of hatching, they'd leave the nest and follow their parents around the flats. But the chances were small that both would survive the summer.

Several years later, I have mixed feelings about my nest hunt with Rick. Though grateful for the rare opportunity to see crane eggs in the wild and to observe, first-hand, how remarkably well camouflaged both parent and nest can be, I have no doubt we harassed the nesting pair during our prolonged search. I suppose I rationalized that I'd been invited by a wildlife manager to view the nest, so that must make it OK. But it's not something I would do again.

I've also gradually come to worry about the harm that's done to animals in the name of science and wildlife management. Is it all right to risk injury to individuals, if the goal is to better understand and manage, and perhaps even protect, the populations to which they belong? Wildlife scientists emphasize the health of populations, not individuals. They accept that some small percentage of the animals they're catching, counting, handling, measuring, banding, collaring, and sometimes drugging will die because of the researchers' own well-intended actions. But is the knowledge that's gained from nest surveys or satellite-transmitter banding or radio collaring worth the cost of lives, even if only a small percentage of the studied animals die because they happen to become part of a study?

Sometimes it becomes too easy to say "it's for the good of the species" or a particular population, when the knowledge gained may benefit us humans more than the animal being studied.

◆

Barbara Carlson, as much as anyone, has been protective of the Anchorage refuge's cranes, especially its nesting pairs. As president and executive director of Friends of the Anchorage Coastal Wildlife Refuge, or FAR, she has worked hard to keep them from being harassed and otherwise harmed by humans. Yet she can understand why I once desired to get an up-close look at a nesting sandhill's eggs. She too has felt the urge to walk through the refuge and count nests and eggs, all for the good cause of learning more about cranes and the refuge's importance to them. In the end, she chose to do otherwise.

Carlson began to closely observe the refuge's cranes from her bluff-top home in 1999, independent of any group, and she continues to watch them each year. From 2007 to 2011, she also organized, coordinated, and supervised FAR's annual snow goose and sandhill crane survey. Initially, she admits, "We talked about going down there [on the flats], and it was tempting because we would have been able to get more information, for example, how many eggs were in each nest." But the survey design team—which included Carlson; Fish and Game biologists Tom Rothe, Michael Petrula, and Rick Sinnott (who apparently had changed his mind about the wisdom of tromping around the flats while looking for nests) and ornithologist Vivian Mendenhall—eventually decided that would unduly stress the cranes and perhaps lure other people, or animals, to the nest sites.

"We went back and forth, back and forth," she recalls, "about how it would be great to be able to get the size of the clutch as part of the data, but eventually settled on 'first, do no harm.'"

Instead of ground surveys, FAR chose to look for nests and observe crane families from atop the bluffs that overlook the coastal wetlands, in teams outfitted with binoculars, spotting scopes, and data sheets. The goal: to collect information on the cranes' first arrival, their peak numbers when migrating through the refuge, and then, later in the season, nest locations, chick emergence, and colt survival to fledging and fall migration.

What Carlson and her allies have learned holds great surprises. For instance:

I'd wager that few Anchorage residents realize that several thousand sandhill cranes may pass through the Anchorage refuge on their annual migrations, or that groups of up to four hundred birds have been observed during their stopovers. As she explains, "Cranes and other species migrate in and out of the refuge in waves, so absolute numbers are very difficult [to determine]. Unless you happen to post yourself overlooking some prime habitat at just the right times, and actually spend several hours watching, you may think few cranes come through."

The number that stays for the summer is substantially smaller. Carlson guesses that between forty and one hundred sandhills inhabit Anchorage's coastal flats between Potter Marsh and Point Woronzof. Those include anywhere from eight to twenty-eight breeding pairs, which produce an estimated twelve to thirty-six chicks. The remainder are nonbreeding adults and juveniles. Colt survival varies greatly from year to year, "depending on availability of food, weather, tides, [human] disturbance, and predation." One year Fish and Game biologists could verify only a single colt's survival; another year, twenty-two made it to the fall migration.

"Sandhill cranes have their work cut out for them," Carlson says, "simply avoiding and fighting off animal predators in the refuge." Those include eagles, hawks, owls, river otters, foxes, coyotes, bears, and dogs. Bald eagles seem especially adept at killing cranes of any age. "Twice," she notes, "I have witnessed eagles devouring adult cranes."

Humans, too, occasionally kill the refuge's cranes, during fall waterfowl hunts. Bow hunting is allowed throughout the refuge, while guns are permitted in certain areas.

Besides the hunting, Anchorage's cranes suffer from human harassment, both intentional and accidental. It happens that the refuge's most important crane habitat occurs in wetland meadows near the bluffs. There they have access to freshwater springs, a variety of foods, and ground that's elevated enough it isn't flooded by Cook Inlet's highest tides. What this means is that human activities along the edge of bluffs, as well as in the wetlands, can sometimes disturb or otherwise harm the cranes.

Carlson's list of human-related threats includes trash, aerial lines that can entangle birds, and possibly effluent from the city's wastewater treatment plant. Of the latter she says, "While we have no evidence to prove that Anchorage's minimally treated wastewater is a problem to wildlife, it cannot be a good thing."

She also names hikers, bicyclists, dog walkers, and people flying paragliders and kites or riding motor vehicles—including the occasional airboat. In years with prolonged winters, such as 2013, even cross-country skiers may unwittingly disturb early arriving cranes. Carlson suspects that many people who explore the flats—and walk their dogs there—have no idea they're bothering the cranes. But they are.

"It's easy to observe obvious disturbance," she says, "for example when a crane emits an alarm call, or flies away from a nest, or feigns injury to draw away a predator. What most people don't understand is that cranes can be stressed and not display it overtly. What cranes are doing is important to their survival and that of their broods, and threats take away from the energy and focus that they need.

"During the time of spring migration, people should not be out in the ACWR in any numbers nor have dogs out there. Nesting and brood-rearing season are also times when sandhill cranes need their space, mainly mid-April through October."

Feeding both Carlson's hopes and concerns is the city's new Campbell Creek Estuary Natural Area (CCENA), a sixty-acre plot of upland forest and coastal wetlands adjacent to what she considers "the very heart" of the Anchorage Coastal Wildlife Refuge.

Purchased by the Great Land Trust in 2010 and later transferred to the municipality, the natural area is intended to provide additional protections to fragile coastal habitat and wildlife. For that reason, Carlson says, "FAR has worked diligently with the municipality, the trust, and others to implement a master plan honoring FAR's mission 'to preserve the integrity and biological diversity of the ACWR.'"

Most of the CCENA will remain minimally developed, but some trails and overlooks and a parking lot were completed in 2013, when the area was officially opened. Visitors are allowed to walk down to the margins of the estuary's wetlands, but they're discouraged from doing so when cranes and other migratory birds are present. While they applaud the protection of this land, Carlson and other refuge advocates worry that it will draw increased people to the estuary and that some will be lured into more sensitive wetlands important to cranes and other animals. Time will tell whether this preservation effort has the unintended consequence of disturbing the area's breeding cranes.

"FAR embraces the opportunity to help Anchorage and the Great Land Trust do this right," Carlson says. "If we do, future generations may be able to stand on one of the overlook platforms and focus their binoculars and scopes on a bonded pair of sandhills as the cranes sit on their nests and later as they raise their colts while listening to the primordial sounds of other crane pairs defending their territories with unison calls east and west along the coast."

On their sandhill crane website, Christy Yuncker Happ and George Happ describe the "schooling" of colts, from their earliest days until they're ready to fly south with their parents. Based on more than a dozen years of observing and documenting the behavior of the "crane couple whom we know as Millie and Roy," they've concluded that the "core curriculum" of sandhill crane colts consists of three subjects: feeding, dancing, and flying, all of which appear essential to the birds' survival. I've already touched on the omnivorous eating habits and complex dancing of cranes, so here I'll simply add a few of their observations about "flight training."

"Flying," they note, "requires strength, coordination, practice, and flight feathers. From the early days, colts walk about with their parents and flap their tiny rudimental wings. Preflight training involves running, flapping, and then, as the wing feathers fill in, bounding to facilitate gliding. Both dance training and preflight training prepare the youngsters for the first flights and the fall migration. By late summer, the family often takes increasingly longer day trips and even overnights in nearby ponds."

Sometimes, though, even the best flight training isn't enough to ensure a colt's ability to join its parents on the long passage south to wintering grounds.

In fall 2012, several people who monitor the Anchorage refuge's breeding cranes noticed that a colt they'd tracked for much of the summer seemed unable to fly. Inspection of the bird through high-powered spotting scopes revealed that several primary and secondary feathers were missing from its left wing. And the pattern of absent feathers suggested a predatory attack.

By early October—considerably later than they would normally depart—the colt and its parents remained stuck on Anchorage's coastal flats. It was then that I was invited into the loop of concerned crane watchers and their chain of e-mailed messages. The big question: what, if anything, could or should be done to help the injured crane? The general consensus, as expressed by FAR's Barbara Carlson, was that any attempt to rescue the colt only be made "if and when the parents are forced to abandon it to save themselves."

Wayne Hall and Marilyn Houser were among those to regularly observe the crane family. On October 10, I joined them on the broad, grassy knoll they call Peat Point. Through spotting scopes and binoculars we watched the parents repeatedly encourage their colt with short flights. The young crane ran and hopped and vainly flapped its wings, one clearly smaller than the other and misshapen. It was a hard, sad thing to watch.

The next day, too, "The adults took flight several times, circling, calling, and landing back near the colt," Wayne reported. "The colt did not leave the ground at any time. Adults were observed feeding the colt."

The morning of October 13, Carlson noticed ice on refuge ponds. That afternoon, Wayne and Marilyn watched the cranes for about forty minutes, until "visibility dropped due to snow." All three were seen feeding together. No flights were attempted.

The next afternoon, Marilyn watched as "an adult male dressed in camouflage and wearing a sash of shotgun shells came down the hill with his two unleashed Labrador retrievers. . . . He glassed the area on several occasions. The two adult SACR [sandhill cranes] took flight while he was looking in their direction. The colt attempted to fly but was not successful. The adults circled the colt in the air, landed, and all three resumed feeding."

Carlson noted on October 16, "I have seen no more cranes coming through the refuge the last few days. The latest crane stragglers I recall seeing in years past was about October 27."

The instinctive urge to fly south must have been intensely strong, yet the parents remained faithful to their wounded colt. The next day Marilyn observed the crane parents flying four different times during her fifty-minute watch, "calling, circling, and returning to the ground each time. The second time the pair took to the air, the disabled colt was clearly visible, running after the two adults, attempting and failing to get aloft."

The e-mail updates then abruptly ended. On October 26 I contacted Marilyn to get the latest news. Her response: "It came to a sad conclusion. The adults were observed leaving by a homeowner on Shore Drive a week ago Thursday [October 18]. Observations that Thursday, Friday, and Saturday yielded no more sightings or crane calls. It is entirely possible the colt had succumbed at that point or it had been injured and become more disabled by its repeated attempts to get aloft, making it easier for the adults to leave. There's also the possibility the colt was killed by a hunter . . . Three hunters were observed in the marsh on Thursday [the day the adult pair departed].

"I am going to try to get a group together to look for remains of the colt. We're looking at the first weekend in November."

On November 4, I joined Wayne and Marilyn in the area where the colt had been last seen. Temperatures were in the twenties, the flats were frozen, and no snow covered the ground. We knew the odds were small that we'd find the colt's remains, but were still disappointed when two hours of searching turned up nothing.

It's Carlson's belief that a bow hunter killed the colt.

On the morning of October 18, she happened to be talking by phone with another refuge steward who'd been monitoring the crane family, when the woman noticed two people, apparently hunters, cross the flats below her property. Not long after their passage, the cranes began calling loudly. The woman then spotted the adult sandhill pair. The two birds "flew up out of the marsh and overhead. They called a few times and flew straight down Turnagain Arm, never to be seen again," Carlson recounts. "We speculate that the parents saw their colt die and, unable to do more, they left to save themselves."

As I write these final words it is once again early summer. Anchorage's breeding cranes have returned to the city's coastal margins, they've built their nests, laid their eggs, and spent weeks incubating the embryos inside. Any day chicks will break out of their shells. Some may have already done so. Soon it will be time for the colts' schooling, their survival training, to begin. Another generation will be taught what's good to eat and what dangers to avoid. They'll learn how to fly and how to ride thermals high into the heavens and how to find wintering grounds far to the south. Just as importantly, they will be taught how to dance like a crane, a complex and marvelous thing. And those that survive will learn how to speak in primal voices that turn our faces and attention to the skies, and evoke in us humans something that might be called awe.

NESTING GOSHAWKS

There is much that I love about poet and essayist Gary Snyder's eloquent and thought-provoking book, *The Practice of the Wild*. It's among my favorite and most marked-up books, filled with underlined and highlighted sentences and paragraphs, notes scribbled in the margins. One part that I especially love touches on the idea that "the world is watching." As Snyder explains it, a person cannot venture anywhere in nature without his or her movements being noticed by each creature that inhabits a place, from bug to bird to bear. The wild world is indeed watching, paying attention. But more than that, all natural systems—whether woodland or coastal sedge flats or alpine tundra—have their own form of intelligence, just as individual creatures do. The information passed from one part of the system to another represents that intelligence.

We humans so often think we've cornered the market on grand intellect and higher consciousness, but we actually know so little about the way the wild Earth works. And most of us have such a narrow, anthropocentric notion of intelligence, based on our human understandings. Why not imagine greater possibilities? Both the world and our species would benefit if we'd only take a humbler approach to life.

I'd come across that "world is watching" passage while rereading *The Practice of the Wild*, one of several books in my personal library that explore the notion of wildness. Those valued references complement my own explorations of Anchorage's wild spots, from my own backyard to our city's coastal refuge, wetlands, and forests. More than ever, I appreciate the wild nature to be found within and around our community.

The moose and bears and ravens that inhabit our city are especially important, because they're impossible to ignore. Their high-profile presence reminds us that the natural world is just as much a part of the Anchorage Bowl as big box stores and office buildings, movie theaters and malls, parking lots and high-density housing developments. But for every moose and grizzly, there are myriad other life-forms all around us daily that speak of larger mysteries, from the chickadees that visit our feeders to the mosquitoes that pester us, the spiders that crawl across our ceilings, the moths drawn to our porch lights, and the fireweed that lights up our city in summer.

As you might guess, I'm one of those people who needs to spend considerable time outside, immersed in nature. Though I love my trips into deep wilderness, I've also come to savor my regular walks through Anchorage's natural spaces.

One place that became a favorite when I lived on the Hillside was Bicentennial Park and the adjacent Campbell Tract. Though I go there less frequently since I moved to west Anchorage, for years I regularly walked the Bicentennial Park/Campbell Tract trails (now and then heading off trail), for any number of reasons: exercise, solitude, solace, discovery, simple happiness. It became one of the places where I tracked the changing of the seasons; where I expanded my sense of community by learning more about the Anchorage Bowl's forest residents; and where I sometimes met friends out on their own adventures.

On one especially memorable walk through Bicentennial Park, I discovered a nesting pair of northern goshawks. Because I'm more of a songbird fancier than a raptor enthusiast, I had to overcome certain prejudices to learn more about the pair, for instance my dislike that they eat the birds I love the most. Even given that harsh reality, my first close and extended encounter with goshawks proved a thrilling surprise and gave me an education that came with an adrenaline rush.

As predators near the pinnacle of the food web, goshawks are wily hunters who've carved out a niche in the northern forest that demands patience, stealth, and impressive maneuverability. They're ghostly in a way, appearing suddenly as if out of nowhere.

Though they're large raptors, with wingspans of three and a half to four feet, they fly swiftly and quietly through the forest, with great dexterity. Once I'd watched a goshawk chase a raven through the woods at breakneck speed, both birds twisting and turning and somehow managing to avoid hitting the trees through which they raced. It seemed as marvelous a flying exhibition as anything I'd ever witnessed.

Besides being secretive, goshawks are exceptionally fierce, in both hunting and parenting. They're known to plunge through branches and thickets, if necessary, to capture prey (which in Alaska ranges from songbirds and shrews to grouse, waterfowl, and snowshoe hares). And when rearing a family, they're ferociously protective, as any person who's unwittingly stumbled into their territory can attest. Over the years local media have recounted several stories about the goshawks that have sometimes nested along the bike trail near Alaska Pacific University, attacking unsuspecting bicyclists, joggers, and walkers.

I first happened upon the Bicentennial pair in mid-March. Hearing a series of piercing, high-pitched screeches, I followed the calls into an opening within the birch-spruce forest. Less than thirty feet away, a pair of hawks sat side by side atop a broken-off, beetle-killed spruce. The white stripes above their eyes, their intensely red irises, blue-gray backs, white, streaked undersides, and large size, all identified the two as goshawks. The smaller of the two—in the case of goshawks, the male—flew off after only a few moments, but the other remained in place, eyes fixed upon me. Barely moving, we watched each other several minutes. Then I changed my position along the trail and the female flew off, shrieking loudly.

I figured the two must have a nest nearby so I returned in early April to search for it. Winding among the trees, I found a kill site on a mound of snow. All that remained were a few gray feathers, some small bones with gristle attached, and splotches of blood. Grabbing one of the feathers, I later asked a biologist what bird it came from; she identified it as a mallard's.

A few minutes later, I made a second discovery: a large platform of branches and twigs built in the crook of a birch tree, some thirty to forty feet above the ground. I couldn't see any evidence the nest was being used, but it perfectly fit the guidebook description of a goshawk nest.

I'd been wandering through the woods for nearly an hour without any sign of the goshawks. But as I began to leave the nest tree, one of the birds swooped past me, flying low. It wasn't so close that I felt attacked, but clearly the hawk was checking me out. The bird settled upon a birch branch and sat there quietly, barely moving except to occasionally swivel its head or preen its soft breast feathers.

Several minutes later I heard loud shrieking from back up the narrow footpath I'd been following. From what I've observed, the female is the screamer; the male has something of a guttural bark or cluck. Backtracking, I found her perched on a birch limb about a dozen feet above the ground, a small ball of bloody flesh in her right talon. She watched me closely as I approached, but showed no inclination to either leave or attack. Had she been calling to her mate, wishing to share a meal? Or was she issuing me a warning?

The male eventually approached to within several yards of the female and for a while we all stayed put, watching one another. Then I retreated a hundred feet or so and "hid" behind a birch, hoping they might join each other. But the goshawks weren't fooled, nor were they as impatient as me. Both remained in place until I finally left the woods.

I returned to the nest site a few more times. Though I never saw nestlings, the hawks became increasingly aggressive. Especially the female. Every time I approached the nest, she eventually noticed and attacked me. Mouth opened wide in a piercing scream, she dived legs first, both wings and talons extended in a maneuver that biologists call "stooping." I wore a hat to protect my scalp, but though she came within a foot or two of my head, she didn't seem intent on grabbing some flesh, that I could tell. Still, I did quite a bit of ducking.

Each time, the female escorted me out of her territory, shrieking all the while and stooping occasionally, as if to emphasize her willingness to raise some hell for the family's sake. The male goshawk appeared every time but once, but he generally kept his distance, apparently content to watch his mate go crazy with fury. From what I've read, he's the hunter and provider, out grabbing food for mom and nestlings. The two seemed to have clearly defined family roles.

Unwilling to become a regular disruption, I purposely didn't go back too often. Of course if I had the goshawks' best interests in mind, I probably wouldn't have returned at all. But I wanted to learn more about these fierce neighbors and couldn't be sure such an opportunity would ever come again. Though I may have been simply rationalizing my intrusion, the hawks appeared to be handling me OK. In fact it almost seemed that momma goshawk had begun to recognize me and understood I meant no harm. The last time I visited, she didn't chase me nearly as far through the woods.

On that last visit, I approached to within fifty feet of the nest tree and then watched for an hour without noticing any sign of the goshawks, uncertain whether the female was on the nest or out hunting with her mate. If she was around, she had to hear or otherwise sense "the signal" of my leaf-crunching approach.

Leaning against a birch tree on that warm and breezy May afternoon, I listened with great pleasure to the songs of ruby-crowned kinglet, dark-eyed junco, red-breasted nuthatch, varied thrush, and boreal chickadee. And I thought about what Gary Snyder had written about the watching world. The forest's songbirds must have been aware of my passage, just as they must be aware of the goshawks' presence. Yet they go about their lives, announcing their own territories and seeking mates, starting their own process of building families, even with death lurking in the shadows, silently and fiercely waiting. There's a certain faith, a hopefulness, in that.

Finally the goshawk appeared. From the nest high above, she stooped at me, screaming. I reminded her I meant no harm and told her I'd be leaving soon, for whatever that was worth. Then I walked around the nest tree, hoping to see some movement above. The goshawk mom dive-bombed me a couple more times, as she must, and I ducked when necessary. In the pauses between her shrieks, I could hear kinglet and junco, still singing brightly and steadily in the woods nearby.

ARCTIC TERNS, THE WORLD'S GREATEST LONG-DISTANCE FLYERS

Midsummer in Anchorage is a raucous time at the city's lakes and along its coastal perimeter, as the eggs of shorebirds, seabirds, and waterfowl hatch and avian offspring make the rapid transition from nestling to fledgling.

With families to watch and feed and protect, now is the brief but exhausting time of aggressive parenting. And among the waterbirds that seasonally inhabit Anchorage's landscape, there are no more protective parents than Arctic terns. They are fierce defenders of their young, as anyone who's approached their nesting grounds can attest. Over the years I have seen them fearlessly attack gulls, ravens, humans, a northern harrier, even a crane that wandered too close.

Long fascinated by the ferocity and beauty of these amazing long-distance flyers, one year I entered the Anchorage Coastal Wildlife Refuge on an early July day, seeking further glimpses into their lives.

Crossing a meadow of sedges, I skirted some ponds inhabited by several families of Canada geese, mallards, and American widgeon, goslings, and ducklings clustered about their parents on an early morning swim. Gulls screeched loudly as they circled and swooped above the ponds and their green perimeters, while families of violet-green swallows cut arcs through the calm air in their hunt for insects. In the distance, a fuzzy, gangly sandhill crane chick—already bigger than an adult goose—followed its parents, mimicking their slow, deliberate pace. Noticing me, one of the cranes called loudly—*roark . . . roark*—in its rusty-door-hinged way and the cinnamon colt disappeared into the sedges.

A hundred yards away or more, a couple of Arctic terns hovered above small tidal guts that wind through the mudflats. I sat upon the bleached trunk of a cottonwood that had been carried here by Cook Inlet tides and I watched the terns through binoculars. They are such handsome, streamlined birds that seem to carry themselves through the air with effortless grace on their slender wings.

Such flying talent is needed for their fantastic migrations. Arctic terns are the world's long-distance flying champs; some members of their species make annual migratory flights between the high Arctic and Antarctica. Though it was once assumed that such round-trip flights covered about twenty-five thousand miles—an amazing distance in itself—in 2010 an international team of researchers reported that some terns (which breed in Greenland and Iceland) annually fly twice that distance while following S-shaped routes, apparently to take advantage of prevailing winds. Over the course of a lifetime, a long-lived tern might travel one and a half million miles, the equivalent distance of three round-trip visits to the moon.

When observed, migrating terns have been seen traveling singly and in small groups of under twenty birds. In high winds they tend to travel low, right along wave tops; in calmer weather they may fly four- to five-hundred feet—and perhaps higher—above ocean waters.

Arctic terns leave Antarctica in March and begin to arrive in southernmost Alaska the latter half of April. Researchers say they breed throughout the state's coastal areas, from the southernmost Panhandle to the Arctic Coast, and west out the Aleutians. They breed inland as well, though their interior distribution is not as well documented.

According to Buzz Scher's *Field Guide to Birding in Anchorage*, terns that spend their summers locally arrive from late April into early May. Mates will breed sometime in May and chicks hatch in June, reaching fledging stage in July. Most parents and offspring will then begin their southern migrations sometime between late July and mid-August.

As I sat on the cottonwood that July day in the coastal refuge, a tern flew in and perched on another, nearby bit of driftwood. Every so often the bird made a cheeping sound, one note at a time. Had the watcher become the watched?

Studying the nearly motionless bird, I admired the tern's sleek form, its black cap, and striking blood-red bill and feet, which contrast so sharply with the white cheeks, neck, and breast, the pale gray wings and back.

After several minutes, the bird lifted off and headed farther out onto the mudflats, where it joined another hovering tern. Mates, perhaps, engaged in hunting. I decided to follow. In a matter of moments, an alert was sounded. The two terns approached, yelling loudly in shrill, raspy voices. In field guides, the tern's alarm call is usually described as some variation on *keee-eer*, though to my ears it sounds closer to *eee-aagh* or *kee-aagh*.

Soon other terns joined the couple. I counted a handful, then ten, then a dozen. It seemed as if they had appeared out of nowhere. I must have been getting close—but to what? I couldn't imagine the terns would try to raise a family out on the mudflats, where the inlet's highest tides would swamp their nests. Researchers have learned that terns will sometimes defend feeding territory. Was that the explanation? Or did they indeed have nests—or chicks—hidden among the salt-tolerant grasses and goose tongue plants that grow along the mudflats' meandering gullies?

My walk onto the mudflats was shortened when a pair of terns started dive-bombing me. Uttering clicking sounds, the birds came straight for my head, then lifted or swerved at the last moment. Occasionally they swooped in close enough for me to hear the whoosh of their fast-moving bodies.

Arctic terns have been known to defecate on intruders and peck heads or hands uplifted to ward them off, sometimes drawing blood. In his pocket field guide *Alaska's Birds*, author Bob Armstrong reported once being hit in the forehead by a tern. "It hit, drew blood, and made me more cautious," he advised.

Somehow my baseball cap didn't seem enough protection. As the swooping birds increased their attack, I retreated back to the cottonwood. Almost immediately, the terns dispersed. Keeping my distance, I scanned the coastal flats. Though some terns continued to fly across the mudflats, others hovered above the pond, hunting sticklebacks and sculpins.

Flying in place, with its long, forked tail spread wide for balance, a tern on the hunt lifts its wings high above the body and beats them rapidly. Seen from below, the body is mostly white. And in that hovering whiteness, with the blood-red beak and black skullcap, the bird becomes a heavenly apparition.

If angelic, however, the tern is undoubtedly an angel of death. Sometimes hovering at thirty feet, other times just a few feet above the water, the tern zeroes in on its prey. Closing its wings, it then goes into a dive and plunges into the water with a splash. Terns also feed by skimming the water, delicately picking prey at or near its surface. If successful at either plunge or skim methods, the bird emerges with a fish, or insect, or crustacean, which it quickly swallows or carries to its mate or young.

Still intrigued by the terns' mudflat attacks, I returned to the refuge later in the week. Crossing the flats seaward from the sedge meadows and ponds, I noticed that most of the terns flew above, or near, the pond and surrounding marsh, though they occasionally made forays out to the mudflats. As long as I avoided the area I entered a few days earlier, they left me alone.

Playing a hunch, I returned to the spot where I'd been dive-bombed. Again, one loudly *kee-aaghing* tern zoomed toward me, quickly followed by another. Others were drawn by the alarm, but they hovered and swooped high above me. Only a couple birds actually attacked.

Confident that this was a nesting pair, I skirted the tidal gut, looking closely among the grasses and goose tongue that grow above its banks. Finally I found it: an oval nest of dried plants and mud, nestled into a patch of goose tongue. Inside the grassy bowl were two eggs, beige oval forms speckled with dark brown spots.

It seemed late in the season for unhatched eggs. Curious to know if they were still being incubated or had been abandoned, I leaned in close, extended a finger and gently touched one egg: still warm. Then I quickly backed off, so the parents would return.

Though their mottled color matched guidebook descriptions, the eggs seemed large for terns. Maybe they belonged to a mew gull. I'd seen one from afar, sitting near this locale. But with my attention turned toward the terns, I hadn't kept close track of the gull's movements. Perhaps it abandoned the nest as I approached. That would also explain why the terns had temporarily eased their attacks—their nest and offspring weren't being threatened.

Whether this was a gull or tern nest didn't seem so important; clearly, some birds, for whatever reasons, were nesting out on the mudflats, risking the tides. I'd solved the riddle.

I turned toward shore to make my retreat, still checking the ground but moving faster. The terns escorted me across their territory, again diving at my head. One of them let loose and splashed my shirt with watery guano. Finally they left, attention turned to other potential intruders.

One final foray, this time to Potter Marsh, a prime place to observe Arctic terns from either roadside pullouts or the boardwalk. Through binoculars, I watched terns circle and loop, heads down as they searched for food. Finding it, they hovered and dived, or skimmed gracefully across the water, opening and dipping their beaks.

Several times terns lifted from the water with fish crosswise in their bills. It was hard to tell whether they'd caught sticklebacks, sculpin, or salmon fry. The birds circled and set down behind a wall of reeds. Were they feeding their families?

Seeking a different angle, I walked south along the Seward Highway. Sure enough, I saw two young terns perched on a log, fifty yards or more from the road. In between feedings, they preened their feathers, stretched, and flapped their wings. From this distance, their plumage didn't look much different from their parents', raising the question of how close they were to flying.

The answer came a few minutes later, when the fledgling terns joined their parents in the air. In flight, the youngsters were less streamlined than the adults. Their tails were shorter and less forked, their head caps were a mottled black, and their bodies had more grays and browns. The fledglings returned to the log after a brief test flight. It would be a while yet before they were ready to hover and hunt.

The adults continued flying, looking for more food. And ever the protective parents, they would yell and dive-bomb and harass whatever stranger came too close to their young, until the entire family headed south together.

CAMPBELL CREEK'S SILVERS

On a bright, calm morning in late August, I stood above a culvert and peered at the dirtied waters of Campbell Creek, looking for salmon. Coho had been returning to the creek for several weeks, bound for spawning grounds across town, and I'd come to the western fringes of Anchorage hoping to see some ocean-bright fish.

Ship Creek may be the city's best-known salmon stream, but thousands of silvers also swim up Campbell Creek each summer. A small number are native to the stream, but most are hatchery fish, part of a Fish and Game stocking program begun in the early 1990s.

Whether hatchery-reared or natural residents of the creek, the salmon are wild when they return to their city roots after spending much of their lives surviving and growing in the ocean. As they spawn and then die, the salmon's eggs and flesh will feed grizzly and black bears and a variety of other local predators and scavengers, from rainbow trout and Dolly Varden to eagles, ravens, and humans. (Anglers may legally fish for coho in portions of the creek between Dimond Boulevard and the confluence of its North and South Forks beginning in late July; exact dates vary, depending on the location.)

About an eighth of a mile to my right, the creek was sparkling clear as it poured out of Campbell Lake, with its expensive waterfront homes, floatplanes, and numerous "Keep Out" and "No Trespassing" signs.

Here, at the edge of the signed private property, the creek had begun its winding path through Anchorage's coastal flats and its waters were thick with mud and silt. Still, as my eyes adjusted to the light and the water's murkiness, I could gradually make out the shadowy, green-gray shapes of six, then ten, then fifteen or more salmon, their sleek bodies undulating slowly in the current. In a few weeks, maybe less, most would be dead or dying. But for now they were bursting with life and the desire to produce more life.

Standing there, appreciating the salmon and their passage through Anchorage, I recalled a walk I'd taken the previous September, through the rushing waters of Campbell Creek's South Fork, counting salmon with local sport fish biologist Dan Bosch.

Bosch and I began our salmon survey at a footbridge crossing near Campbell Creek Airstrip Road. For the next several hours we would travel through some of Anchorage's wildest woodlands in Bicentennial Park and the Campbell Tract.

Because we'd be walking down the creek itself, we wore chest-high waders. Our other gear included rain jackets, day packs with lunch and extra layers of clothes, ballcaps and sunglasses to cut the glare and help us see the salmon, and "tally whackers" to track the coho numbers. Dan would count the live fish; I would do the dead ones.

Because we might share the stream with fishing bears, Dan also carried a shotgun loaded with slugs. Earlier in the summer, while counting king salmon in Campbell Creek's North Fork, he'd been charged by a grizzly with two cubs. No harm came of it, but the brown-haired, mustachioed biologist with a deeply tanned and freckled face figured you can't be too careful. For that same reason, Dan packed something to announce our presence as we passed through the thickly wooded forest: cigars. Lighting up, he explained, "The only times I smoke are when the bugs are bad or I'm in bear country. I like to give bears the chance to use all their senses."

Taking a puff, Dan recalled that a day earlier, while surveying the North Fork for cohos, he saw "lots of bear sign, but no bears. That's what I call a good day."

The first stretch of stream channel was mostly straight and narrow, its bottom covered with cobbles and boulders; in other words, it's poor spawning habitat. Preferring to place and fertilize their eggs in pea-sized gravel, silvers rarely come this far upstream, so we were likely to miss few, if any, fish.

The creek's cold, crystalline water splashed noisily as it ran fast and hard down the channel, in depths that ranged from ankle to knee to midthigh deep. At higher levels, Dan said, this upper creek can be "more of a stumble than a stroll." Even today, stepping carefully upon the cobbly bottom, I occasionally tripped and once spun 180 degrees before regaining my balance. Still I fared better than Dan's previous volunteer counter; that poor guy fell into the creek three times.

After many days, perhaps weeks, in fresh water, the cohos had lost their silvery, ocean-bright sheen. Their bodies were crimson to purple, with gray-green heads. That, of course, simplified our job. Red and purple forms are much easier to spot along the brown and gray creek bottom.

Less easy to see were the creek's rainbows. As with the salmon, there's a small native population, supplemented by hatchery fish. Most of the trout are less than a foot long, but now and then Dan would hear about an angler catching one in the twenty-inch range.

"Some guys fish this creek almost exclusively for rainbows," he told me. "To think we have something like this, right in Anchorage—it's amazing."

We spotted a half-dozen salmon during the first fifteen minutes, but then went nearly a mile without seeing any. By the time I found the first dead fish, about and hour and a half into our walk, Dan had already counted seventy-four live ones. Most were paired up and swimming in pools or beneath cut banks, where the current was slower.

In these upper reaches, Campbell Creek flowed through spruce-birch-cottonwood forest. In places, the banks were thick with alder, scarlet fireweed, purplish highbush cranberry bushes, tall brown grasses, and patches of devil's club—the plant's bright red clusters of berries raised above platter-sized leaves that glowed golden on the gray, overcast day. Still, the woods were opening up, as leaves dropped from trees and bushes. In July, said Dan, "it's like a wall of green" along each bank.

Though we were paralleling Campbell Creek Airstrip Road, there was no sound or other sign of traffic; only the forest and the loud splashing of creek water. Still, evidence of human use was scattered among tracks of moose and mink. We passed boot prints, trails, fire pits, and—even here—bits of trash: plastic bottles, aluminum cans, candy wrappers. In one logjam we discovered the remains of a small, wrecked, rubber raft. By day's end we would find three more, lower in the drainage.

The nature of the creek changed as we approached the Campbell Creek Science Center: there were more meanders, some nearly bending back on themselves, and a greater mix of deep pools, white-water riffles, and shallow stretches of water. Passing near the center at midday we saw a few people, the only humans we'd notice until nearly at the North and South Forks' confluence, a distance of several miles. So far we had counted 179 live coho and one dead.

Between 12:30 P.M. and 3:30 P.M. we walked the stretch of creek that's farthest from roads and other human development and our coho count jumped to 633, all but 9 of them living. Here, finally, we found signs of bear: tracks and scat. And the chickadees we'd heard throughout our walk were joined by other wildlife. A northern harrier glided silently past, disappearing among spruce trees. Three magpies chattered loudly in their raspy way. Mergansers and mallards swam in the creek, here underlain mostly by sand and silt. The creekside habitat too, had changed: spruce-birch-cottonwood forest gave way to more open patches of grassy meadows, interspersed with dense alder thickets and black spruce bogs.

As we neared the end of our traverse, the creek took us back to "civilization." We passed a tent camp, then started to see houses, part of a neighborhood south of Tudor Road. We also started to meet people along the creek or on nearby trails. Almost inevitably they wanted to know, "Did you see any bears?"

Finally we reached the forks' confluence, where a large number of salmon had schooled up. Over the last short stretch of creek between the confluence and our stopping point at Folker Street, Dan counted more than 2,000 salmon. Our total for the day had grown to 3,235 living salmon and 34 "morts."

At a viewing platform that overlooks the creek, a crowd had gathered. There were kids and elders, street people and business people, Native and non-Native, black and white and Asian.

The stretch of creek below the forks is open to coho fishing until October 1, but hardly anyone was doing that because the salmon were far past their silvery prime. Some people talked, others napped or read books. But most looked toward the water and the mass of red, finned bodies swimming within it, as if entranced by this surge of wild energy passing through midtown, driven through Alaska's urban center by ancient instincts and desires that, for all we've learned about salmon, largely remain an enigma.

ON THE TRAIL, FINDING LYNX

Friday evening, month of April. I had come to celebrate Alaska's change of seasons with a walk along my favorite forest path, the Turnagain Arm Trail. Cut across a wooded hillside, the route predates Anchorage by several years. It was built in 1910 as a telegraph line and later served as a winter mail trail. Nowadays, it's a popular hiking trail on the city's fringes, in Chugach State Park.

I've hiked here, off and on, since the late 1980s. Over the years, the trail has become one of my important local landmarks. It's where I note the passing of seasons and continue learning about the plants and animals that inhabit Anchorage's wild edges. Even when nothing special happens, it's a place of solitude and great contentment. And there's always the possibility of surprise.

The entire trail is nine and a half miles long, but ambling along at a leisurely pace I normally do only the first mile or two, then turn around. In the early nineties I began keeping a "TAT journal" to record observations and discoveries, but many are etched deeply in my memory as well. Numerous spots have become personal mileposts, even the trailhead, where one summer I watched the furtive passage of a young black bear through dense foliage, a fleeting forest shadow. Along another stretch, Mom and I looked for four-leaf clovers during a July visit, then surprised—and were surprised by—a browsing cow moose with calf. Just beyond the one-mile marker, I once met a short-tailed weasel in November, its seasonal camouflage of white betrayed by an unusually warm and snowless winter.

The woods were nearly free of winter's grasp that April evening. Only patches of white slush remained scattered through the mostly brown and gray forest. Here and there, green sprouts poked through leaf litter. Gray, fuzzy catkins softened the ends of willow branches and spring's first mosquitoes buzzed slowly through the air.

It was a splendid evening to take a forest walk, with temperatures in the forties, a faint swirling breeze, and the sun bright in an azure sky. By the time I reached my turnaround point, I'd been serenaded by the welcoming *fee-bee-bee* songs of black-capped chickadees and scolded by loudly chattering, twitching red squirrels. I'd watched bald eagles spiral above Turnagain Arm's mudflats and flocks of gulls skim the chocolaty water.

As I headed back to the trailhead just before 9:00 P.M., the forest edged toward darkness. My mind was drifting among memories of other hikes when I noticed movement near the base of a large cottonwood, one hundred feet ahead. Putting binoculars to eyes, I saw what appeared to be a furred, beige foot. I imagined that it belonged to a snowshoe hare, in the midst of its seasonal color shift.

After making certain I had marked the spot in my mind, I advanced up the trail, then looked again. A familiar yet surprising form took shape amidst the tangle of bushes and branches: the face and body of a cat. A shot of adrenalin surged through my body. Could I really be so lucky as to meet a lynx? Several had been seen around Anchorage in recent years, as their numbers rose in response to booming populations of snowshoe hares, a favorite prey. But local sightings had dropped off and state wildlife biologist Howard Golden confirmed that lynx numbers were declining, in response to the hares' down cycle (the hare population peaks every eight to twelve years, then plummets as overgrazed food supplies dwindle).

Even when abundant, lynx are secretive forest creatures, so I considered the possibility that this feline was a house cat gone feral. Shifting position to gain a different perspective, I then spotted the telltale sign: tufted ears tipped in black. I had hoped for so long to see a lynx in these woods. Now that it had happened, I could barely contain my glee.

Hopeful of an even closer look, I resumed walking slowly up the trail. There was no reason to hide, because the lynx had already seen me, but I did my best to appear casual, nonthreatening. When I stopped again, the lynx filled the field of my lens. Even knowing where it sat, I could see how well it blended with the forest. Perfect camouflage, the cat's fur was tawny, grizzled, a blend of white, brown, and gray-black hairs. The face was whitish beige with thin black streaks outlining the mouth, as if delicately painted by a makeup artist. Sleek, black whiskers sprouted from the face and black-edged ruffs flowed along the lynx's face like huge, bushy sideburns.

Caramel-colored eyes watched me intently, prompting me to wonder how often the lynx saw people along the trail. Far more often than hikers noticed lynx, I'm certain.

The wild cat sat on its haunches, crouching low to keep me in view as I shifted positions. Its eyes were alert, yet showed no alarm. I sensed caution, but not fear. Once the lynx blinked, then closed its eyes slightly, as if sleepy. It seemed willing to remain still indefinitely and I had no pressing need or desire to leave. Fifteen minutes or more passed and I began to question whether I might be keeping the cat from its evening hunt—or a mate, perhaps. The courting season for lynx begins in March and extends into April.

I was the one who finally yielded. Brightened by this unexpected pleasure, I resumed my walk, not looking back. On returning home, I would describe the meeting in my journal. But already I was recalling details, firmly imprinting the lynx on my memory and connecting it with this spot. Already, it had become part of my relationship with this forest, this trail: a Friday night, month of April . . .

VALLEY OF THE EAGLES

We spotted the first bald eagle at Milepost 16 of the Haines Highway. White head and tail showed it to be an adult, at least five years old. (Lacking the species' characteristic plumage, immature birds have a darker, mottled look.) The eagle wasn't doing anything spectacular. It wasn't soaring, or diving or feeding, simply sitting in a cottonwood, motionless except for its head, which swiveled our way as the bus slowed.

Inside, a shout of "there's one, on the left" had stirred a flurry of activity. Some passengers grabbed for binoculars or cameras, while others put faces to windows. It seemed an unusual thing, to be among nine Alaskans all intently focused on that one bird. Each of us had seen bald eagles before, many times. This wasn't anything new or especially exciting. But it wasn't the eagle that stirred us up. It was what the bird portended.

We pulled over and spent a few moments of that early December morning in the company of the eagle, our greeter to one of the world's great wildlife feasts. Then, anxious to attend the banquet, we continued up the road toward the heart of the forty-eight-thousand-acre Alaska Chilkat Bald Eagle Preserve. Within five minutes, we were surrounded by bald eagles. Dozens of them roosted, like feathered holiday ornaments, in the cottonwoods that line the highway. In one tree I counted twelve eagles. Others sat immobile on the Chilkat River's snow-covered flats, circled and played in the sky, or picked at salmon carcasses.

Two miles away, on the Chilkat River's opposite banks, were more cottonwoods and even larger concentrations of roosting eagles. Some trees held thirty, forty birds. In all, hundreds of bald eagles were visible, as well as smaller numbers of ravens, gulls, mergansers, and magpies. It was a sensory overload, for ears as well as eyes. In a talkative mood, the eagles chattered in a nonstop cacophony of high-pitched screeches and trills. They have weirdly high voices for such large, predatory birds, not at all in keeping with their image.

Each autumn and early winter, for as long as anyone can remember, thousands of bald eagles have congregated in the Chilkat Valley, at the northern end of Alaska's Panhandle. Attracted by a late fall run of chum salmon, they come from an area of more than one hundred thousand square miles. The majority reside in Southeast Alaska (two hundred to four hundred are year-round residents), but tagging studies have shown that others, usually younger birds, travel here from British Columbia, the Yukon Territory, and Washington state.

This meeting of eagles, the largest in the world, is centered in a five-thousand-acre Critical Habitat Area called the Bald Eagle Council Grounds. Here, for much of the winter, warm-water springs keep sections of the Chilkat River from freezing over, thus giving eagles easy access to a large supply of spawned-out chum salmon carcasses at a time of year when food is normally scarce. "Warm," of course, is a relative term. The spring waters that percolate into the council grounds are, by most standards, quite chilly: 39°F to 43°F. They originate in an alluvial fan reservoir, an accumulation of boulders, gravel, sand, and glacial sediments at the Chilkat's confluence with two tributary rivers, the Tsirku and the Klehini.

From spring through early fall, water accumulates in the Tsirku Fan to create a huge underground reservoir. When air temperatures drop in winter, the reservoir's subsurface waters are minimally affected. Feeding the Chilkat from below, they keep a five-mile stretch of river open long after surrounding waters have frozen. Fortunately for the eagles, the upwelling groundwater aerates and cleans the river bottom to create exceptionally good salmon-spawning habitat. Lucky, too, that chums choose this open water to spawn, and that they enter the river through January; few of Alaska's salmon runs occur so late in the year. Sockeye and coho salmon also migrate up the Chilkat in winter, but they don't concentrate in the spring-fed portions of the stream and are therefore usually hidden from the eagles by ice.

Equally lucky are eagle watchers. The Bald Eagle Council Grounds are easily visible from the Haines Highway. And they're only a short drive from the town of Haines, which offers year-round visitor services. It's this unusual convergence of variables—winter, open water, nearby comfort—that makes the Chilkat experience unique.

Large numbers of eagles normally arrive by October, with a population peak between mid-November and early December. Most leave by January, when salmon carcasses dwindle and the open river gradually freezes. Eagle numbers vary considerably from year to year, depending on the availability of food, which in turn depends primarily on weather and the strength of the salmon run. Since the late 1970s, when researchers began doing aerial surveys, annual peak counts have ranged from 1,000 to 4,000 individuals. In 1984, the U.S. Fish and Wildlife Service recorded a "modern record" of 3,988 eagles.

In the late 1980s, when I first visited the preserve, two surveys were flown each year, weather permitting. Of course it was impossible to count every eagle. And some years, weather prohibited flying when their numbers were highest. Federal eagle specialist and Chilkat census taker Mike Jacobsen admitted, "In any given year, peak numbers can be missed."

To supplement the flyover censuses, state park ranger Bill Zack would conduct weekly ground counts; less exact, they at least provided an index by which trends could be measured.

Some people claim that the Chilkat Valley once supported as many as 8,000 to 12,000 bald eagles. But after an intensive four-year study (1979–82), wildlife biologists Erv Boeker and Andy Hansen concluded that the Chilkat's eagle population "appears to be at the carrying capacity of its habitat. . . . It is likely that present population size and productivity are similar to presettlement levels."

What that level is remains uncertain. Though he'd counted as many as 3,700 eagles, Boeker was convinced "a lot more than that use the Chilkat. Birds move in and out."

Once the tour bus had parked on a designated turnout, we eagle watchers were turned loose into overcast, calm, 20°F weather. The ground rules were simple: stay out of traffic and off the flats, where the eagles feed, keep tripods off the pavement (again because of roadway safety concerns), and don't do anything to harass the birds. No trails or viewing decks or other visitor facilities had yet been built (those would come later in the 1990s) so visitors watched, photographed, and videotaped the eagles from either the turnouts or the narrow wooded corridor between road and river channel.

Armed with camera gear, spotting scopes, and binoculars, we quickly dispersed, as though some distance from each other would enhance our closeness to the great raptors. North America's second-largest birds of prey—only the California condor is bigger—adult bald eagles generally weigh nine to fourteen pounds (females of the species are largest) and have wingspans of seven and a half feet. Though they often seem to glide slowly through the air, eagles can fly up to thirty miles per hour and reach speeds of one hundred miles per hour when diving.

As I walked to a neighboring turnout, it became clear that the Chilkat's eagles had adapted well to motor vehicle traffic. They paid little or no attention to the mechanized roar of cars and trucks that rumbled past. Human traffic was not so universally tolerated. My presence unnerved, or perhaps merely annoyed, a few of the eagles, who left their cottonwood perches with slow-motion waves of their wings. Most, however, simply nodded their heads or stared impassively as I walked past.

Several roosting eagles sat with their wings extended downward. This "relaxation posture" helps them dry out feathers that get wet when they fish for salmon bodies. In winter's cold, these bald eagles feed almost exclusively on dead or dying salmon. Capturing active fish requires a high-energy expenditure that they can't afford. The choicest foods are fish carcasses that have been partially eaten—which eliminates the need to tear through tough skin—or recently submerged. Fish exposed to the air soon freeze and become inedible.

An opening in the trees allowed me a good view of the flats. Less than ten yards away, chum salmon swam in one of the river's open channels. Many had already spawned; their bodies decaying, they slowly fanned their tail fins while awaiting death. Along the river bottom were the carcasses of two already dead. A third carcass, pulled up on the riverbank, was surrounded by three eagles. Only one ate; the others watched and waited their turn. Also watching in nearby cottonwoods were a dozen more eagles.

The feeding bird tore off a chunk of flesh, swallowed it, then quickly looked around, making certain that no competitors were trying to cut in. Three times spectator eagles left their roosts and swept low over the gravel bar. The feeding eagle ducked its head, but kept its grip on the salmon and the challengers flew off. Finally a rival came in with wings and talons extended. Both the feeder and the two nearby observers screeched loudly, but they jumped clear and yielded to the newcomer. They'd been displaced, a biologist would say.

Though it looks combative, displacement behavior is, in some respects, a cooperative thing. Studies have shown that injuries rarely occur during such confrontations, because eagles "attack" those rivals most likely to yield a carcass without a fight: smaller or less ravenous birds. And through their body language, food holders apparently show whether or not they'll aggressively defend their meal. Displacement, or pirating, can therefore be a highly efficient way of procuring a meal, often preferable to hunting.

Over the next forty-five minutes, the ritual was repeated four more times. An eagle fed for several minutes, then was chased from the carcass by a hungrier bird. Within an hour, all edible parts had been consumed and five eagles had shared in the meal. Whether they had all been adequately fed is hard to say. In their studies of the Chilkat eagles, Boeker and Hansen found that "food holders typically are displaced before feeding to satiation."

What neither they nor anyone else had yet determined were the food requirements of Chilkat eagles. But studies elsewhere have shown that at subfreezing temperatures, eagles consume 10 percent or more of their body weight daily. For a fourteen-pound eagle, that's one and a half pounds of chum per day.

Despite all the available prey, there was surprisingly little feeding out on the flats. Most of the eagles sat motionless, as though patiently awaiting their turn in the buffet line. This, too, is typical cold-weather behavior. Washington researchers found that eagles along the Nooksack River spend more than 90 percent of their time perching, 4 percent eating, and 3 percent flying. The reason is simple: to conserve energy.

At night, or even in daytime when the weather is harsh, Chilkat's eagles abandon the river flats and roost in cottonwoods or nearby old-growth sprucehemlock forest. And on rare occasions, extended cold spells have driven them from the valley entirely. In November 1986, subzero temperatures caused most of the Bald Eagle Council Ground's river channels to freeze. Already stressed by wind, extreme cold, and a small chum run, the eagles had their salmon supply almost entirely cut off. The obvious solution: look elsewhere for food. In October, 1,124 eagles had been counted; on November 20, when numbers should have been at, or near, their peak, only 510 were seen. Exactly where the eagles went is unknown, but biologists agreed they probably scattered to warmer saltwater areas where herring and other winter foods could be found.

Energy conservation isn't quite as critical when the weather is mild and food abundant. In September and October, Chilkat's eagles are more likely to be spotted soaring or engaged in a form of play called "talon locking." Flying in pairs, the birds face each other and lock talons; one bird on top of the other, they tumble downward in a freefall.

Chilkat's eagles are now considered a local, state, and national treasure. But not so many decades ago they were hunted as vermin, because of the widespread—and mistaken—belief that their appetite for salmon and small game posed a threat to commercial fishermen and trappers.

From 1917 to 1952, more than 128,000 of Alaska's bald eagles were killed for territorial bounties of one or two dollars. Many were taken in the Chilkat Valley. The bounty on eagles ended in 1953; six years later Alaska gained statehood status and shortly after that its eagles gained federal protection through the National Bald Eagle Act of 1960. Still, some killing continued.

The Chilkat gathering, though recognized as unique, didn't receive any special protections until 1972, when the five-thousand-acre Critical Habitat Area was established. Any activities that might threaten the eagles were prohibited within the new sanctuary, but surrounding eagle habitat remained open to resource development.

For much of the next decade, conservationists and developers fought over the need for additional safeguards. In 1977, then-governor Jay Hammond proposed a state park within the Chilkat Valley, but local opposition killed the plan. Two years later, the state signed a long-term timber-sale contract with a Haines lumber company, allowing more than ten million board feet to be harvested annually. The trees to be clear-cut were mostly in the Chilkat Valley, thereby threatening the river, its salmon, and its eagles.

What had been a largely local issue soon gained nationwide attention. In response to a growing public outcry—and one United States senator's proposal to establish a national wildlife refuge—Hammond in 1980 declared a moratorium on logging in the Chilkat Valley. He also directed $250,000 in state funding to the Chilkat bald eagle study already started by Boeker and Hansen (and cosponsored by the National Audubon Society and the U.S. Fish and Wildlife Service).

Additional protection for the Chilkat eagles was finally secured when an advisory committee crafted a compromise acceptable to all parties. And in June 1982—two hundred years after the bald eagle had been chosen as America's emblem—Governor Hammond signed legislation that established the Alaska Chilkat Bald Eagle Preserve. Managed by the Division of State Parks with the help of a twelve-member advisory council, the preserve is off-limits to mining and logging but open to such traditional uses as fishing, hunting, berry picking, and trapping. Chilkat is therefore unique among Alaska's state park units, in that its primary mission is to protect wildlife and wildlife habitat.

Dave Cline, the National Audubon Society Alaska representative who played a crucial role in the preserve's creation, later commented, "I know of no other resource controversy in Alaska where loggers, miners, commercial fishermen, conservationists, and borough, city, federal, and state officials all signed" an agreement that settled an issue.

Once deeply divided over the need to protect the Chilkat eagles, the community of Haines now overwhelmingly supports the preserve for a simple reason: it makes good business sense. With traditional resource industries like logging and mining in decline, Haines has become increasingly dependent on tourism. And Chilkat's eagles are a big draw.

A half-hour drive from the council grounds, this small coastal community is the gateway to the preserve. Not surprisingly, business owners now emphasize the town's eagle connection. "The preserve was created for the eagles, not tourism. It just so happens to be along the highway—but that fact makes it a tourist attraction," Ray Menaker once told me. A longtime Haines resident, Menaker served on the advisory board for a decade and became one of the preserve's strongest advocates. "A lot of people who didn't like the idea originally have become gung ho, because of the added tourism in winter and late fall. The preserve has been a fortuitous thing. It's put Haines on the map. This is where the eagles are."

Haines and its surrounding mountains, lakes, rivers, and ocean have plenty to offer the summer tourist. But there's little reason, besides the eagles, to visit during the off-season. Though still comparatively small, winter use of the Chilkat preserve grew sharply during its first decade, thanks largely to documentaries, magazine articles, and even a live broadcast, televised via satellite to a worldwide audience in 1986.

"That show was seen by millions of people," Menaker said. "Afterward people called in from all over the place."

During the preserve's "high exposure time" in the 1980s, ranger Bill Zack once counted three hundred people watching eagles. But numbers are usually much smaller and most visitors are amateur and professional photographers who stay in Haines for periods of a few days to a few weeks.

Twenty-one highway miles from Haines, cradled between the road and the Chilkat River, is a community with even closer ties to Chilkat's eagles: the Tlingit Indian village of Klukwan.

Klukwan's people have coexisted with eagles for centuries. Their small community sits adjacent to the council grounds, which they first named, and many of their rituals and artworks are bound to the eagles' presence. Yet they have mixed feelings about the preserve. Village leaders have occasionally talked of building an eagle-viewing center and museum. But many residents have remained leery of tourism, fearing that they, like the eagles, would be put on view.

In November 1994 I returned to the Chilkat Valley for the third time in eight years, but my timing was lousy: the weather was the stormiest it had been all season. More than two and a half feet of snow fell during my five-day stay, and when the snow eased off, high winds kicked up a ground blizzard and drove wind-chill temperatures to minus 40°F. Wicked stuff for both eagles and eagle watchers.

Heavy, drifting snow kept me in Haines for two days. Two other days were only marginally better, but I dug out the rental car and headed for the Bald Eagle Council Grounds. Winds and below-zero chill had driven eagles off the flats and into the trees. A couple of hundred roosted in cottonwoods along the highway, but most had fled to the relative comfort of old-growth Sitka spruce and hemlock in neighboring Haines State Forest. Nearly all the eagles sat immobile, hunched over, though a few hardy birds picked at partially frozen carcasses on the riverbank.

Yet for all the gloom and cold, one morning I caught a break in the weather. Ranger Bill Zack was kind enough to give me a ride to the preserve through still unplowed streets, and we found the valley rich with birds: mergansers, ravens, gulls, chickadees, magpies, Steller's jays. And lots of eagles. More than I'd ever seen. Zack told me that 2,137 eagles were counted on the year's first survey flight. And the salmon return looked healthy. Two pieces of good news.

We walked along the highway to a spot that offers a panoramic view of the council grounds. Then Zack offered his binoculars and challenged me: "See how many you can count."

First I scanned the flats, where hundreds of eagles sat on stumps, snags, boulders, and snow-covered ground, and counted 590. Next, the cottonwoods. Eyesight beginning to blur, I slowly swept across the distant trees, trying to somehow keep track of the tiny, dark shapes. I estimated 360 more, 950 in all, seen from a single spot. Zack and I traded glances, then smiles. The count simply confirmed what we both already knew: It's truly a place of wonder, this valley of the eagles.

PART III

BACKCOUNTRY ENCOUNTERS

IN THE COMPANY OF BEARS

1.

I used to have nightmares about bears. They entered my dream world in the mid-1970s, shortly after I'd come to Alaska, and they roamed the forests of my subconscious for many years after. A geologist then, just out of graduate school, I spent my first Alaskan summers in some of the state's wildest, most remote grizzly bear country. And each year, usually toward the end of the field season, phantom grizzlies would stalk me, chase me, attack me. They lurked in my dream shadows, ominous and haunting. I now sometimes wonder if those nightmares were omens. Perhaps they spoke of things to come, of a summer afternoon many years later in Shuyak Island State Park, at the northern end of Alaska's Kodiak Archipelago. . . .

Five of us had spent the morning in kayaks. After several hours on the water, we were ready to stretch muscles and explore one of the many small islands that border Shuyak's northern coast. The islet we chose was inhabited by Sitka black-tailed deer; from the water, we'd seen several feeding in open meadows. It was also home to a brown bear female with three tiny cubs. We had spotted them, too, earlier in the day, though the bear family had since disappeared into the forest.

I'd seen many grizzlies over the years, but that was my first sighting of brown bears, the coastal cousins of griz. Alaska's brown bears tend to be more chocolaty in color and have less distinctive humps and shorter claws than their inland relatives. On average they're much larger animals, mainly because they have access to more plentiful, energy-rich foods, especially salmon. A large male grizzly may weigh six hundred to seven hundred pounds in fall, when it's fattened for hibernation. But the largest brown bears are twice that size. And nowhere do brown bears grow larger than on the Kodiak Archipelago, home to the subspecies *Ursus arctos middendorffi*. Even here, researchers say, adult females rarely reach seven hundred pounds, though this mother bear appeared much bigger.

We beached our kayaks, then split up. I joined Sam, one of the expedition's guides, and together we explored a game trail that began in a meadow but soon bordered a thick stand of spruce. Sam called out to announce our presence: HOOYAH . . . HOOYAH. Eventually the trail petered out, where the forest reached the island's edge. We were faced with a simple choice: return down the trail or cut through the woods. Sam chose the trees and I followed despite some misgivings. He was the guide, after all.

The spruce were twenty to thirty feet high, spindly, and densely packed. We couldn't easily see more than ten to fifteen feet ahead, sometimes less. We were walking slowly and talking loudly, when my worst nightmare came true: a bear charged out of the forest's shadows. She must have tried to hide her family in this stand to avoid the two-legged invaders of her island. But we had entered her sanctuary and threatened, however innocently, her offspring. Retreat hadn't worked, so her only remaining option was to defend her cubs by force.

Things began to speed up and, simultaneously, move in slow motion around me. Less than twenty feet away, the bear was a blur of terrible speed, size, and power—a dark image of unstoppable rage. Her face was indistinct, and I sensed, more than saw, her teeth and claws. In two giant bounds the bear reached Sam, five feet in front of me. Somewhere, amid the roaring that filled my head, I heard a cry: "OH NO." I felt certain Sam was about to die, or be seriously mauled, and feared that I might also be attacked.

The last thing I saw was the bear engulfing Sam in a violent hug. Then, despite everything I'd learned about bears, I turned and ran, breaking one of the cardinal rules of bear encounters. But my instincts were strong and they urged me to get out of sight, out of the woods. Climbing one of the slender trees wasn't an option, and without any weapon, there was nothing I could do to help Sam.

The only question was whether the bear would come after me after it finished with him. I ran out of the forest onto a narrow stretch of beach; I had to find the other three members of the party, get Sam's rifle from his kayak, and try to rescue him.

Back in the forest, Sam was doing his best to survive. As the bear charged, Sam would tell us later, he ducked his head and fell backward. Falling, he saw the bear's open mouth, her teeth and claws. Hitting the ground, he curled into a fetal position to protect his head and vital organs, and offered the bear a shoulder to chew on instead. And with the bear breathing in his face, he played dead.

The brown bear grabbed Sam, woofed at him, and batted him a few times like a kitten playing with a mouse. But she struck him with her paws, not her claws. There was no sound of tearing flesh. And when, after several moments—or was it minutes?—she got no response from her victim, the bear ended her attack just as suddenly as she began it. The threat removed, she left with her cubs.

I remained on the beach, listening and looking for any sign of the bear, when, incredibly, I heard Sam shout: "The bear's gone. . . . I'm all right."

Though uncertain where the bear had fled, I returned into the woods and rejoined Sam. Miraculously, he was uninjured, except for a small scratch on the back of his hand, which he got when falling backward into a small spruce. For someone who had just been attacked by a fiercely protective mother bear, Sam seemed to be taking the incident much more calmly than I. Perhaps, I would learn later, this was because he had lots of experience in such matters. He'd been "false charged" by bears three times previously.

"Thank goodness it was a friendly bear," Sam said with a wry grin after recounting his story. "It wasn't looking for a fight; it was trying to make a point: 'Leave me alone.'" Hours later, when we rehashed the attack with others in our group, he would add: "I felt no sense of aggression or panic. I believe animals can sense a person's energy. If you're projecting aggression, or if the adrenaline is flowing, they know it. I was very calculating as to what I should do." It turned out he did everything right once the bear attacked. Listening to Sam's story, still pumped with adrenaline, I could only shake my head and marvel at our escape.

Heading across a meadow to warn the others, we spotted the sow a hundred yards away, still greatly agitated. She stood up, ran around in circles, then stood up again. She kept looking down the island, and we guessed that she had seen or smelled our companions. The bear stood one final time, fell back to all fours, turned sharply, and loped into another, larger spruce stand. Strung out in a line, the three cubs ran hard to keep up with mom.

We rendezvoused with the others, quickly retold our story, and left the bears' island. Back in camp, we talked for hours about the encounter and second-guessed ourselves. We agreed it was foolish to visit the island, given our earlier bear sighting, even more foolhardy to cut through the woods. I was reminded, again, to question authority and trust my own judgment.

The encounter also raised questions about firearms, which may be carried in all of Alaska's state parks. I have never brought a gun into Alaska's backcountry; I'm not a firearms expert, have no desire to be, and believe that guns cause more trouble than bears. Like Sam, I also believe that guns change a person's "energy," change the way a person relates to wild places, wild creatures. They offer security, but they also can prompt people to take chances they ordinarily wouldn't, sometimes resulting in confrontations that might have been avoided. The usual result is injury or death, often for the bear.

For a while, after the Shuyak attack, I questioned my philosophy. It's often said that bears, like people, are individuals. Each one is different, unpredictable. As Richard Nelson, an Alaskan writer, anthropologist, and naturalist whose philosophy I greatly respect, comments in *The Island Within*: "All it takes is once in a lifetime, the wrong bear in the wrong place. Without a rifle (and the knowledge of when and how to use it), the rest of the story would be entirely up to the bear. . . . It's my way of self-preservation, as the hawk has its talons, the heron its piercing beak, the bear its claws. . . ."

But as time has passed, I've become more convinced than ever that it's right, for me, to walk unarmed in Alaska's backcountry. It would be different, perhaps, if brown or black bears preyed on people. But they rarely do. In a sense, my choice is a symbolic gesture of respect to the animal and its world; I'm only a visitor in the bear's realm, passing through and intending no harm.

On Shuyak, we provoked the attack. A mother was being crowded, and she wanted to eliminate what she perceived as a very real threat. She was protecting her cubs, no more, no less. Playing dead, removing the threat, proved the best thing to do, not fight back. Shooting her would have been a tragedy.

Bears continue to walk the forests of my dream worlds, but no longer are they a shadowy menace. This makes good sense to me. Over the years I've come to believe that the Shuyak bear was a messenger of sorts—and a gift in my life. Her attack was more fearsome than anything I'd imagined or dreamed. Yet the encounter ended well for both humans and bears. The bear's sudden and overwhelmingly powerful presence taught me lessons about foolishness and the need to pay greater attention to my own intuition. And, in a curious way, her brief passage through my life led to new pathways. In the years since the attack, I have spent many, many days in the company of bears and have learned them to be surprisingly tolerant of people—much more tolerant than we humans are of them, certainly. Bears, especially the brown/grizzly, have been guides as I reconnect with my own wild spirit. Now I welcome their appearance in both my waking life and dreams.

2.

During the summer of 1999, I flew by charter plane across Cook Inlet to the upper Alaska Peninsula, the heart of brown bear country. It was fifth time I'd camped along the shores of Kamishak Bay's McNeil Cove in the company of other bear lovers. We had barely finished storing away food and setting up tents among tall meadow plants, when a family of brown bears came ambling down the narrow sand beach that fronted our camp. The bears were walking slowly, without menace, eating as they went. Still, they were moving ever closer. In the lead was a large female with a beautiful milk chocolate–colored coat that had not yet begun to shed. And trailing her in single file were four little cubs. Darker than their mom, the cubs had been born in January or February. Only a pound or so at birth, the largest of the four in late July weighed twenty-five to thirty pounds. The runt of the litter weighed only half as much, with the cute appeal of a real, live teddy bear.

In most places, the steady approach of a brown bear family would be cause for concern, perhaps even alarm, because females with cubs are notoriously aggressive. The five of us who watched the bears—soon to be joined by a half-dozen others—would likely have announced our presence by talking loudly, maybe while waving our arms and slowly retreating. We would have crowded together, to increase our size, and worried that the bears might invade our camp. Someone in the group might have reached for a firearm or pepper spray. None of that happened, however. Not here, with this particular female.

Newly arrived at Alaska's McNeil River State Game Sanctuary and accompanied by a Fish and Game bear biologist, we watched calmly and quietly from the edge of camp while the mom and her cubs foraged among sedges that grow where beach sand gives way to expansive mudflats. We talked in whispered tones of our good fortune, as the bears came to within one hundred feet, then eighty, then forty. It was clear that their approach had nothing to do with us. It just so happened that the mother's beach foraging had brought the family in our direction. The cubs looked toward us now and then with an apparent mix of curiosity and anxiety, but their mom hardly paid us any heed as she hungrily gulped down clumps of green blades.

One of dozens of brown bears to congregate at McNeil each summer, this female was recognized by sanctuary manager Larry Aumiller as Snow Bear. Known to be highly tolerant of humans and comfortable in their presence, she understood, in her own ursine way, that we presented no danger to her or her cubs.

McNeil's staff had for many years named nearly all of the sanctuary's adult bears, at least the regulars who come back summer after summer. Some people criticized this practice, but Aumiller, who had run the McNeil program since 1976 (and would eventually retire after his thirtieth season), noted that wildlife researchers often use naming to identify individuals: "With more than eighty or ninety adult bears here, you need a way to keep track of different ones. Naming them is almost like a mnemonic device, to help you remember them. It doesn't imply human characteristics or qualities." In Snow Bear's case, the name had been bestowed several summers earlier, while she sat upon a patch of snow. Now in her prime, she weighed five- to six-hundred pounds. That's a good-sized female. McNeil's largest males weigh twice that.

Snow Bear was only one of several females to bring new litters to McNeil River that summer, but she and her cubs would dominate our conversations over the next four days. Partly that was because she and her family frequently foraged near camp; but it was also because four-cub litters are so rare. Over the past quarter century, only four females had shown up here with four cubs. The usual number is two.

Brown bear cubs are usually weaned from their moms during their third summer, at age two and a half. The chance of a cub surviving that long at McNeil are fifty-fifty, Aumiller told us. Some drown; others starve or are killed by disease, falls, or other bears. The runt's odds were even slimmer. A few days later, during a swim across McNeil Lagoon, he lagged behind the others and for a few moments we were unsure he would make it to shore. He did, but took far longer to recover than his siblings. We found ourselves rooting for him to make it, a natural human response to underdogs.

Established in 1967 and managed by the state's Division of Wildlife Conservation, McNeil sanctuary protects the world's largest gathering of brown bears. The focal point of this gathering is McNeil Falls, where bears come to feed on chum salmon. During the peak of the July–August chum run, dozens of brown bears congregate. As many as 144 individual bears (adults and cubs) have been identified along McNeil River in a single season. And in July 1997, biologists counted 70 bears at the falls at one time. (That record would be topped in 2011, when staff identified 80 bears in a single count.)

Even more impressive than the number of bears, perhaps, is their acceptance of a human presence. Every day from early July through late August, ten visitors plus sanctuary staff spend seven to eight hours at the falls, while stationed at two gravel pads (one atop a knoll, the other right below it). "Think about it," Aumiller said. "You've got this group of people standing in the middle of forty, fifty, sixty bears. You're very close to where they want to be. And they tolerate you." Some will eat salmon, take naps, nurse cubs, or even mate within a short distance of the visitor viewing pads.

The high degree of tolerance shown by McNeil's bears may be Aumiller's greatest legacy. More than anyone else, this naturalist with dark, silver-speckled hair, sparkling eyes, and an easy smile demonstrated that bears can become habituated to people without also becoming food conditioned. And he showed that such people-tolerant bears—Aumiller calls them "neutrally habituated"—are safe to be around. As he once explained it, "At McNeil, humans are neither a threat nor a source of food. Over time it became clear from their actions that the more tolerant bears were perceiving us as neutral objects, maybe as innocuous as a rock or a tree."

Before the McNeil experiment, most people—including many so-called bear experts—believed that habituated bears, particularly grizzlies, are extremely dangerous. McNeil has proved the opposite is true, *if* food is removed from the equation. For that reason, all human food is stored and meals are prepared and eaten in a sturdy cabin that's off-limits to bears. The sanctuary's bears-come-first philosophy has also been a key to its success. Visitor numbers are restricted and human activities are kept as predictable as possible. As a general rule, people aren't allowed to wander outside the well-defined campground area without being accompanied by sanctuary staff.

Reflecting on the lessons he'd learned at the sanctuary, Aumiller readily admitted that living with bears is not an easy thing, but McNeil is proof of what's possible when humans are willing to compromise: people and bears can indeed peacefully coexist, often in close company. "What goes on here is still news to a lot of people. They don't think it can happen. But it does. McNeil shows that if you learn about something that's different from you, and begin to appreciate it, then you'll figure out a way to keep it in your life. You'll learn to coexist."

The number of bears gathering at the falls was down in 1999, reflecting a poor return of chums. Unless a sudden surge of fish arrived, the run would likely be the smallest on record. In a good year, bears fishing the falls in late July and early August will pull one hundred or more salmon from McNeil's blue-green waters every hour. The hourly counts on August 1 were dismal by comparison: eight, ten, five, twelve. . . .

With little food to go around bears were less tolerant of each other as they competed for prime fishing spots. There was more tension, more fighting, and fewer scraps for the adolescents and females with cubs that roam the river's perimeter. The best fishing spots were hogged by large, mature males weighing up to one thousand pounds or more and bearing numerous pink scars from battles won and lost.

The lord of the falls that year, as he'd been since the early 1990s, was a hulking, dark chocolate brown male named Woofie. In his late teens, Woofie had a huge "fish gut." He also had a huge head, legs, and rear end, rippling muscles—and a long pink slash of a scar that cut diagonally across his left side. Given Woofie's reputation, it seemed natural to ask: what happened to the other guy? Or was the scar a leftover from his earlier, less dominant days?

Among the largest of McNeil's bears, Woofie showed an aggressive, intimidating personality among his own kind, though like many mature males he tended to shy away from people. A decent salmon fisher, he seemed to prefer bullying other bears and stealing their fish. Typically he would arrive at the falls, take in the scene for a few minutes, and then walk nonchalantly, in his swaggering way, to his chosen victim. With Woofie's reputation well established, most picked-on bears gave up their catch without a fuss. Occasionally, however, there was much growling, snarling, baring of teeth, and even front-leg jabs to the chest.

With little hope of snagging fish at the falls, many adolescents and females with cubs had taken to wandering the coastal mudflats, where they fed on sedges and other greens or chased salmon in tidal channels.

Once while we watched from a remarkably close distance, Snow Bear rolled over onto her back to nurse her cubs. With her in this most vulnerable position—legs extended and her more sparsely furred belly and groin area revealed—I could more easily see, or at least imagine, the physical likeness between human and bear.

As David Rockwell explains at great length in *Giving Voice to Bear*, many Native American tribes—including some of Alaska's "first peoples"—have attached great meaning to the physical similarities of our two species. Bears, like people, can easily stand on their hind legs; they can even walk upright for short distances. And when a bear is standing, the animal's front legs hang at his sides like arms. As anyone who's seen bears catch and eat salmon knows, they are surprisingly adroit when using their front paws. Even more impressively, Rockwell notes, "in captivity they have been known to peel peaches." And there's this fact: skinned bears look eerily human.

Such resemblances, combined with similarities in diet and behaviors (strong maternal instincts, problem-solving abilities, playfulness) have led many Native groups to feel a special kinship with bears. Tribes throughout North America traditionally believed the bear to be half human, or that humans were descended from bears.

I like that notion, just as I've come to relish the shape-shifting myths that tell of bears becoming humans or humans becoming bears, transformations back and forth. Something about those stories resonates. They hold a certain magic. And here things start to get tricky. How do you talk—or write—about such things without seeming New Agey? Without trivializing something that holds great power? Or without "stealing" from other cultural traditions?

I don't know the answer, so I usually steer clear of such dilemmas, keep my more mystical leanings under wraps (except with dear friends who've come to accept my occasional ecstatic outbursts). But here I'll recklessly plunge ahead: bears, I've come to realize, are one of my totem animals. Though I come from a different cultural tradition, this white guy of European descent, Lutheran upbringing, and scientific training nevertheless finds meaning in the Native American notion of totems; and I've come to understand and identify them in my own, personal way. A totem animal is one that has caught or demanded my attention; one that "speaks" to me; one with which I sense some special connection or an inexplicable fascination. A teacher. A messenger. A guide. Bear is one. Squirrel, chickadee, wolf, and spider are others.

Who can comprehend, let alone explain, such things? Shamans and other mystics, perhaps. But as weird as it seems, there's something to the kinship/totem idea, even for a recovering, born-and-bred fundamentalist Christian and ex-geologist educated in the sciences. This fascination with bears and the desire to know them better is worth pursuing. Bear brings me closer to wildness, closer to myself.

As to how and when the seeds of this bonding were planted, I can't say for sure. I recall no special interest in bears during my boyhood years in Connecticut. Bears weren't part of my world, though it seems they must have occasionally roamed through the woodlands my friends and I explored. What I knew of them I learned from sensationalized outdoor-magazine stories and "bear tales" sorts of books, namely that bears are dangerous, unpredictable, blood-thirsty critters that can—and will, if given the chance—tear you limb from limb.

Not until I came to Alaska in 1974 did I see a bear in the wild. And it wasn't until the late 1980s—after I'd left Alaska, switched careers from geology to journalism, and then returned to work at the *Anchorage Times*, eventually to become the newspaper's outdoors writer—that I truly became a passionate student of *Ursus*. My education accelerated dramatically, and my affinity for bears deepened immeasurably, both during and after my first trip to McNeil in 1988, which I've had the good fortune to visit several times.

Taught by both the bears and Aumiller, I've been changed by McNeil, as so many others have been transformed. I've come to understand bears as complex, amazingly adaptive, and intelligent creatures. And I've learned, as Aumiller learned years earlier, that bears are much more accepting of us, than humans are of them.

As the sanctuary's "take-home" lessons took hold, my fear of bears gave way to respect and reverence. Yes, bears—especially grizzlies—are large, powerful, and sometimes fiercely aggressive animals, particularly when protecting their young or food. They have the strength and "tools"—their teeth and claws—to do great harm. They can be dangerous. But they're not bloodthirsty killers of humans and rarely prey on people. If that weren't true, we would have plenty to fear when passing through bear country.

And, I've learned, they carry a power that goes far beyond their physical strength and size and ferocity.

Shortly before 11:00 P.M. my last evening at the sanctuary that summer of 1999, I stood above the sand beach in gray light that was dimming to darkness. The land and seascape beyond our small defined campground had once again become a place only of bears, gulls, eagles, ravens, ground squirrels, foxes, and salmon. Watching from camp's edge, I counted twenty-nine bears scattered from the mouth of McNeil River to the outer mudflats of Kamishak Bay. And I heard the sounds of night: the screech of gulls and eagles, the loud splash of bears chasing fish, the melancholy three-note call of a golden-crowned sparrow in alder thickets behind camp.

The bears were distant silhouettes. I saw one family with two cubs, another with three. And then I saw Snow Bear, still with her four. I was cheered by this, even while knowing the chances were small that they would all make it through the summer.

The wildness deepened with the darkness as we humans ducked into our tents and sleeping bags, hiding from the night, the cold, the rain. Thick clouds shrouded the landscape as salmon moved through tidal flats toward McNeil River and bears hunted the salmon as they've done for centuries.

3.

Mid-August, the Brooks Range. Two years after meeting McNeil's brown bear quadruplets, I traveled alone deep into the Arctic to explore Alaska's northernmost mountain chain. For two weeks I had been keeping watch for bear. Partly that was to ensure I didn't have any surprise encounters with a grizzly. Unlike their coastal relatives, grizzlies don't easily adapt to being around other bears. Or people. Researchers guess that's because they rarely, if ever, gather in large groups to feed on concentrated, energy-rich food sources. So they haven't evolved the social behaviors to be in close company with each other—or, by extension, with humans. My previous experience with northern grizzlies in remote wilderness had been this: upon seeing, smelling, or otherwise sensing *Homo sapiens*, most skedaddle with little or no hesitation. They want nothing to do with us hairless bipeds.

Still, if you surprise a grizzly (or any bear, for that matter) at close range, all bets are off. The bear must make a split-second decision. It may flee; or it may choose to forcefully eliminate the perceived threat by attacking. Happily, surprise encounters are rare in the vast tundra expanses of Alaska's northernmost mountain chain.

There was another, deeper reason that I'd been keeping watch: I wished to share the landscape with bear. In one respect, I had been doing so since arriving in the Brooks Range. Whether or not they're visible, or physically present, grizzlies regularly pass through the valleys I'd been exploring. These "barren ground" grizzlies are almost constantly on the move in their search for food, not nearly as abundant here as it is along Alaska's southern coastline. For all its beauty, most of the Arctic is a place of scarcity—except for its mosquitoes. The living is not easy, especially for a large predator.

In the course of my Arctic explorations that summer, I'd seen plenty of bear sign: tracks (some of them fresh), scat, and tundra diggings, where a grizzly had hunted ground squirrels. But no bears. So in my journal I asked: would seeing a grizzly make my trip here more memorable? Is it not enough to know that bear frequents these valleys and ridges? I knew the answer even as I wrote the question. I wouldn't be disappointed if I left without seeing a grizzly. But a sighting of a bear would inevitably enhance my stay here.

Stretched out in camp, I imagined a grizzly walking across the tundra. Sitting on a tundra bench. Watching. Watching me? Might bear seek me? Am I becoming bear? Certainly I'd begun to feel a more ursine presence within my psyche in recent years. Allowing my thoughts to roam, I asked myself again why I'd come to this Arctic wilderness and its high alpine. What did I seek? Adventure? Revelation? Transformation?

Adventure was undoubtedly part of the draw. So was the wild beauty of this place. Since I'd first come here more than a quarter century ago, the Brooks Range had become my favorite wilderness. It's a place where wildness is manifested in wave after wave of rocky, knife-edged ridges that can be reached without climbing expertise, and which stretch to the horizon and beyond; in glacially carved basins that grow lush in midsummer with the rich greens of tundra meadows and the vibrant purples, yellows, magentas, and blues of alpine wildflowers; in wolves, Dall sheep, caribou, bears, and wolverines; in an unpeopled landscape where one can still travel for days—perhaps even weeks—without seeing another person, or even signs of humanity.

Not coincidentally, the Brooks Range is where I saw my first wild bear, in 1974 while working as an exploration geologist. A chocolate-colored grizzly, the animal stood several hundred yards away, busily digging into the tundra for roots or perhaps ground squirrels, while I collected rock and sediment specimens from a mountain stream. I was deeply stirred by the presence of the bear; but what moved me initially was the grizzly itself, rather than anything it implied about wildness or vast, undeveloped landscapes. That recognition would come later, in bits and pieces, along with a passionate interest in the animal and a desire to know it better.

But more than adventure or memories were at play. I also sought answers. I wanted to better understand what wildness means to me. And what "sacred" means. I wanted to embrace the wild other that roams this Arctic world and also lurks inside, still mostly hidden.

Keep searching and questioning, I encouraged myself. Sleep on it. Dream it. What's important? What's here for me? What's the essence of this journey? Stay open to possibilities and revelations. Let the landscape speak. Pay attention to its inhabitants: animal, plant, rock, creek, mountain.

❦

Three days after I raised so many questions—and probed possible answers—in my journal, bear came to me.

Like the previous four, that August day had been gray, raw, windy, and wet, so I'd spent most of the morning and afternoon hunkered in my dry tent and warm cocoon of a sleeping bag. Finally braving the storm, I grabbed my bear-resistant food container, ducked under a small tarp, and slowly relished a meal of granola bars, cheese, oatmeal, beef jerky, and pressed, ground coffee. Then, in my usual way, I scanned the landscape.

Across the creek, on a gentle rise, I turned my attention to a couple of dark, hulking shapes. That was nothing unusual; I'd seen dozens of "bear boulders" over the past two and a half weeks. But there was something about one of the rocks. Exactly what, I couldn't say. Maybe it was the boulder's dark chocolate brown color, or the fact that I hadn't noticed this particular boulder before among several other familiar ones.

After shifting my gaze to another part of the valley, I pulled it back across the creek. And darned if that chocolaty boulder hadn't moved. A couple of minutes earlier, it sat in an open meadow. Now it was beside a willow thicket, near the bottom of a gully. Just to be certain, I hurried back to the tent and grabbed my binoculars. Normally I carry them everywhere, but with the weather being so poor, I figured I wouldn't need them.

By now the boulder had moved again, so I was all but certain what I would see. The glasses confirmed it: a chocolate grizzly bear was grazing on tundra plants directly across Giant Creek, maybe an eighth of a mile away. Well, this was what I'd wanted, but miles from the nearest human on a dark and utterly dreary day, I couldn't help but recall the saying: be careful what you wish for.

The bear's shape suggested an adult: heavily muscled body, large belly, and massive head. From here the grizzly easily looked large enough to be a male and that's what I guessed the animal to be. The bear worked his way uphill, out of the thickets and back into the tundra meadow, and I found myself encouraging that movement. *Good bear; stay away from my camp.*

The wind and rain didn't seem to bother him a bit. In fact he moseyed along, munching as he went, as if he had no cares at all—which at that moment, and likely most moments in his adult life, was probably true. From what I could tell, he was consuming both greens and wildflowers. *Maybe*, I thought, *when the bear leaves I'll go inspect where he's been grazing and find out what he's been eating.* But I knew that high, rain-swollen creek waters might prevent that.

Scribbling notes in my journal, I lost track of the grizzly. Ten or fifteen seconds passed before I relocated him, though he wasn't hiding. That's how well he blended in. Out in the open, sprawled among some cobble-sized rubble, he faced directly into the wind-driven rain. An after-lunch nap?

The grizzly hadn't looked my way once that I could tell, though almost certainly he was aware of me, the purple-and-green tent, or my beige flapping tarp. From my own hikes, I know the tarp stood out, even from a distance. Flailing about in the gusting wind, it had to be even easier to spot. If the bear *had* noticed me or my shelters, what did he think? Or sense? What did his instincts tell him? Had he encountered humans before?

For the moment, at least, I was much more interested in the bear, than he in me. That was good, just the way I wanted it. Though pleased to be sharing the valley with the grizzly, I wished to do so at a distance. Even having one this close to camp made me a little nervous. One thing seemed certain: the grizzly's experience of this valley was not enhanced by a human presence. Many residents of the nearest village would likely shoot the bear if they found him this close to camp, or even crossed paths with him on trips through the mountains. Whether or not he'd had any past encounters with humans, the bear showed no anxiety about my presence.

❧

It was *cold* out there. Both fingers and toes were tingling. My small field thermometer read in the upper forties, but with the gusting winds, the chill was probably closer to freezing. Classic hypothermia weather. Even protected behind a shelter and cloaked in several layers of clothing—wind shell, fleece jacket, capilene shirt, nylon pants, wool cap with rain hood pulled over it, and fleece gloves—I started to shiver. Meanwhile the bear, lying on an exposed bench and faced into the wind, showed no discomfort at all. If he wasn't chilled on a day like this, did he overheat on the bright, sunny, warm days of summer (which admittedly seemed to be few and far between here)?

The bear napped more than an hour before rising. Immediately, he resumed feeding. He did little else for the next two hours except chew mouthfuls of tundra greens. He barely lifted his head, except to see where the next patch of food might be, and seldom had to take more than a few steps to get there. He continued to ascend a rocky rivulet surrounded by low-lying but lush green plants, until reaching a rubbly pile of lichen-bearded boulders. He then topped a brownish knoll that apparently had little to tempt him, and ambled to another lush swale, where he resumed his feasting.

It appeared the grizzly had entered the late-summer phase that biologists sometimes call hyperphagia: an almost around-the-lock gorging, in preparation for winter's months-long fasting. At one point the bear found a spot so luscious, all he could do was sprawl in the midst of it.

The more I watched the grizzly, the more confident I became that he was a heavily muscled mature male, perhaps in his prime. He had little to fear, except, perhaps, for a larger bear—which seemed unlikely in that place—or hunters bearing guns. That was one good thing about the weather: no hunters were likely to come this way today.

By the time I'd finished dinner, my stinging-cold toes cautioned me not to stay out too much longer. At least five hours had passed since I first spotted the boulder that turned into a bear. Over that time it became clear that much of what he grazed upon was Richardson's saxifrage, also commonly known as "bear flower" for good reason. The grizzly seemed to be consuming it all: flowers, stems, and leaves. An eating machine, indeed. And havin' a ball. Again he sprawled out, head swiveling back and forth, mowing down those plants. It must have been the closest thing to bear heaven, if you don't have access to berries or salmon.

Once, then twice, the bear's attention was diverted. He stared down into the creek a few moments, then resumed eating. As unlikely as it seemed, the thought struck me that perhaps backpackers had come over from a neighboring valley and were headed down Giant Creek. Or, even less probable, that Nunamiut hunters had come up there, unnoticed by me in the howling and drum-beating cacophony of wind and rain. *Don't you dare shoot that bear,* I silently warned the imagined hunters.

I put away food and cook gear, hauled some stuff back to the tent, then returned for a final look. The grizzly was again on the move. Heading slowly toward the creek bottom, he stopped intermittently for snacks along the way. I took down the tarp and retreated to the tent with binoculars and sitting pad, setting up on the downwind side. Glancing at my watch, I saw it was 8:30 P.M.

Just once that I could tell, the grizzly looked toward the tent. Then, still headed downstream—and away from my camp—he disappeared into thick brush that lined the creek. I lost sight of him for several minutes. Finally he reappeared, going up a gully that led to a side valley. Moving beyond a thicket of shoulder-high willows, the grizzly headed out onto open tundra, walking slowly but steadily in a gait that was part swagger, part waddle. He came to a rise and topped it, body disappearing bit by bit till he was gone.

I'd spent six hours, maybe more, in the company of bear. It's one thing to do so at a place like McNeil, where you walk among bears in a guided group, within a structured system. It's quite another while alone, deep in the wilderness. I felt a vague emptiness in my gut as the bear disappeared, a sadness to go with my joy in this gift, this opportunity to gain an extended peek into a grizzly's solitary life.

You could say nothing special happened that day. The bear didn't do anything unexpected or threatening, so the story of my encounter with that Arctic grizzly won't ever grip friends and new acquaintances the way my bear-attack story inevitably does. And I had no epiphany. Yet it was everything I could have asked for, and more.

There's little that could have kept me outdoors in such bleak weather, yet while engaged with the grizzly I largely forgot my own discomfort and moved more deeply into the raw power of that Arctic alpine valley. Even before it ended, I knew that wet, blustery day in the Brooks Range would remain as memorable to me as that long-ago afternoon on Shuyak Island. There I was an unschooled intruder. Here I had slipped into the bear's world without threatening him or otherwise affecting his behavior, that I could tell. Though each on his own path, we shared something that August day: a valley, a storm, an awareness of place.

Ending the vigil, I crawled into the wind-whipped tent, curled up inside my sleeping bag, and drifted into a deep sleep. Body calm and spirits lifted, I moved through those mountains with bear.

CROSSING PATHS WITH PORCUPINE

The August sun teased us briefly on our fourth morning deep in Alaska's Arctic wilderness. Then it retreated inside a gray fortress of clouds, leaving behind the sort of raw, windy, and bitingly cold day that makes a person reluctant to leave the warm comfort of a sleeping bag. Still, by midday Andrew and I had squirmed from our synthetic cocoons and wrapped ourselves in many layers of clothing, ready to continue our explorations of the Central Brooks Range, Alaska's northernmost—and wildest—mountain chain.

Moving deliberately, we ascended a side valley north of camp, along the southeastern flanks of Three River Mountain. Rarely have I explored a place that so clearly shows how erosional forces wear mountains down. Rocks that ranged from the size of peas to refrigerators had been heaped into great piles along the valley bottom. Some were scoured from the surrounding hills by masses of ice. Others were torn loose by frost action, running water, and gravity. Huge landslides had been funneled through gullies and creases. I counted more than a dozen large tongues of rocky debris on just the valley's west side. Some stones were dark gray, wearing thick coats of lichens. How many years, decades, centuries, must pass for lichens to completely encrust a boulder? Others were freshly broken, making the textures and minerals of sandstones and conglomerates easy to read. Even as we hiked up valley, the clatter and bang of falling rocks echoed around us.

Two sets of stepped waterfalls cascaded hundreds of feet, their clear splashing waters silver pendants against the mountain's dark, broken body. Stepping close to one, I watched the water drop in sheets and streamers, through red and brown rock that had been fractured and folded, rusted and worn. The water and spray washed over brilliant green mosses that glowed in the gray afternoon light, then crashed into a pool that fed a sinuous tundra brook.

In the valley's upper basin was a rock glacier: a huge debris pile, nearly a half mile long and hundreds of feet wide, left by melted glacial ice. As we neared its base, Andrew spotted a "standing rock." About two feet wide and three feet high, the black, rectangular boulder reminded him of the monolithic obelisk in Arthur Clarke's *2001: A Space Odyssey.*

Andrew stood beside the waist-high rock, closed his eyes, and laid his hands upon its lichen-crusted body. A minute or two later, he removed his hands but remained still and silent.

"What sort of revelation did you have?" I finally asked.

Turning toward me, Andrew smiled mischievously. "The obelisk wants two cheeseburgers, a large fries, and a large Coke." After a long pause, he added, "Did you expect something profound?"

A longtime resident of Alaska whose personal journey had taken him to the Lower 48 in something of a midlife crisis, Andrew had returned north on vacation and for several days joined me in these mountains, hoping to gain some clarity and direction. While wandering through this primordial landscape, homeland to the Nunamiut Eskimo people, he constantly imagined ancient and sometimes sacred cultural remains. A jumbled, uplifted mass of tundra became a burial ground. A volcanic dike became a wall built by the Nunamiut. Boulders became signposts or sculptures—or obelisks with bizarre desires.

Andrew and I may joke about his imaginings and visions, but I knew something serious was going on (though in this instance I think his standing rock mirrored his own appetite for city food). An environmental engineer in his professional life, he's an odd mix of scientist and mystic, a guy who's highly sensitive to people's emotions, environmental toxins, Earth energies, and other intangibles.

Though at first blush I was here simply for the adventure of wilderness exploration, I too wished to learn more about myself—and my deepening relationship with wildness. I hoped to discover more of the mystery that is so much a part of these Arctic mountains, which I've loved since my first journey here in the mid-1970s. What would I take away this time?

I didn't have to wait long for some answers.

Not far from his standing rock, Andrew made an even more amazing discovery. At least it was to me. Crossing the base of a bouldery talus slope, he happened upon a porcupine. If I hadn't seen the animal myself, I'm not sure I would have believed it. Porcupines are woodland creatures. So what the heck was this one doing up here, at least a dozen miles, one mountain pass, and more than two thousand vertical feet from the nearest forest? As I told Andrew, "This guy took a major wrong turn—or several wrong turns—somewhere along the way."

As is often my habit, I instinctively attached a gender to the animal. Instead of "it," the porcupine became "he." If someone were to quiz me, I couldn't have explained my reasoning; it was an intuitive thing.

The porcupine was probably just as startled, if not more so, to meet us. Showing no desire for a closer look or whiff, he headed for a pile of dark, lichen-encrusted boulders at a fast waddle. In his retreat the porcupine stopped once, twice to look back. Each time he stood hunched on back feet, golden-brown quills swaying in the up-valley wind, black head and eyes studying us, as if asking himself, *Who are these guys?* This deep in the wilderness, we might have been the first people he had ever seen. Or smelled. With poor eyesight, members of the species depend on their superior senses of smell and hearing while maneuvering through their world.

A few strides later, the porcupine dropped from sight. Hesitant to harass him, we held back, watched from a distance. Finally, despite Andrew's teasing protests, I was unable to resist the desire to observe this remarkable rodent a few minutes more and crossed the talus pile. But the porcupine had vanished, hidden among the jumble of rocks. Almost certainly he would remain under cover until he no longer sensed our presence.

All sorts of questions ran through my head. *How long has the porcupine been in this high valley? Is he lost? How long can he survive in this barren, rock-strewn landscape?* Porcupines feed on green plants, flowers, and the inner barks of trees, but the meager alpine meadows here at 4,400 feet consisted mostly of lichens and mosses, with only a few clumps of grass and an occasional flower. I couldn't imagine that this tundra would sustain him for long, especially with summer fading.

I entertained the notion that this porcupine, like us, was on something of a vision quest. Perhaps our searching paths had brought us together. Whatever the case, I wished the porcupine well in his travels and hoped he would find his way home or at least to less harsh surroundings. Porcupines aren't hibernators, so if stranded here by an early snowfall it seemed unlikely he would endure the winter.

Later, returned to camp, I jotted down some notes about the encounter in my journal and also made a mental note to learn more about the territorial and travel habits of porcupines.

Back in Anchorage, I checked several sources, including the pocket field guide *Alaska's Mammals*, the state's "Wildlife Notebook Series," and legendary biologist Adolph Murie's *Mammals of Denali*. I managed to glean all sorts of fascinating natural history facts from this research. For instance, Alaska's far-north porcupines are descendants of tropical species that migrated from South America (a long-distance migration that must have been among the slowest ever). When pursuing a mating partner, males will fight each other with tooth and quill if necessary. The victor then splashes the lucky gal with his urine. If she's not interested, the female porcupine simply shakes off the pee and leaves. If ready for romance, she invites the male to mount her, and curls her tail over her quilled back to lessen the chance that their bonding will leave the male in great pain.

After a gestation period of about seven months, a single porcupette (yes, that is truly what newborns are called) is pushed out into the world. The baby's thirty thousand or so quills are soft during birth, but harden within a half hour. If not eaten by a lynx or wolverine or other predator, or trapped by a human, or run over by an SUV, the porcupine can expect to live five to seven years.

There's lots more of course, but here I'll add only one more observation: though they roost and often eat in trees, porcupines are rather slow, awkward climbers.

All of this is interesting stuff, and some is fascinating. But nothing that I found helped me to understand the porcupine's presence in so barren a place as the upper reaches of a Brooks Range valley where greens of any sort are few and far between.

Summer 2005. Nearly four years had passed since our Arctic encounter with porcupine. Andrew had returned to live in Anchorage and, though still searching, regained some direction and stability in his life. Meanwhile I was on the cusp of some major shifts of my own.

In early July, continuing my wilderness education in downtown Anchorage, I attended an event that drew hundreds of people from around the state and nation. Among their numbers were environmentalists, poets, scientists, Native activists, historians, politicians, wilderness guides, park rangers, nature writers, and grassroots organizers. All carried a deep love for the Earth and our world's many forms of wildness. They also brought a deep appreciation for ANILCA (the Alaska National Interest Lands Conservation Act) and the people who spearheaded the nationwide preservationist movement that produced the Alaska Lands Act.

The year 2005 marked the twenty-fifth anniversary of ANILCA, frequently heralded as the grandest wilderness-preservation legislation in U.S. history, if not all of human history. The 1980 law protected more than one hundred million acres of Alaska's federal wildlands—an area larger than California—in parks, preserves, monuments, wildlife refuges, national forests, and wild and scenic rivers. The act also added fifty-five million acres to the nation's wilderness system and protected the subsistence rights of Alaska's rural residents on federal lands. Much of my favorite mountain range is protected by "units" established through ANILCA, including Gates of the Arctic National Park and Preserve, which straddles most of the Central Brooks Range region that Andrew and I had explored years earlier.

Though December 2 marks the date that President Jimmy Carter signed ANILCA into law, midsummer seemed more suitable for a silver-anniversary observance, since that's when Alaska's wildlands and waters burst with life. An early July gathering also made it possible for Jimmy and Rosalyn to celebrate both ANILCA and their own fifty-ninth wedding anniversary in Alaska. It was a sweet confluence of the personal and political.

To those of us who hadn't been part of that landmark 1980 moment—and the decade-long preservationist push that preceded it—the gathering presented an opportunity to meet ANILCA's many heroes: from eighty-year-old Jimmy Carter to pioneering Alaska conservationist Ginny Wood and Athabascan chief and orator Jonathan Solomon. Then we joined the rest in honoring those visionary people and the Alaska Lands Act itself.

We came to see, in these bitterly partisan times, that ANILCA was a true bipartisan victory, made possible only because conservatives and liberals, Republicans and Democrats, Natives and non-Natives, joined together in service of something greater than themselves. And we were reminded by Cecil Andrus, interior secretary under President Carter, that ANILCA was a coast-to-coast grassroots victory. "The people won the battle," he reflected. "It wasn't just for Alaskans, but for all Americans."

Whether a veteran of the effort to protect wild Alaska, or new to that ongoing struggle, everyone in the sold-out crowd of five hundred was given the chance to reflect upon the "perfect storm" of events that made ANILCA possible. Panelists and speakers shared stories about the 1968 Prudhoe Bay oil discovery, the subsequent "freeze" of federal land grants to the state, and the 1971 Alaska Native Claims Settlement Act (ANCSA), all of which set the stage for the Alaska Lands Act.

We learned too that ANILCA, though immensely successful in protecting wildlands and waters, was hardly perfect. Speaker after speaker told us that unfinished business remained. "As much as it settled, ANILCA left much to be done," said Allen Smith, The Wilderness Society's former Alaska regional director. Some examples: ongoing battles to protect the Tongass National Forest's old-growth forest and the Arctic Refuge's coastal plain, plus an expansion of Alaska's designated wilderness areas in places that deserve such safekeeping.

Another idea that surfaced again and again was that of vigilance. A key player in getting ANILCA passed by Congress, retired Ohio Representative John Seiberling urged the crowd, "You must stay organized . . . as [deceased Arizona congressman] Mo Udall used to say, there are no final victories."

Everyone who attended the ANILCA celebration took away something a little bit different. For me, a nature writer, the frequent evocation of writers and poets served as both an inspiration and a reminder of the need to be engaged: politically, socially, spiritually. Edward Abbey, Wallace Stegner, Henry David Thoreau, John McPhee, William Wordsworth, John Muir, Mary Oliver, Nora Gallagher, Wallace Stevens, M. Scott Momaday . . . the list went on and on. Given my bias, it should come as no surprise that two of my favorite presenters were Alaskan writers who are also activists of the highest order: Kim Heacox and Richard Nelson.

Through his own photography and both his words and those of others, Heacox emphasized what an astounding achievement ANILCA is. He also reminded us of the need for maintaining an attitude of both gratitude and restraint. And quoting the poet Mary Oliver, he asked us to consider her powerful words: "Tell me, what is it you plan to do with your one wild and precious life?"

Nelson, a Sitka resident and former Alaska State Writer, urged us to remember and to say, "again and again," that the lands protected by ANILCA "are *public* lands." As such "they are locked *open*," in contrast to private lands, "the ultimate lockup." In his spellbinding way, he told how conservation activism had opened his eyes to the "immeasurable gift of democracy" and the fact that conservation is "the ultimate form of patriotism. We are patriots for the American land."

As much as anything, Nelson said, ANILCA is "a promise we made to shining lakes and twisting rivers . . . to forests and tundra . . . to caribou, grizzly, wolf, wolverine . . . to eagle, crane, raven . . . to the unendingly mysterious land of Alaska."

Variously playful and reverential, Nelson both issued a call for action and chanted a glorious song of praise. "Wildness," he enthused, "is the heart and soul of Alaska. It is the defining characteristic of Alaska." Respected as a cultural anthropologist as well as a nature writer and wilderness advocate, "Nels" shared the beliefs and attitudes of his Native Alaskan teachers, both Eskimo and Athabascan. He explained that his time with the Koyukon people who live along the Brooks Range's southern edge opened him to a deeper understanding and appreciation of wild landscapes and creatures: "Because of them, I've come to see that there's a lot more to the natural world than what can be seen and heard and touched. The world is filled with power and spirit. Every animal, every part of the landscape, has a soul."

Among the animals that Nels evoked was one the Koyukon call *dikahona*, the "stick eater." The porcupine. "You know how porcupines wander around all over?" he asked. "Well, to the Koyukon people, the power of the porcupine is to know the land."

Fireworks went off inside my head while I furiously scribbled notes. So, the porcupine we met hadn't been "lost" or disoriented at all. If Nels and the Koyukon people were right, he'd been on something of a walkabout, learning more about the lay of the land, his homeland. I again resolved to do more with this.

Several more months passed. Then, one winter morning in the solitude of my home, I went to a bookshelf and pulled down Nelson's highly acclaimed work, *Make Prayers to the Raven: A Koyukon View of the Northern Forest*. Paging through the book, I turned to the chapter he devoted to small mammals and found its section on the porcupine. Here's part of what the Koyukon taught Nels: "No one can predict when a porcupine will be found, because they wander everywhere; and so they usually turn up unexpectedly.

". . . At the end of summer, porcupines become restless and begin moving widely. . . . During the first half of winter they still travel around a good deal, leaving their distinctive tracks as a testament to their slow, rather aimless explorations."

And this: "Porcupines are great wanderers despite their labored gait, as anyone knows who has followed their tracks winding almost endlessly through the forest. They are given a special power to know the landscape, I was told, and this is why people should never set traps for them (no further explanation was given). Beyond this, their familiarity with the geography is described as a kind of 'understanding,' as if their comprehension of the terrain is really just a metaphor representing something much greater."

Nels then quotes one of his Koyukon teachers: "Porcupines know all the country. Even though they're low to the ground they really know the land. They're powerful animals. My old man said, 'The whole of Alaska is just like something inside the palm of a porcupine's hand.'"

I like the idea, the *awareness*, that the humble, plodding porcupine is more powerful and wise than we humans can possibly imagine. And I was again reminded that sometimes we must go beyond Western science to gain a more profound understanding of the creatures with whom we share the Earth.

Sitting at my desk after reading about porcupines in *Make Prayers to the Raven*, I recalled my most recent encounter with *dikahona*: the previous fall, along Alaska's Parks Highway.

Unfortunately for these poor-sighted wanderers, their travels through Alaska's more populated areas often take them across roads. Over the years, I've seen more splattered porcupines on Alaska's highways than any other critter. Once or twice I've seen entire families smashed and bloodied. Although that's partly because of their slow-moving ways, I think it's also because they prefer to wander at night, or in summer during those parts of the day when the light is dimmest and fast-moving drivers don't see so well either.

It was September, which the Koyukon say is a season of widespread porcupine movement. I caught a flash of the animal while cruising the Parks at sixty-five miles per hour; he was eating greens along the highway's shoulder, only a foot or two from the driving lane. With memories of other squashed porcupines flashing through my head, I braked my Toyota and did a U-turn.

The porcupine must have seen, or heard, or otherwise sensed my approach, because he was in slow but steady retreat by the time I walked across the highway. When he finally stopped to look back, I smacked my hands loudly and the porcupine waddled away at a pace that can only be described as swiftly for his kind.

I've learned over the years that interfering with nature, even with good intentions, can do as much or more harm as good. But sometimes I can't help but meddle. (As a friend once told me, "That's what we humans do: we meddle in everything.") Now, as then, I believe that chasing the porcupine from the highway was the right thing to do, and that his instincts carried him far from pavement. We can never have too many porcupines—or other life forms—who *really* know the land. Just as we can never have enough off-the-beaten-path wanderers who sometimes go on trips that may, in some inexplicable way, give us greater vision and a better understanding of our world.

LOOKING INTO WILD EYES

Dark clouds and thick fog cloaked the Alaska Range and surrounding lowlands, as if some gray, sodden blanket had been dropped over the landscape. There was no hope of seeing The High One, 20,320-foot Denali. And in all this soupy grayness, there seemed to be little chance of seeing the wildlife for which Denali National Park is famous.

Given the weather and the hour—7:00 A.M. on a Saturday—the fourteen people on our bus might understandably have been grumpy. Or asleep. Instead, we were talking, laughing, sharing stories, and taking turns on "wildlife watch," one or more of the group alert for memories not yet captured. In short, we were a happy bunch, spirits refusing to be dampened by dank circumstances.

There was good reason for our brightness: members of our small community had spent anywhere from two to six days in the heart of one of America's great wilderness parklands. Only two of us were Alaskans. The rest—four couples and a family of four—came from Iowa, New York, and Paris. Strangers to each other a few days earlier, we were now like one giant family on holiday.

We'd been staying at a backcountry lodge, with many of the comforts of home: heated rooms, hot showers, cushy beds, great food. And the lodge's employees (most of them, too, from outside Alaska) had been eager to make our experience the best possible.

But the people on this bus could have found such luxuries almost anywhere. What had made this trip so memorable were the subarctic wilderness and its wild residents. Beyond the reach of cell phones, TV, newspapers, and the Internet, we'd been humbled by the immensity of tundra-topped hills and vast rolling lowlands, the glimpses of faraway, snowcapped peaks tucked beneath stubbornly persistent clouds. We had seen snow-white Dall sheep, big-antlered caribou and moose, migrating sandhill cranes loudly roarking overhead, swooping falcons, and, best of all, berry-crazed grizzly bears.

Even the sighting of a grizzly a mile or more away was something to be shared at dinner. Others told how they spontaneously broke into loud song when a trail took them into dense alder thickets, simply because a bear might be in the area.

Bears happen to be one of my great passions. In fact one reason I had come here was to present a program on Alaska's bears. My interest is that of a writer, naturalist, and animal lover, and I make no claims to special expertise. But once people know that I've studied bears, spent considerable time in their company, and even been charged by one, they pepper me with questions, ask me to share my stories, and tell me theirs. Everyone, it seems, has a bear story.

One of the grizzly's gifts to us humans is that the animal demands we pay attention to our surroundings when passing through their homelands. In doing so, we take notice of things we might ordinarily miss: berries, flowers, diggings in the tundra, animal droppings. We move out of our heads and into our bodies. Into present time. All of this is good.

To most people, no other North American animal symbolizes wilderness and wild ferocity as much as the grizzly. Except, perhaps, the wolf.

It turns out that Denali is among the best places to see wolves in the wild. But they're not seen nearly as often as grizzlies and few people at the lodge had sighted or heard any during their stay. The dark, foggy day of our departure would be their last, best chance.

Joe, a railroad engineer from America's heartland, was especially hungry to see a wolf. Even the briefest, most distant glimpse would do. He kept his eyes trained on the landscape until the gray shroud grew so thick almost nothing could be seen. Finally the veil began to lift and someone in the back of the bus announced, "OK, Joe, time to get serious again."

Minutes later, came a shout: "Wolf up ahead!"

Fifty yards in front of the bus, a black wolf nonchalantly walked down the middle of the road.

Martin, our driver, shut off the engine. Almost immediately the wolf stopped and looked our way, then turned and approached. The murmur built. People pulled down windows and reached for cameras, videos, binoculars. As the wolf got close, Martin recognized him as the Toklat Pack's alpha male.

The wolf paused, stepped forward a few feet, paused again. He looked directly at us, his bright yellow eyes shining fiercely with intelligence. The stark contrast of dark body and bright, piercing eyes was hypnotizing to some, unsettling to others. Later, someone would comment that the eyes reminded her of a horror film. Others would remark on the wolf's great calm, his easy manner. He was clearly comfortable around buses and people, but there was no question he belonged to another, much wilder, world.

Several minutes passed, then the wolf continued down the road and turned back onto the tundra. The bus was filled with an electrified hush before the driver restarted the engine. Then everyone began talking excitedly. This was the encounter people would share years and decades from now: a few minutes spent looking into the gleaming eyes of wolf, which somehow reflected back a deeper, wilder, more ancient part of ourselves.

SEEKING CARIBOU, TOUCHING THE ARCTIC REFUGE'S COASTAL PLAIN

Standing on a rocky, windblown perch at the edge of Alaska's northernmost mountain range, I looked north across a vast, green, undulating plain, hoping—half expecting—to see caribou. Five others joined me in the search, binoculars pressed tightly against their eyes. Time passed and one by one the binoculars dropped, as my friends wandered off to discover other Arctic delights and mysteries: golden poppies, bleached bones, wolf tracks, golden eagles soaring against a cerulean sky. I stubbornly lingered atop the unnamed marble mountain that rose, like a giant cone, from the Achilik River Valley.

That north-south trending drainage is one of the corridors used by members of the Porcupine Caribou Herd as they migrate through the Brooks Range to and from the Arctic National Wildlife Refuge's coastal plain. We'd come hoping to intercept caribou on their way to southern wintering grounds. We knew that most of the herd's one hundred thirty thousand caribou were already far to the south and east, but dreams die hard, so a few of us kept imagining that thousands—or at least hundreds—of late-departing migrants would suddenly surge into our valley and pass beside our tents in a thunder of bodies. Yet by trip's end, we would see only a couple of stragglers, each wandering alone upriver.

Though we missed the animals, their signs were everywhere, of every kind imaginable. Hoofed tracks marked the ground wherever it was soft. Clumps and tufts of brown and white hair hung from willow branches. Sun-bleached bones and antlers lay scattered on gravel bars, tundra wetlands, and craggy limestone ridges. Hundreds of deep, rutted trails crisscrossed the lowlands and hills. Even in the caribou's absence, the sense of their presence, their spirit, was overwhelming. As Glenn, visiting from California, suggested, "It's a little like being in someone else's house when they're not at home."

I'd come north also expecting to spend a day, maybe more, exploring the Arctic Refuge's coastal plain: calving ground for the Porcupine Caribou Herd and political battleground between those who want to probe its hidden depths for oil and gas and others, like me, who wish to keep this landscape preserved forever as wilderness. Listen to Alaska's politicians and you get the sense that only "outsiders" want to "lock up" the coastal plain. Another instance of environmental extremists spreading lies, and Lower 48 special interest groups—not to mention the federal government—meddling in local affairs, or so the argument goes. In fact some polls had shown that nearly half of Alaska's residents wanted the area to remain wilderness.

As it turned out, my friends and I spent most of our time in the mountains, where the hiking was easier, the scenery more spectacular and diverse, and the mosquitoes less ferocious. Our group of six ventured onto the coastal plain only once. Most stayed a half hour or less before retreating to camp. Glenn and I stayed a bit longer. Still, we hiked no more than a mile or two beyond the Brooks Range foothills before being chased back by swarming mosquitoes and wet feet.

The coastal plain isn't a pleasant place to explore by foot (which is probably why float trips are so popular here). Tundra walking is made difficult, if not torturous, by biting bugs, abundant marshlands, and sedge tussocks—unstable, mushroom-shaped mounds of plants. Tussocks can be avoided by hiking along the large, braided stream channels that dissect the plain, but there's no escaping mosquitoes. Or soaked feet. And the meandering network of river channels makes stream crossings—or tundra detours—inevitable.

Stumbling through wetlands and harassed by mosquitoes, with no caribou, grizzlies, or other animals in sight, I could understand why some people so easily dismiss this landscape as desolate or barren. From a narrowly human perspective, the coastal plain is a remote, flat, monotonous, harsh, and expensive-to-reach place that few people would ever hope, or wish, to visit. In winter, it's draped in darkness and subzero cold, wracked by blizzards; in summer, it's bug-infested swampland.

Yet even in my discomfort, I noticed wolf tracks pressed into the sandbars, the buzzing trill of a savannah sparrow hidden in the knee-high grasses. They were reminders that the coastal plain's true importance has nothing to do with humans. These lands and waters are breeding, nesting, spawning, calving, feeding, and denning grounds for polar bears, muskoxen, wolves, voles, loons, ducks, shorebirds, snowy owls, Arctic grayling—dozens of species in all.

Crossing back to the foothills, I stopped for a moment and once more imagined the pounding of hooves: the beating of the refuge's biological heart, a place throbbing with life during the short Arctic summer. Barren and inhospitable to our kind, perhaps, the coastal plain is a homeland to our wild northern kin. Those of us who venture here would do well to show gentle manners and respect, as when we step into someone else's house—even if they are not at home.

FOURTEEN WAYS OF VIEWING ALASKA'S WILD, WHITE SHEEP

1.

The image is a sentimental favorite, a portrait of two wild sheep that's suitable for framing or getting published in a book. A Dall sheep ewe and her lamb gaze directly at the viewer, only their white upper bodies and heads visible behind gray, lichen-splattered rocks. The faces of both appear calm. Inquisitive. Yet their large golden eyes, erect ears, and pursed lips also suggest caution. And maybe some uncertainty. There's a sense that the sheep will bound away if the human they're intently watching steps any closer or makes some sudden, awkward move.

The ewe-lamb pair were captured in this picture while perched on a steep hillside that looms above the Seward Highway south of Anchorage. They were among a half dozen or so sheep visible from the highway that day, yet high enough on the cliff face and far enough from Windy Corner—a place known for its sheep-viewing opportunities—that most travelers missed their presence.

Unlike those who rushed past on their way to farther destinations, I'd come looking for these animals, which I knew to be extremely tolerant of people. Armed with a high-quality camera, a newly purchased telephoto lens, and a burning desire to get some close-up wildlife shots, I painstakingly ascended the steep wooded and rocky slope, hopeful the sheep would allow me near them.

Though I'd come to Anchorage in the early 1980s to work as a sports writer, I had other long-term (and at that point largely unspoken) ambitions: to someday be the newspaper's outdoors writer; and to supplement that writing with my own photography.

Eventually I would delve into the nature, the life stories of Alaska's Dall sheep. But on this day I was less interested in observing their behaviors and habits than sharing their company and, especially, getting their pictures. In that regard, the day proved a heady success. A mix of mature ewes, adolescents, and lambs, the sheep allowed me to briefly join their company. At times we came within fifteen or twenty feet of each other, their curiosity a match for mine, or so it seemed. Perhaps they were bewildered that some foolish human would risk his life to walk and stumble along such steep and crumbly slopes.

2.

The Brooks Range is where I saw my first wild sheep, while working as a geologist in the mid-1970s. During one day-long traverse I made in bright sunshine and energy-sapping heat, two short-spiked ewes appeared atop a ledge, like some far north mirage. Less than fifty feet above me, the sheep seemed more inquisitive than wary when I slowly passed beneath them. And why not? Deep in the Arctic wilderness, dozens of miles from the nearest road or village, I may have been the first human they'd ever met. The two continued to watch until I walked out of sight, my mood brightened and body enlivened by the surprise encounter with luminously white animals.

3.

After I'd become the *Anchorage Times'* outdoors writer in the mid-1980s, I began making springtime pilgrimages to Denali National Park, to view and photograph wildlife and collect notes for stories. Each May I would camp in Denali's entrance area and drive the park road, which before the Memorial Day weekend is open to private vehicles for its first thirty miles. One gravelly stretch of road just beyond pavement's end at mile fifteen passes beneath Primrose Ridge, a gentle east-west trending hill whose southern flank faces the road.

In spring, Dall sheep rams congregate on that sun-drenched slope, which is among the first to green up. Initially I was happy enough to watch the faraway rams through binoculars. But one year I decided to get closer. Grabbing my daypack and camera gear, I headed uphill, occasionally stopping to study their response to my approach. Some of the rams faced my direction and through binoculars I could see they watched my slow progress.

A mile or so of hill climbing brought me to within one hundred feet of several rams. Some lay on the tundra, others grazed. None retreated or showed signs they were disturbed by my presence. Among them were some large-bodied and full-curled males that photographers and big-game hunters alike would consider trophies. (These, of course, were protected from hunting as long as they remained inside the park's wilderness.)

This was before Denali's managers formulated a more stringent set of rules to govern the behavior of wildlife-viewers and photographers. So a few steps at a time, I gradually moved closer to the rams, careful not to alarm them. Body pulsing with excitement, I stopped now and then to take their pictures, amazed by both their beauty and their calm acceptance of my presence. Eventually I sat and the rams moved around me, sometimes approaching closer than I would have dared to try. I changed rolls of film, scribbled notes, took in the grandeur of the day, considered what they made of me, thanked them for their tolerance. Some of their portraits, too, would eventually be framed and hung on walls or appear in publications.

4.

It can be argued that Dall sheep, as much as 20,320-foot Denali, grizzly bears, wolves, or vast tundra expanses, are perfect symbols of what famed biologist Adolph Murie called the parkland's "wilderness spirit." The snow-white mountain sheep are what drew naturalist-hunter-author Charles Sheldon to the Denali region in 1906. And their preservation, as much as anything, inspired him to seek park status for this wildlife-rich part of Alaska, a quest that led to the creation of Alaska's first national park—then named Mount McKinley—in 1917.

Later in the park's history, severe Dall sheep declines in the 1930s and '40s caused great alarm and forced park officials to confront wildlife-management policies that favored one species (sheep) over another (wolves). Thanks largely to Murie, the sheep crisis—and the species' eventual recovery—ultimately led to a strengthening of ecosystem rather than favored-game management in Denali; here, all native species would be protected. It also led to Murie's northern classic, *The Wolves of Mount McKinley*.

Nowadays, an estimated twenty-five hundred Dall sheep inhabit Denali National Park and Preserve's alpine heights; based on 2008–9 surveys and those done in the mid-1990s, park biologists believe sheep numbers throughout most of the park to be "fairly stable" entering the 2010s. The large majority live on the park's northern side, in both the Alaska and Outer Ranges. Because the Denali

Park Road borders some of the sheep's prime habitat, visitors have an excellent chance of seeing these animals, though usually from a distance of several hundred yards to a half mile or more. They are most often seen as tiny white dots on the upper flanks of tundra-covered hills, though occasionally they can be spotted near or even on the road. Visitors willing to climb hills are more likely to see the sheep up close, though park regulations prohibit people from approaching closer than seventy-five feet.

A small percentage of Denali's Dall sheep actually cross the road on seasonal journeys between the park's two mountain ranges. These migratory sheep spend their winters in the Outer Range, where snowfall is light and high winds often keep exposed ridges free of snow. In May or June they form groups of up to sixty or seventy animals and cross wide lowlands to reach the Alaska Range's northern foothills for summer's green-up. There the sheep remain until late August or September, when they retrace their steps. Biologists since Adolph Murie have known that a portion of Denali's sheep migrate, but it remains unknown why some do and others don't.

5.

With a nod of thanks to all of those who've studied *Ovis dalli* and shared what they have learned, I'll now present a potpourri of natural history facts and figures about the white, wild sheep which is named after American naturalist William Healy Dall and inhabits mountain ranges throughout much of inland Alaska and neighboring western Canada.

Adult male and female members of the species live apart except during the early winter mating season, which occurs in November and December. Just prior to the rut (and occasionally throughout the year), mature rams butt heads in fierce battles that scientists say determines their place in the band's social order and, consequently, its breeding order. Facing each other, two rams rear up on their hind legs, then charge and clash horns with a loud bang that's been compared to that of a baseball bat slammed into a barn door. Adult females too will sometimes knock heads, apparently to determine social rankings.

Ewes produce a single lamb in late May or early June. As the birth approaches, a pregnant ewe will go off by itself and head for steep, rugged terrain where predators are less likely to be. Lambs usually do fine their first summer, when food is abundant, but half or more may die their first winter, depending on the season's severity. Sheep that survive their first couple of winters may live to between twelve and fifteen years. Mature rams in their prime may weigh 200 pounds or more, ewes 110 to 130 pounds on average.

Both sexes of adult sheep have horns, though only males grow the large, sweeping, and outward-curling horns so often seen in photos. As rams mature, their horns gradually form a circle when viewed from the side, reaching a full curl in seven to eight years. The amber-colored horns are male status symbols; large mature rams can sometimes be seen displaying their horns to other sheep as a sign of their dominance. Those of females are shorter, slender spikes that resemble the horns of mountain goats, which sometimes cause people to confuse the two species. But goat horns are shiny black and sharper than sheep horns and goats also have more massive chests. Besides that, their ranges rarely overlap, goats being most common in coastal mountains while sheep largely remain inland.

Unlike the antlers of moose and caribou, horns are never shed; they continue to grow throughout a sheep's life. Horn growth occurs only from spring through fall; winters are marked by a narrow ridge or ring. So, much like a tree, the age of sheep can be determined by counting their "annual rings," also called annuli. Though rams may live into their midteens and ewes their late teens, biologists consider twelve to be very old for a wild sheep.

Dall sheep are grazing animals that feed on a variety of plants, including grasses, sedges, willows, and herbaceous plants; in winter they survive on lichens, moss, and dried or frozen grass. They prefer to stay up high, in places that combine open alpine ridges and meadows with steep slopes, because their hill-climbing skills make it easier to escape predators in such sheer, rugged, mountainous terrain. Wolves are the most efficient predators of sheep, but grizzlies, coyotes, lynx, and wolverines sometimes successfully hunt the species and golden eagles prey on young lambs.

6.

In the early 1900s, when prospectors and pioneering mountaineers were lured into the Denali region by gold and summit fever, respectively, easterner Charles Sheldon came north to the Alaska Range on a different sort of quest: a big-game hunt. What Sheldon found proved far more valuable than any trophy animal. Denali's wilderness and wildlife sparked the idea for a park-refuge unlike any other in the nation.

By all accounts a skilled hunter, passionate naturalist, devout conservationist, successful businessman, gifted writer, and astute political lobbyist, the Vermont-born and Yale-educated Sheldon was passionate about all species of mountain sheep, which he believed were the noblest of wild animals. He studied and hunted them throughout their North American range, finally pursuing his passion to the most remote part of the continent, in search of Alaska's fabled white sheep. For a guide he chose Harry Karstens, a transplanted Midwesterner known to be a first-rate explorer and woodsman (and who would later become the first superintendent of Mount McKinley National Park).

Accompanied by a horse packer, Sheldon and Karstens lived off the land while they explored the Alaska Range's northern slopes. By mid-August they had seen hundreds of sheep, but all were ewes, lambs, adolescents, or young adults. Finally, while hiking Cathedral Mountain alone on August 17, Sheldon discovered a band of mature rams, including nine with "strikingly big horns." In great and dramatic detail, he described his solo stalk of those "Big rams!" in *The Wilderness of Denali*.

Locating a spot along the edge of a canyon where he could hide from the sheep while watching them—and taking aim with his rifle—Sheldon waited until his body had grown calm, after the exertion and excitement of his stalk. Confident that the rams had not detected him, he then sat up, braced his elbows against his knees, placed one of the sheep in the rifle's sights, and pulled the trigger. As the shot echoed across the mountain, the ram fell, its back broken. Alert but bewildered, the remaining rams milled about, looking in all directions. Taking advantage of their confusion, Sheldon spotted one sheep that seemed to be looking directly at him, but was frozen in place. He shot that one, too, and it rolled into the canyon between them. Several other rams then made a dash for the chasm, but one paused at its edge and Sheldon dropped that one, too.

Other kills followed, also described in considerable detail. In the end, Sheldon killed seven "fine" rams with only eight shots, this by someone who described himself as "an indifferent marksman." In a matter of minutes, his earlier discouraging quest to "collect" several trophy rams had become a grand success. In short measure he'd filled his quota for the U.S. Biological Survey, which would add the skulls and skins of four rams to its study collection in the national museum. And he'd added three "reasonably good trophies" for himself (regulations at the time allowed him to keep up to four rams besides those taken for the survey).

The rain that had been falling when Sheldon stalked and began shooting the sheep had stopped. Exhilarated by the entirety of the hunt, Sheldon sat peacefully and smoked his pipe, while taking in the beauty of the landscape, "intensified by my wrought-up senses."

7.

Given what I knew of Charles Sheldon—legendary champion of Alaska's wild sheep and Denali's wilderness—his account of the killing spree stunned me when I first read it.

I understand the inherent unfairness of using contemporary standards to judge people who lived in other eras, under different value systems and moral codes. In his time, Sheldon was considered a consummate conservationist. And by most accounts, he worked harder than anyone to get the homeland of these sheep protected. He is celebrated for his wilderness advocacy, especially his role in getting the federal government to establish Mount McKinley National Park, later to become Denali National Park and Preserve. Still, both the actions and attitude he exhibited that long-ago day disturb me.

Except for catching and killing fish (and I don't do much of even that these days), I am what's called a nonhunter. I don't directly kill other animals for food, or clothing, or other reasons. But contrary to what some of my Alaskan critics say, I am not an "anti." I do not oppose the respectful and humane hunting and killing of animals for food or other subsistence purposes. It seems more honest, in a way, and arguably more ethical than buying meat at the store, especially given what we know about the awful lives of most farm animals that become our food. But as I've noted elsewhere, over the years I've become intolerant of trophy hunting. To me such blood sport is unacceptable, a selfish and harmful act fed by pride and ego.

Can I accept Sheldon's behavior? Given the context, I suppose. Yet I'm bothered by his excitement and self-congratulatory tone (I read false humility in the comments about his marksmanship) and especially his cavalier attitude toward the sheep he killed. Sheldon suggests no sense of regret or sadness that he took their lives. Yes, he obeyed the hunting laws. But to kill seven rams for science and personal satisfaction seems the epitome of overkill, no matter how healthy the local sheep population may have been.

End of commentary, back to Sheldon's story.

8.

To his credit, Sheldon painstakingly recovered the animals he'd killed. One by one he butchered the sheep and hauled their meat, skins, and skulls down the mountain, then treated them for preservation, took measurements, and studied the stomach contents. Once reunited with his companions, he packed his specimens out and returned east. His trip had been a resounding success.

Sheldon's main work was now complete. Several of the sheep he'd killed and collected would be studied by scientists and displayed in the American Museum of Natural History. But he recognized the need for a longer stay, to better understand the sheep's life history. So before leaving, he built a cabin along the Toklat River.

The following August, Sheldon returned for a ten-month stay. Besides studying sheep, he gathered facts on other species, large and small: moose, grizzlies, caribou, foxes, birds, even voles. He paid close attention to the landscape, the wildlife habitat, and the changing weather and seasons, and he made friends with many year-round residents. He was astounded by the abundant wildlife on the Alaska Range's north side, but also fearful of the damage done by the market hunters who supplied wild meat to the region's towns and mining camps; hunters who, if uncontrolled, would someday threaten Denali's wildlife populations.

Along the way, Sheldon fell in love with the Denali region and he began to envision a plan for its preservation as a park and game preserve. In a journal entry dated January 12, 1908, he even named this park-refuge: Denali National Park. Though he never again returned to Denali country, it remained an inspiration for this dream.

Back in New York, Sheldon shared his Denali vision with fellow members of the Boone & Crockett Club, a politically influential group of big-game trophy hunters and conservationists. His colleagues responded enthusiastically, but momentum for the new park-refuge lagged until Congress in 1914 mandated construction of a railroad from Seward to Fairbanks. The preferred route would pass through the heart of the Denali region.

With new urgency, Sheldon pursued his dream. Joined by equally enthusiastic allies—among them were newly appointed Park Service director Stephen Mather and prominent artist, explorer, and hunter Belmore Browne—Sheldon helped to draft legislation establishing a Mount McKinley National Park. He also won the backing of Alaska's lone delegate to Congress, James Wickersham, who realized such a park could be a major tourist attraction and boost the territory's economy.

With new momentum and little opposition, bills to establish the park were introduced to the House and Senate in 1916. Congress passed the legislation in February 1917 and later that month, President Woodrow Wilson signed it into law. Shaped roughly like a parallelogram, the original Mount McKinley Park protected twenty-two hundred square miles of prime wildlife habitat, primarily north of the Alaska Range, where Sheldon had met the Dall sheep that would help to define his life and conservation legacy.

9.

Traffic slows to a standstill. Cars, pickups, and RVs begin pulling over to the side of the highway. Binoculars and cameras (and by the second decade of the twenty-first century, smart phones) are grabbed. And a crowd begins to gather, as both tourists and Alaskans maneuver for a better look at the Dall sheep that feed less than one hundred feet away.

The sheep pay little attention to the human spectators. Continuing to feed on grass and willows, they sometimes wander close to the road and show no outward signs of fear, even when people approach to within thirty feet or less. It's a scene that's repeated dozens of times each summer, along one of Alaska's busiest stretches of highway.

Tens of thousands of Dall sheep inhabit the state's mountain ranges, from Southcentral Alaska to the Arctic. They're prized wildlife symbols of three national parks: Denali, Wrangell-St. Elias, and Gates of the Arctic. But nowhere are they as accessible to the public as the Windy Corner area of Chugach State Park, a half hour's drive from downtown Anchorage and the only place in the world that people can watch Dall sheep while both are standing near sea level.

Ewes, lambs, adolescents, and young adult sheep inhabit steep cliffs and grassy meadows above the Seward Highway for much of the year, coming closest to the road between mileposts 106 and 107. Peak viewing occurs in summer, after the ewes have given birth. The best time to see the sheep is usually early morning, though they're sometimes visible throughout the day. As many as fifty have been spotted from the highway, but twenty or fewer is more the norm. Only rarely are the older, big-curl rams present; they seem to prefer backcountry solitude to busy highway corridors.

While the sheep's high visibility is a guaranteed treat for wildlife lovers, it has long proved a management headache for Chugach State Park personnel and state troopers. Drivers who slow down or stop to watch and photograph the sheep may ignore designated turnouts and park instead along narrow highway shoulders, despite "No Parking" signs. Or, even worse, they'll slow almost to a stop on the highway itself. And as crowds gather, people pay less attention to traffic patterns.

As former Chugach superintendent Al Meiners once described it to me, "When people see wild sheep three feet from the road, they just go nuts. Other senses tend to shut down and you get people doing foolish things, like slamming on their brakes right on the highway. It's real dangerous, because you have other drivers coming screaming around that curve at fifty, sixty miles an hour, and here's a traffic jam. I went down there once to study the problem and ended up directing traffic."

State officials have talked for years about ways to better address the Seward Highway's "sheep jams." Some improvements have been made, for instance widened pullouts, but the problems persist. Now I've learned that a major highway redesign is in the works. Plans for Windy Corner include a widened road with passing lanes, parking lots on both sides of the highway, informational signs that present responsible wildlife viewing behavior, a pedestrian tunnel, and perhaps some sort of barriers to better separate people and sheep.

10.

Given my love for both wildlife and wildlands, it was perhaps inevitable that I would write about Chugach State Park's Dall sheep, as well as photograph them, after becoming the *Times'* outdoors writer in 1984. A few years after I'd gained that coveted position, I met with Dave Harkness, the state biologist responsible for managing the Anchorage area's wildlife, to learn more about Windy Corner's sheep. Dave told me that biologists weren't absolutely certain why sheep would congregate in such large numbers along a busy highway, but suspected a mineral lick, where they were likely getting salt and other essential minerals from the soil (those suspicions have since been confirmed). He also believed that the cliffs contributed to their tolerance of human traffic: "The sheep know they have an easy escape route if they need it. In a few minutes, or even seconds, they can be out of view."

Harkness further noted that the Windy Corner sheep frequent an area that was—and remains—off-limits to hunting, which would help to account for their tame behavior: lambs learn early that people don't pose a threat. Yet, he added, "Come August and September, the sheep are vastly different creatures; they're not as accessible or visible. It's hard to say whether they equate danger with different times of the year."

Neither Harkness's successor, Rick Sinnott, nor the Anchorage area's current wildlife manager, Jessy Coltrane, have noticed such a seasonal shift in the sheep's behavior. And in a conversation with me, Coltrane questioned why the animals would suddenly become more wary during that time of year. I can offer one possibility: sport hunters.

The one obvious danger that Alaska's Dall sheep face in late summer and fall is human hunting. Of course it's difficult, if not impossible, to know whether sheep make that seasonal connection. But if Harkness was right, it's telling that they become "different creatures" when the killing season begins, or at least did so during his watch. Yes, sheep are protected at Windy Corner and on neighboring terrain. But parts of Chugach State Park's backcountry are open to sheep hunting from early August through early October, including one area less than five miles away, as a sheep rambles. Could the skittish behavior that Harkness observed be mere coincidence? I for one can imagine that sheep might somehow learn to associate that time of year with a need for greater caution.

On the other hand, it's strange that neither Sinnott nor Coltrane has witnessed such behavioral changes in the two decades or so since Harkness retired. And there's this to consider: as Coltrane points out, the great majority of Chugach hunters have always targeted full-curl rams. Why would the killing of rams make ewes and young sheep more cautious, especially since mature males generally keep to themselves?

It is true that any permitted hunter could kill ewes in Chugach State Park from the mid-1990s into the 2000s, though since 2009 only archers have been allowed to take them. (Coltrane says that the hunting season begins after lambs have been weaned.) Between 2010 and 2012, hunters killed thirty-nine full-curl rams and only three ewes in the park and some adjacent lands. The paradox is that no ewes could be hunted when Harkness was manager, yet that's when Windy Corner's sheep apparently were most guarded during the hunting season. Could he have misread their actions? Could Sinnott and Coltrane simply have missed the seasonal shift? Or perhaps some other circumstance has changed. Such enigmas reflect how little we actually know about Dall sheep (and other animals), including—and especially—their inner lives and communication with each other.

Before moving on, I'll add a few additional observations about Chugach State Park's sheep and the hunting of them. Over two thousand sheep were annually counted in the park from the late 1980s through the 1990s, about double their number in the early 1980s. Wildlife managers correctly suspected that was more than the sheep's habitat could indefinitely sustain and Sinnott added new hunts, including the ones for ewes, in the mid-1990s to trim their numbers. The park's sheep population plummeted in the early 2000s, perhaps because of overgrazing and severe winters, though no one knows for certain. By 2007, about nine hundred sheep remained. Since then the population has rebounded slightly, to about a thousand animals.

Because, in Coltrane's words, "We micromanage the hell out of 14C [the unit that includes Chugach State Park]," managers are confident that the human kill didn't contribute in any substantial way to the sheep decline. And the allowable harvest has been lowered as sheep numbers dropped. In 2002, for instance, Coltrane says hunters killed fifty-nine full-curl rams and twenty-three ewes in 14C, mostly in the park; in 2012 they took thirteen rams and no ewes. For now the park's population seems stable.

One more thing: Sinnott says that nowadays "there are more sheep more of the time at Windy Corner" than during Harkness's time. That's good news for wildlife watchers. And increased highway headaches for park managers and troopers.

11.

When I lived on Anchorage's Hillside, I could sometimes watch Dall sheep from my front yard. Even through binoculars, they were small white dots on the green or brown slopes below a Chugach landmark called Rusty Point. I always considered it a remarkable thing, to watch wild sheep move about their alpine homelands while I stood in my own suburban neighborhood, with its houses, roads, gardens, garbage pickup, and lawn mowers.

12.

Though my geology career ended in the 1970s, I've periodically returned to the Central Brooks Range in the years since then, as writer, adventurer, and wildlands advocate. Now largely protected by 8.2-million-acre Gates of the Arctic

National Park and Preserve, it has remained my favorite wilderness, a largely unpeopled landscape where one can spend days, even weeks, without seeing obvious signs of humans; a place where knife-edged ridges stretch in waves to the horizon and beyond and glacially carved basins grow lush with tundra plants in summer; a place enriched by free-roaming grizzly bears, wolves, wolverines, sheep, and other northern animals.

In August 2008, I traveled to Gates on a ten-day solo trip. My visit got off to a rough start, with a broken tent pole and wintry weather, raising worries and dampening my spirits. My second day in the range was mostly rainy and gusty, so I stayed inside the tent except to cook and stretch muscles on a short hill climb. That hike proved to be exactly the tonic I needed. Step by step my worries washed away while I gently slipped into the magic of those wild and ancient mountains. It was as if the harsh, rugged surroundings somehow eased me into a more tranquil state of being. The shift was subtle, until finally a thought hit me brightly: *Wow, it's great to be back.*

Near the end of my ascent, I happened to spot four sheep with short, spiked horns in a creek bottom below me. One looked small enough to be a lamb, its horns barely nubs. Unaware of me that I could tell, they moved steadily yet leisurely up valley, the smallest one prancing playfully at times among the boulders and meadows. Looking through binoculars, I then spotted three more sheep on a neighboring ridge.

Once atop the hill I hunkered down out of the wind and pointed my binoculars east, across a broad river valley. Scanning the distant hills, I first found a group of five sheep, resting on a dark slope. Then two more. And on another mountainside, nine sheep were scattered across the tundra. They were too far away to tell if any were mature rams; I thought about this because all of the sheep across the valley were on national preserve lands, where trophy hunting is allowed.

By the end of my walk, I'd counted thirty-one sheep. As I noted in my journal, "Not a bad sheep-hunting day," at least for a guy armed only with binoculars.

A few days later, while exploring the upper reaches of a stark valley enclosed by huge marble walls and towering spires, I was surprised to discover a group of four sheep, hundreds of feet above me: two ewes, each with a lamb. Upon noticing me, they immediately headed for even higher ground and within minutes topped a mountain pass at least sixty-five-hundred feet high. Few plants grew in this high basin; so what could have drawn the sheep to this barren place? Had they taken refuge here to escape some danger or were they simply passing through? Or did they have some other motive that I could never hope to guess?

I made an equally odd discovery while on another walkabout: a bleached ram's skull, its massive horns still attached. The horns nearly made a full curl and both they and the skull were well preserved. What struck me as weird was the skull's position. It sat upright on a tundra bench, facing north, with no other skeletal remains, body parts, or hair nearby, as if someone—or something?—had carried the skull to this spot and placed it carefully on the ground.

The horns' annular rings showed that the ram lived to be six years old and I tried to imagine how one in its middle-aged prime might have died. Deep inside the park's wilderness boundary, he couldn't have been killed by a sport hunter, at least not legally. Park rules do allow residents of the area to lawfully hunt animals for subsistence purposes throughout Gates of the Arctic. But would such a hunter have left this beautiful head? And this locale seemed remote, even for someone aided by plane or snowmobile. There are many easier places to hunt.

Neither a grizzly nor wolves were likely to kill a ram during the peak of its life, unless the sheep was injured or otherwise infirm. Could a ram be so severely wounded during the rut's head-butting battles that it would become easy prey for a bear or wolf? Or starve? Maybe the animal died in an accident of some sort, an avalanche or a fall. Were there clues that I was overlooking? I reluctantly left the spot, filled with questions about the ram's life, its last days and hours.

13.

My final day in the Brooks Range in 2008 I spent several hours in the company of three middle-aged sheep hunters, while we waited for the chartered plane that would take us out of the mountains. The men had killed two large rams during their weeklong stay. Besides the horns, they packed out nearly 150 pounds of meat.

Two of the hunters were brothers. Dean was a life-long Wyoming resident, while Aaron had lived in Valdez for about ten years. Both were blue-collar guys; one had worked in Alaska's mining industry, the other in petroleum. Glen, the oldest of the three and likely in his sixties, was employed as a nurse in rural Alaska. No one asked what I did for a living, though they correctly surmised that I live in Anchorage. Dean asked what drew me to the Brooks Range, "Hiking and taking photos and stuff?" I told him, yeah, that was pretty close, adding that I like to hike and explore and relish simply being in the wilderness.

Sensing our different political leanings and wildlife-management philosophies, the hunters and I largely steered clear of those topics during our three and a half hours together. But I did learn something about their lifestyles and especially their passion for hunting (after this trip, Aaron would hunt for brown bear on Kodiak Island and then moose on a river float through Interior Alaska).

Maybe because this was his first sheep-hunting trip and he'd "bagged" a big ram, Dean enthusiastically described both the trials and rewards of their Arctic expedition. He shot his trophy from 250 feet, while clinging to "a precarious perch." Glen had outdone him, though, taking down his ram from 700 yards away—nearly four-tenths of a mile—a distance that seemed unbelievable to me. When I expressed my amazement, the trio insisted it was true and explained that Glen had little choice. The ram had detected the hunters, so he had to shoot or lose the opportunity.

All three guys were amiable and I hope they found me the same. Though normally I wouldn't have chosen their company, thrown briefly together in the wilderness I enjoyed our time together and gained a greater appreciation for the effort and skill needed to successfully hunt Dall sheep. Though sad for the sheep, I did appreciate the hunters' willingness to share their stories with me. Yet I was bothered by the long-distance gamble that Glen took; what if he'd been slightly off target and only wounded the sheep and the animal somehow escaped, only to die much later from the wound or its weakened condition? Was losing the opportunity really worth the risk of the sheep's suffering? The men seemed humble enough and they were taking home some meat, but nothing that they told me that day changed my strong opposition to such "sport" hunting, which to me involves the needless killing of wild animals for the adventure and the challenge, some personal satisfaction, and a trophy.

14.

Nearly three decades have passed since I stalked the Falls Creek sheep on that steep hillside above the Seward Highway. Nowadays when I venture into the Chugach Mountains, I carry only a small, point-and-shoot digital camera, or none at all. And when I watch Dall sheep it's usually from afar, through binoculars. Because of my own habits and favorite haunts, the place that I most often see them is along the rock-and-tundra-quilted flanks of Wolverine Peak, on a south-facing slope below the ridge that leads to Rusty Point.

Besides its southern exposure and abundance of rocky knobs and cliffs, that hillside must produce plenty of sheep food, because they can be found there throughout much of the year. One time I counted seventy-two animals scattered across the slope, a mix of ewes, lambs, adolescents, and young adults. More commonly I'll spot anywhere from a handful to a couple of dozen sheep. Now and then some large, full-curl rams (or nearly so) also congregate here, keeping to themselves as older males do. Even when no sheep are present, I can gaze at their paths, which crisscross the hill, and imagine their comings and goings.

Over the years, Wolverine Peak and Rusty Point have become two of my favorite hiking destinations, for any number of reasons: the terrain, the views, the easy access to high country, the exercise, the wildlife. For Rusty Point especially, nostalgia and solitude also draw me back. I still recall looking up there from my Hillside yard, watching those sheep. Over time, that distant rocky hilltop began to feel an extension of my own neighborhood.

Though I've moved to another part of town, Rusty Point remains a special spot to me, but apparently few others. Though it's easily reached from the path to Wolverine Peak, to get there a hiker has to leave the main route and ascend untrailed tundra. Because most hikers like to stay on the trail (a good thing) and because Wolverine's summit is the main attraction, few people visit Rusty Point. That makes it all the more appealing to me.

After reaching the point, I find a comfortable spot among the rocks and grasses and wildflowers, remove my pack and sweaty shirt, add layers of dry clothing, eat snacks and drink water, write in my journal, and take in the world immediately below me: mountains and city side by side, and then the landscape that stretches far beyond Anchorage, more than one hundred miles north to 20,320-foot Denali and another hundred miles southwest to Mount Iliamna. Eventually rested enough, I gather my belongings and follow the ridgeline, looking for signs of sheep. Almost always I'll find their scat, piles of small brown pellets, and clumps of coarse white fur. Occasionally I see the sheep themselves, grazing or resting on the slopes below. There is something wondrous and reassuring about this, to be up high in their rugged domain, to be walking where sheep walk and otherwise lead their wild and largely mysterious lives that sometimes overlap with mine, however briefly.

MEETING A LEGEND: WOLVERINE

"C oya! COY-AH! Come here, girl," I shouted across an alpine basin to my middle-aged hiking partner, a white-and-brown collie mix who loved to roam the mountains. Once we ascended out of the forest and into high-country tundra, Coya ran as much as she walked, especially when chasing down the high-pitched chatters of Arctic ground squirrels. Rushing wildly across broad tundra bowls, she never quite reached the squirrels before they ducked into their dens, which seemed to drive her nuts but was a relief to me.

Coya and I had been rambling through Alaska's Chugach Mountains for several hours and it was almost time to return to the car. But before descending from a wildflower-brightened ridge, I wanted to sit a spell. Plopped comfortably on tundra grasses and mosses I nibbled on snack food, jotted notes in my journal, and soaked in the beauty of that early August day.

Most of our hike had been devoted to a five-mile walk up Wolverine Peak, a 4,455-foot mountain that is part of the Chugach's Front Range. Visible from nearly all of Anchorage, it's one of the most popular hill climbs in Chugach State Park, the city's half-million-acre "backyard wilderness."

After gaining the summit, we stayed briefly on top. Coya happily munched on a rawhide chew stick while I put binoculars to eyes and vainly swept the surrounding hills and valleys for signs of wildlife. Like my squirrel-obsessed dog, I keep my senses attuned to the presence of animals, though I'm more interested in less-common species, from the small and handsome Lapland longspur to the large and fiercely powerful grizzly.

Once more ready to ramble, we dropped down along the undulating ridge-line that connects Wolverine Peak with Rusty Point. Few other hikers follow this untrailed route, giving us lots of solitude even on a Saturday that was prime for hill-climbing: temperatures in the sixties, a slight cooling breeze, and blue skies free enough of clouds and haze to see 20,320-foot Denali, gleaming white far to the north.

Coya roamed just below the ridge, while I stayed on its spine. Now and then I called her closer before she wandered too far.

My path took me past jagged outcrops and meadows speckled with the whites, yellows, purples, blues, and pinks of alpine wildflowers. I'm always amazed by the variety and delicate beauty of flowers that thrive in these high, harsh places and I keep an informal record of the species I encounter. That's one reason I finally stopped and sat down: to list in my journal the many wildflowers, few birds, and one mammal—yes, ground squirrels—I had noticed that day. All are among the pleasures that keep drawing me back to these hills. A list doesn't capture the joy, but it can be a reference and stir memories.

I couldn't easily track Coya's movements from that spot, so I called her in, had her lie beside me. Notebook in hand, I was reaching into a bag of locally grown carrots and sweet peas when Coya stood and took a few steps, sniffing nose raised into the air.

"Hey, get over here," I said sharply, certain she had caught the scent of yet another squirrel. I didn't want her running off again. She hesitated, sniffed once more, and then reluctantly returned to my side, still distracted.

Moments later, a dark, mostly brown animal stepped onto the ridge right in front of us, no more than ten yards away. Though the size and color of a young grizzly bear cub, it was built closer to the ground, with a much longer coat and a bushy tail that stretched nearly one and a half feet.

The animal's appearance was so sudden and unexpected, my mind tricked me into imagining an entirely different mountain critter, the hoary marmot. The choice seemed a strange one, because that grizzled alpine rodent is mostly gray. And though much larger than its cousin the ground squirrel, even the biggest of marmots is considerably smaller than what stood before us. I'd never met a marmot on this or neighboring Chugach peaks. But past encounters in other mountains apparently made it the one stocky, short-legged, and long-tailed critter that best fit this high ridge.

The illusion lasted only a moment, before the fantastic truth rang through both my brain and body: *Wolverine!*

Just as suddenly, what had been an ordinary alpine hike took a turn toward more mysterious, astonishing realms.

●

There's no better place in North America to encounter a wolverine than Alaska, which wildlife experts say has a robust population. Yet in more than three decades of wandering the state's wild landscapes, I had seen a wolverine only once before and then while flying in a helicopter. That earlier sighting occurred in the 1970s, when I worked on a geology crew. Someone in the copter spotted the wolverine loping up a mountain spine. I saw it for mere seconds, but can still picture the dark chocolaty body, with creamy streaks along its flanks. In running from our noisy machine, the wolverine seemed more determined to be rid of us than panicked by our presence.

I had always hoped for another meeting with *Gulo gulo*, but recognized the likelihood was small. Without the benefit of radio-tracking technology, even researchers may go long spells without seeing their quarry. In recounting the discovery of wolverine tracks on a trek through Arctic Alaska, renowned field biologist Adolph Murie recalled that years later, those prints with their distinctive five toes and broad rounded form were what he remembered most about that day; the wolverine who'd made the tracks was nowhere to be seen.

Murie further commented that while he'd followed numerous wolverine trails over the years, he'd sometimes gone many years between sightings of the animal itself and added that even experienced trappers "rarely meet them." I will briefly mention here that Murie also noted the resemblance of wolverines and marmots and that one could easily be mistaken for the other; so I don't feel as embarrassed by my initial mistaken identity.

The reason that wolverines are seldom encountered or even seen from a distance is simple: even where wolverine populations are healthy, their numbers are small. Mostly solitary and primarily scavengers, they need lots of ground to make a living. And not just any ground will do. Even more than grizzlies and wolves, wolverines need large expanses of wilderness to thrive, particularly landscapes where they can roam open mountains in summer and retreat to forested areas in winter.

Male wolverines may stake out territories of up to 240 square miles, females a quarter to one-half of that. Within their home ranges "they cover an amazing amount of ground for an animal of their size, much of it very rugged country," Howard Golden told me when I interviewed him after my wolverine encounter. A state wildlife researcher, he had studied wolverines off and on since 1993. "They think nothing of going from a valley bottom straight up and over a ridge and then back down to the next valley bottom. Sometimes they cross remarkably steep terrain, places you'd more closely associate with Dall sheep or mountain goats. Why they do it is beyond me. It's astounding, really."

Besides their small numbers and preference for places that few people go, wolverines avoid our kind whenever possible, a trait that has earned them the reputation of being elusive, even where relatively abundant. Whether instinctive or learned, it seems a wise behavior. Wolverines don't fare well in the company of humans, as demonstrated by the species' substantially shrunken range in the Lower 48.

Wolverines once inhabited a northern band of the contiguous United States from Washington to Maine, with populations in the mountainous West extending south to California, Arizona, and New Mexico. Trapping and the widespread use of poisons largely wiped out the continental U.S. population by the early 1900s, but the species eventually repopulated mountainous areas in parts of the west as human harvest and poisoning programs were curtailed. Nowadays they're a confirmed presence in Washington, Montana, Wyoming, and Idaho, with occasional reported sightings in neighboring states. Even where established, wolverine populations are small and scattered, largely because of dwindling, fragmented wildlands, and it's likely that only 250 to 300 still survive.

Now a new threat looms. Wolverines' sensitivity to heat and females' dependence on deep and persistent snow cover to build maternal dens and protect their newborn make the species vulnerable to global warming. Throughout much of the mountain west, average annual temperatures are rising, and snowpacks are both shrinking and melting earlier in the spring, a potentially devastating combination that raises new questions about the wolverine's future in the continental U.S.

Three times since the mid-1990s, a coalition of environmental groups has petitioned the U.S. Fish and Wildlife Service to add Lower 48 wolverines to its Endangered Species List. In early 2013 the FWS finally announced its intent to list the species as threatened, largely because of shrinking snowpacks tied to climate change, an overdue move welcomed and celebrated by conservationists.

While Lower 48 wolverine populations are squeezed into ever-smaller refugia, an abundance of mountainous wilderness and long, cold winters make Alaska ideal wolverine country. Even Anchorage, the state's highly developed and populous urban center, adjoins prime wolverine habitat. Based on recent, state-of-the-art surveys, state biologists estimate that ten to twelve wolverines inhabit Chugach State Park. That's a reasonable number, they say, given the park's size, and comparable to wolverine densities in more remote Alaska wildlands. Yet only a few lucky people among the legions who annually visit Chugach will even briefly glimpse a wolverine from afar. Many more will see the park's moose and Dall sheep, even its grizzlies and wolves.

The wolverine's appearance seemed to startle Coya as much as me. Or if not surprised, she was momentarily frozen by indecision. Her hesitation gave me just enough time to lunge, grab her collar with my left hand, and then wrap my right arm around her body. In response, Coya squirmed and whined, then tugged hard to break away.

The wolverine, to my great surprise, remained still, as if it too might be uncertain what to do. Perhaps it was equally shocked to find us atop the ridge, or simply puzzled by our presence. I'd always heard that wolverines are naturally wary of people. So why didn't this one lope away?

Several seconds passed before the wolverine moved. Instead of fleeing, it began to slowly circle, dark eyes watching us intently. Now and then the animal briefly paused, lifted its head, and sniffed. Then it resumed a steady, unhurried pace while staying within thirty feet.

I sensed neither fear nor aggression on the wolverine's part, but something closer to curiosity. Golden, the researcher, would later tell me this makes sense, adding, "I would have been more surprised if it ran off." Wolverines are the largest terrestrial members of the Mustelidae family (from the Latin *mustela*, or weasel). Besides several varieties of weasels, this group of carnivores includes minks, badgers, ferrets, martens, skunks, and otters. As anyone who's owned a ferret or met a weasel can attest, they are extremely inquisitive animals.

On the other hand, plenty of people who've crossed paths with wolverines reported that the animals immediately took off running and sometimes didn't stop for what seemed to be miles.

The wolverine appeared calm as well as curious, in striking contrast to frenzied Coya. Yipping and whining, she lunged forward again and again. Keeping my voice low, I ordered her, "Coya, stop . . . Coya, sit . . . COYA. . . ." Still she squirmed and tugged, attention focused on the wolverine. One time she nearly eluded my grasp. I had to tackle her, pin her to the ground, while whispering, "Easy Coya, easy girl. . . ."

Coya's frantic behavior might have been what kept the wolverine nearby. It watched our wresting match as if mesmerized. I wondered what the animal made of all this. Had it ever encountered a dog before? I was sure the wolverine had met humans, because someone had attached a red tag to its right ear. Part of a research project, no doubt. (Golden would later confirm that was so, adding that the animal somehow shed its radio collar.)

I then imagined how the wolverine would respond if Coya got loose. Wolverines aren't especially fast runners. According to Golden, "a person could almost outrun them." Surely Coya could, so the wolverine would likely stand its ground and fight. Any such battle would be a mismatch and not in Coya's favor, though my fifty-pound mutt likely outweighed the wolverine by twenty pounds or more.

Efficient scavengers known for their great appetites—their scientific name, *gulo*, means "glutton"—wolverines have the powerful jaws and the large teeth and neck muscles of an animal that survives by crushing bones and tearing apart frozen meat. And this one's calm demeanor hid a strength and ferocity that's legendary among northern trappers and wildlife researchers. Biologists at Denali National Park once watched a wolverine drag the carcass of an adult Dall sheep—three to four times the wolverine's weight—down a mountain, across a fast-flowing stream, and then back up a steep bank, more than two miles in all.

Wolverines also have been reported to occasionally drive off much larger wild predators, even cougars and bears, while protecting their food caches, though such stories may be more apocryphal than real. Wildlife scientists say wolverines' survival depends on avoidance, not confrontation. Though rarely observed, biologists have documented instances in which mountain lions and wolves have attacked and killed wolverines. And a wolverine would have to be either crazy or desperate to take on a grizzly.

In Alaska, wolves are likely one of the two major "natural [nonhuman] sources of wolverine mortality," Golden said, the other being starvation. Not only are wolves larger and faster than wolverines, they are fiercely protective of both their young and their territories and often travel in family groups. A single wolverine would stand no chance against a wolf pack or even a pair. In fact, wolves killed one of the radio-collared wolverines that Golden had been tracking. Still, he added, a wolverine might hold its own against a single adult wolf, especially a younger one. And most dogs wouldn't stand a chance.

Perhaps her wolfish roots were what got Coya so riled. But her instincts, in this case, would only have led to bloody trouble, so I held on tight. I'd hate to have to intervene in a wolverine-dog fight.

For all my concerns about Coya, I felt no fear in the wolverine's close presence. Despite its fierce nature, a wolverine would likely attack a person only if it felt cornered and threatened, was caught in a trap, or had rabies. And except for a rabid animal, a wolverine would even then almost certainly flee from a human at the first opportunity.

With Coya safely in my arms, I took a closer look at the creature prowling the flanks of its namesake mountain, a circumstance that brought me some additional pleasure. (I would later learn that a hiker making an early ascent of the peak found wolverine tracks on the summit ridge. Suitably impressed, he named the mountain in the animal's honor.)

The wolverine's head was broad and rounded, with small dark eyes and short, rounded ears. Most of the face was dark brown, but a beige band of fur ran across the forehead, between the eyes and ears. Despite the species' legendary fierce and ornery nature, I never noticed the animal snarl or bare its teeth. The tail was dark and the short legs even more so, almost black, with pale brown claws. The stocky, long-furred body was mostly a dark, chocolaty brown, though creamy bands run along both flanks, from the shoulders to the base of the tail.

My overall impression: small, dark, and handsome, the wolverine was one self-assured animal, confident of its place in these mountains.

Despite a passion for wild animals, especially those that inhabit the local landscape, I'd known almost nothing about Chugach State Park's wolverines until wildlife politics brought them to my attention a couple of years before my own close encounter.

In 2007, the Alaska Board of Game voted to open the park to wolverine trapping, thus overturning a ban that had been in place since 1973. A notoriously political body, the board establishes Alaska's wildlife management policies and regulations. For too many years its seven members have shown an alarming tendency to boost hunting and trapping opportunities that primarily benefit urban "sportsmen," often at the expense of wildlife conservation.

Even given its consumptive leanings, the board's wolverine decision caught nearly everyone by surprise, including local wildlife manager Rick Sinnott. He had testified against such trapping because there was evidence that wolverines in neighboring areas were already being overharvested. Chugach State Park had for many years been the region's largest and most vital wolverine refugium, but the board's action would change that.

Also caught off guard were park staff and its citizens' advisory board. Though strongly opposed to such trapping, not one of them testified on behalf of Chugach's wolverines or even attended the meeting.

Within days, I joined several other Anchorage-area wildlife advocates to form "Team Wolverine." Over the next several months, we kept the issue in the local news and generally fueled a local uprising. Admitting their earlier failure, state parks officials joined a broad spectrum of Anchorage residents in requesting the board to reconsider its vote.

Even as the public protest grew, state wildlife managers bewildered by the board's action proceeded with a new, groundbreaking survey of wolverines in the park and surrounding areas. Biostatistician Earl Becker called it a world-class effort that produced "the most precise wolverine estimate in Alaska history." The study provided sharp evidence that some eighteen wolverines inhabited the entire management area, or about thirteen wolverines per thousand square miles. More troubling, it also provided irrefutable evidence that these wolverines were already being trapped at an unsustainable rate.

For all of that, two years went by before the Board of Game restored protections to the park's wolverines. Need I add that it did so reluctantly?

Minutes passed and still the wolverine showed no inclination to leave. Astounded by this behavior, I wondered if anyone else had noticed the animal. I could see at least a dozen other hikers, the nearest a few hundred yards away. None, that I could tell, were looking our way. Even if someone were to gaze in our direction, I doubted he could easily see the small drama that was unfolding. A part of me wanted to shout out the wolverine's presence. But I didn't dare risk breaking the spell.

Finally the wolverine turned and ambled off, its interest in us apparently satisfied. My own interest still roused, I gingerly followed, Coya firmly in hand.

Trying to stay out of sight, I scampered to a large, jagged ledge of rock several feet below the ridgeline. Peering around the outcrop, I spotted the wolverine, standing in a lush, grassy meadow. And it noticed us. Again I expected the animal to run off. Again it surprised me. The wolverine scurried to a large neighboring rock and poked its head around the side, once more watching us intently. Then it again began to circle, this time slowly moving away from us.

The wolverine paused to glance back, then loped farther below the ridge. Stopping once more, the animal lifted its leg against a bush. Though perhaps only relieving itself, the animal might also have been scent marking, which wolverines do by urinating or rubbing abdominal or anal glands on objects. A form of chemical communication, such markings may be used to identify an individual's territory or its food caches. In either case, the message is to stay away.

Watching the animal pee, I considered the wolverine's gender. The lifted leg suggested a male. But Coya frequently pees that way though she's a female dog, so I still couldn't say for certain.

I'm not sure why I didn't identify or perceive the wolverine as either "he" or "she" as I often do when an animal gains my attention and holds it in more than a fleeting way; maybe because I hadn't yet fully processed our startling encounter, or didn't know the species well enough to make such assumptions. Later Howard Golden would identify the red-tagged wolverine as a young adult female. But the notes I wrote in my journal immediately after the experience simply referred to the wolverine as "it." Still, there was no question in my mind that this was another being, worthy of respect.

The idea of wolverine as a "being" and related questions about the respect—or disregard—that we show other forms of life inevitably stirred thoughts of Richard Nelson's writings about Alaska's Koyukon people. Published in 1983, *Make Prayers to the Raven: A Koyukon View of the Northern Forest* explores the way this tribe of Athabascan Indians has traditionally understood and interacted with the "natural world."

Nelson, a cultural anthropologist, explains, "Traditional Koyukon people live in a world that watches, in a forest of eyes. A person moving through nature—however wild, remote, even desolate the place may be—is never truly alone. The surroundings are aware, sensate, personified. They feel. They can be offended. And they must, at every moment, be treated with proper respect. All things in nature have a special kind of life, something unknown to contemporary Euro-Americans, something powerful." Their perception of the world, he adds, extends beyond the physical level, "into the realm of the spiritual."

Over the years, *Make Prayers to the Raven* has become a favorite reference when I've sought indigenous perspectives on Alaska's wildlife. I'm not surprised the book includes a section on wolverines. What is shocking is that the Koyukons have traditionally considered the wolverine "the greatest of all spirits, most demanding of obeisance and respect. It is a dangerous power," even greater than the grizzly.

Though wolverines "stand above" even bears in the spiritual order, they are "small and reclusive, while bears are conspicuous, imposing, sometimes even awesome personages. . . . Wolverine is like the hermit king, more powerful, but less to be reckoned with than the prince who marches through the streets."

Hermit king: what a perfect image.

Despite their reverence for the animals, Koyukons harvested both bears and wolverines. But they did so in highly ritualized ways intended to honor the animals' spirits. By custom, whenever a man trapped a wolverine—women were barred from doing so—the tribe staged formal ceremonies to pay tribute to "the chief of animals."

Dressed in tribal finery, the wolverine was seated in a privileged spot within the trapper's house. Other village men placed food before their deceased guest, gripping the wolverine's paws in respect. The men then feasted and shared stories about *doyonh* (meaning chief or great man). Older women could attend, but not eat the food. Young women and girls were not allowed to participate at all, being more vulnerable to the animal's dangerous powers and the risk of misfortune. "Afterward," Nelson writes, "the carcass was skinned, dismembered, and burned with food for its spirit. Honored this way, *doyonh* would bring good fortune to those who attended."

By the 1970s, such elaborate ceremonies had largely given way to simpler rituals. But at least among the elders who followed older, more traditional ways, the wolverine remained the most powerful of spirits which, if offended, could lead to bad luck in trapping, perhaps even illness or death.

Nelson doesn't try to explain why the wolverine has such a supremely dangerous spirit. To the Koyukon, no such explanation would be necessary. Both physically and spiritually, the animal's role was established long ago in the "Distant Time," and it's been passed from one generation to the next in shared, communal stories. Still, I can't help but question whether the wolverine's ferocity and strength, combined with its reclusive nature, played a role in establishing *doyonh*'s place at the pinnacle of spiritual power. To the Koyukon, wolverine "seems to keep itself a mystery and a stranger. It lurks somewhere beyond seeing, leaving only tracks and having no physical embodiment."

It's in my own nature to seek understanding, to figure things out. Yet the religion into which I was born, Christianity, holds as many mysteries, if not more. The Triune God? A virgin birth? Christ's resurrection and ascension into heaven? Miracles and mysteries all. No explanations were required, only faith, because all came from the Word of God, written in the Bible, my culture's version of traditional stories handed down across the generations.

Now a fallen Christian who's something of a pagan pantheist, I celebrate the magic and mystery inherent in all of nature. Yet sometimes I need reminding: there is so much we don't know, can't know.

It's a puzzling thing that people would trap and kill a being they hold in such high spiritual regard. But the Koyukons were practical, too. They needed the wolverine's fur, which like the animal itself is legendary among northern peoples who endure long and bitterly cold winters. Soft, warm, and durable, the fur is especially valuable because it doesn't "frost up," making it ideal for parka ruffs that protect the head and face.

For most of my life I didn't think much about trapping. But over the past couple of decades, as I've paid closer attention to our species' complicated relationships with other animals, I've grown increasingly disturbed by—and opposed to—trapping, which by its nature causes suffering, often severe and for prolonged periods.

I reluctantly accept the necessity of trapping by people who truly "live off the land" and depend on the meat, fur, bones, and other parts of animals to survive. But few people lead such subsistence lifestyles anymore, even in Alaska. Recreational trapping, on the other hand, seems unnecessarily cruel and therefore abhorrent.

For all of my repulsion to such trapping, I'd like to better understand the relationship of modern, more urbanized trappers to wolverines. What's the appeal of killing such uncommon, beautiful, and spirited creatures to those who don't depend on the animal for their survival?

While talking with Golden after my encounter with the Chugach wolverine, I asked him about that, since his furbearer studies put him in touch with many trappers. For one thing "it's a real challenge and a lot of work" to catch a wolverine, he told me. That naturally increases their allure. "Wolverines are elusive, widely scattered, and cover so much ground it's a real coup to catch one," Golden continued. "For many trappers, it's a once-in-a-lifetime sort of deal. That makes wolverines special. And their pelts fetch a pretty good price."

Along with wolf hides, wolverine pelts bring the best prices of any Alaskan furbearers. They rarely sell for less than $150 and the highest quality wolverine pelts will go for $750. But it's more than just the challenge or the money, Golden explained. "Trappers love these animals, they love to study them, learn about their lifestyles. You have to know a lot about the animals to catch them. The trappers I know have a tremendous amount of respect for wolverines."

Adding to their appeal is what wildlife manager Rick Sinnott called "the legend of wolverine," the belief that they're a formidable and defiant foe that will, if given the chance, wreak havoc on a trapline or cabin. Or worse, that they're viciously evil in some way, as the nicknames "devil bear," "northern demon," and "woods devil" suggest.

Among those contributing greatly to the wolverine's unsavory status was Ernest Thompson Seton, who earned fame as a naturalist, author, hunter-conservationist, wildlife artist and founding member of the Boy Scouts. Seton wrote dozens of books between 1886 and his death in 1946, most of them about animals, Indians, and woodcraft. In *The Arctic Prairies*, he explained to his readers that the wolverine "has an unenviable reputation for being the greatest plague that the hunter knows. Its habit of following to destroy all traps for the sake of the bait is the prime cause of man's hatred, and its cleverness in eluding his efforts at retaliation give it still more importance."

Years later, in *Lives of Game Animals*, Seton wrote, "Picture a Weasel . . . that little demon of destruction, that small atom of insensate courage, that symbol of slaughter, sleeplessness, and tireless, incredible activity—picture that scrap of demonic fury, multiply that mite some fifty times, and you have the likeness of a Wolverine."

Whew, that's some picture of devilish rage. And it's one reason that many conservationists and researchers today say the wolverine—like the wolf and other predators—is still frequently misunderstood and demonized. A major goal of the Idaho-based Wolverine Foundation is to "introduce the wolverine in a science-based context. Our [culture's] image of the wolverine has for too long been based on sensationalism and misinformation."

While Golden knows a lot about trapping, I wanted to hear directly from those who capture wolverines and kill them for their pelts. After several failed attempts, I got that opportunity in Fairbanks, at a Board of Game meeting. Some 360 road miles north of Anchorage, Fairbanks is the urban center of Interior Alaska and the state's third-largest city. Still it's considerably smaller than Anchorage and much more of a frontier town, with a higher percentage of hunters and trappers, state's-rights advocates, and those of a libertarian bent.

Wolverines weren't on the board's agenda, but wolves were. And plenty of trappers came to testify on issues that they believed threatened their lifestyles. During one break, I cornered Randy Zarnke, president of the Alaska Trappers Association. He recognized my name, knew my writings and political leanings, and so was naturally cautious. But he eventually opened up, just a bit. Wolverines weren't common where he ran a trapline and he'd never caught one. But he confirmed that they are special. He began to say they're "trophy" animals but then backed off. In wildlife politics, trophy is an emotionally charged word, one to be avoided. "Trophy isn't exactly it. But they're a highly desired species. When you catch one, you're at the height of what trappers do."

To help make his point, Zarnke used a fishing analogy. "In Wisconsin, where I grew up, we probably caught thousands of perch and crappie, fish like that. They're sport fish, but they're common and easy to catch. Then you have the muskie. You know what that is, right? Well, to catch a muskie [officially the muskellunge, biggest and rarest member of the pike family] was something really special. And one reason the muskie is so highly prized, is its rarity. They just aren't very abundant. It's the same thing with trapping wolverines."

Zarnke's analogy was a good one. Growing up in Connecticut, I caught bunches of sunfish and perch. It was a much bigger deal to catch a rainbow trout or small-mouthed bass, or pickerel—small members of the pike family. But even those paled in comparison to muskies (which don't inhabit Connecticut waters). Fed by stories and photos in sport-fishing magazines, as a boy I dreamed about someday catching a muskie, arguably the greatest freshwater fishing trophy—there, I said it—in North America.

Besides their rarity, wolverines are respected for their strength and perseverance. "Wolves are actually a lot harder to trap," Zarnke confided. "They're super smart, savvy around traps. Wolverines aren't nearly as hard to catch. But once caught, they can be really nasty. And they won't give up. A wolverine caught in a small trap will just tear it apart. Trappers respect that."

I eventually talked to three trappers who had caught wolverines. All agreed the species is revered for its uncommon nature, its ferocity and strength. But there's more to it than that.

The wolverine is "the Holy Grail" of trapping, said Pete Buist, a big, whiskered man and longtime Fairbanks resident who once served on the Board of Game and also headed the Alaska Trappers Association for several years. "Part of it is that wolverines aren't common. Part is the value of a wolverine pelt. And though they're not that difficult to catch, they're really difficult to hold. They're very good at getting out of traps. If the trap isn't big enough or made that well, they'll render it into a pile of parts. When you've caught a wolverine, it's a mark that you've achieved something special."

Sometimes the relationship between trapper and wolverine may become a love-hate sort of thing. A youngish-looking thirty-year-old trapper named Chris (who asked that his last name not be mentioned) said wolverines occasionally "take over" a trapper's line. Besides stealing the bait, they eat the marten and other smaller, easier-to-catch species that are a trapper's bread and butter. "A wolverine can cost a trapper thousands of dollars," Chris said, his voice and eyes suggesting he knew this from experience.

Marty Caress, who ran a trapline for most of his sixty-two years, considered wolverine "unique" among the animals he's caught. "They're real individualistic animals, smart and challenging to trap. They're fierce and can get really nasty when you catch 'em. I've seen one that chewed up everything within reach, it even mowed down three-inch [diameter] alders. It was like those alders had been hydro-axed. Amazing."

Caress, like Golden, had seen a wolverine ascend a steep mountain slope straight to the summit, for no apparent reason. "It's just hard to figure out," he said with a shrug. Upon surprising another one, Caress watched it run "like it was gonna go forever. It went over one ridge, then another. With my binoculars I could see it two miles away, still running. Unbelievable endurance."

I can't recall exactly when I became aware of totems and totem animals, but almost certainly it happened in the 1950s, when I was a young boy learning about the wider world from the edges of rural Connecticut. Either through books or TV (more likely the latter), I discovered that Indians carved these eerily beautiful things called totem poles, which always seemed to contain some sort of animal figures. But totems remained an obscure abstraction until my early forties, when I began to seriously explore some of the world's mystical traditions and do what might be called "inner work." Among their gifts to me, these middle-aged explorations introduced the idea of totems in a deeper, more meaningful way. For the first time I began to sense the magic, the power, they embody.

As I've mused elsewhere, especially when discussing my connection to bears, this is where things start to get complicated for a white guy who was raised a Christian and later trained in the sciences. But the fact remains, I have come to believe that totems are powerfully real, not simply abstractions or fantasies or myths. Some animals have special meaning for me. If I'm open enough, such an animal may become my teacher, my guide.

The question then naturally arose after my startling encounter with the animal: might wolverine be another of my totems, my teachers?

Back in Anchorage I began a search. Wolverines, it turns out, are rarely included on lists of totem animals or spirit guides; another sign, perhaps, of their uncommon nature. I did finally track them down in *Animal Spirit Guides*, written by Steven Farmer, a "shamanic practitioner, ordained minister, licensed psychotherapist, and former college professor with over thirty years' experience as a professional healer and teacher."

I must admit to some skepticism when reading books like Farmer's. As a rule, they're too formulaic, too pat. Still I'm open to the possibilities that lie within. In his introduction, Farmer informs the reader, "when an animal shows up in ordinary reality in an uncommon way or at unusual times . . . it's definitely a sign from that animal spirit guide."

Well, maybe. To say something is "definitely true" in all such circumstances hits me wrong. One of my own rules is that generalities are dangerous. Still, the Chugach wolverine entered my life in an uncommon way. So I went to page 401 and read what it means "If WOLVERINE shows up." The fully capitalized word signified this was not about one animal, but "the spirit of the entire species."

Six meanings followed. Most had to do with caution, assertiveness, planning ahead, or choosing between fight or flight. I tried to recall my circumstances leading up to the encounter. Had I faced some particular crisis, confrontation, or life-changing choices? In truth I had, but I'd already decided what action I would take. Did wolverine's appearance somehow confirm that decision? I don't think so, but could I be sure? Totems can act in mysterious ways. Most intriguing to me was Farmer's section "If WOLVERINE is your POWER ANIMAL:

"You're very shy and prefer to stay in the background and out of the way, rarely putting yourself forward."

This is less true than it once was, but I still fit pretty high on the shyness scale. Then:

"You'd prefer to avoid conflict, but if necessary you won't back down and can become quite ferocious if actually threatened."

"You enjoy camping out and walks in the forest and feel like the outdoors is a second home to you."

And, finally, "You're rather elusive, hard to pin down, and notable for avoiding events that require you to be sociable."

Check. Check. Check.

All of the above fit me well, the latter two exceptionally so. I recalled that once, in graduate school, an acquaintance observed, "You're a loner, aren't you?" I shrugged in response, but his comment hit me hard. I knew that he was right. And though I haven't been such a loner for many years, I still sometimes feel a powerful need to remove myself from people, keep to myself. There's a fine line, I've come to realize, between my desire for solitude and my occasional retreat into solitude's darker twin, isolation.

And I love to roam the mountains alone (though thanks to Coya I've come to enjoy the company of a dog). So whether or not I'm guided by the spirit of WOLVERINE, I think I have some wolverine in my blood.

After stopping to pee, the wolverine angled downhill, loping in a leisurely, almost carefree, way. It reached some grassy swales, then dipped into a deeper gully and disappeared. I watched a few minutes more, but saw no sign of the animal. Then, Coya in tow, I headed back to where I'd left my pack and journal. I needed to record as many details as possible, before they faded. When I finally remembered to check the time, it was after 2:00 P.M. Our time in the wolverine's presence likely lasted ten to fifteen minutes. But this was hardly ordinary time.

Note-taking done, I leashed Coya and headed back toward where I last saw the wolverine, hopeful of another sighting. We began a slow descent, stopping now and then so that I could scan the alpine basin with my binoculars. We hadn't been gone that long, but the wolverine had vanished.

Though the animal was gone, its presence lingers. Wolverine Peak has always been a favorite place of mine, but now the mountain holds new and powerful memories, a deeper significance.

Halfway to the creek bottom, I stopped and finished my snacking, added a few more notes, unleashed Coya. She nosed around, but found no scent that put her on alert. "C'mon girl, let's get going," I finally said.

Coya ran ahead, sniffing the ground and listening for squirrels. I glanced back toward the ridge one final time; a story was already taking shape in my mind, fed by a desire for some greater understanding. Then I too bounded downhill in an easy, unhurried fashion, amazed by my good fortune.

PADDLING WITH PORPOISES

Pffff. Pause. *Pffff.*

I'd heard this sound my first evening at Nuka Island and thought—hoped—it might be a sea mammal. Maybe even a whale. But I hadn't been able to locate its source and eventually decided it must be waves lapping on the shore somewhere. Or my mind playing tricks.

Now I was hearing it again, while paddling across Berger Bay, a funnel-shaped embayment along Nuka's southwestern shore. As far as I knew, I was the only person on that nine-mile-long piece of land, which is roughly shaped—if you stretch your imagination—like a sea otter with too many legs.

Three miles off the Kenai Peninsula's outer coast in Southcentral Alaska, Nuka was added to Kachemak Bay State Park in 1989, but it rarely gets visitors. With the exception of a few abandoned buildings, it's still a wild and pristine place. I came here for both the wildness and the solitude and as a bonus discovered abundant wildlife. In five days I'd seen a black bear, sea otters, bald eagles, harbor seals, cormorants, loons, Steller's jays, kingfishers, and numerous songbirds and sea ducks, most of which I couldn't identify.

Like previous nights, I would explore the bay in my Klepper kayak, looking and listening for wildlife. But mostly I just wanted to spend some quiet moments on the mirror smooth water, in a world that was gray and tranquil. Low-lying clouds and fog shrouded the coastal mountains and the only sound was the muffled roar of waves breaking endlessly on the distant mainland.

I had nearly crossed the bay when I heard the whispered call. *Pffff.* . . .
Pffff. . . . Over there, by Berger Island.

I slowly approached the sound and spotted what looked like a wake. Then, a
hundred yards away, maybe less, I saw a curved back and dorsal fin gently break
the water and disappear. And another. I counted two, three animals. Not large.
Not whales. They were harbor porpoises, also known as common porpoises.

Shivers running through me, I paddled closer while asking myself, *How
close should I go?* I didn't want to scare them off. The sea otters and harbor seals I'd
seen along Nuka Island had all been wary, easily spooked, for good reasons. The
region's otters were hunted by Natives for their pelts, and seals were sometimes
illegally shot or otherwise harassed by commercial fishermen. But the porpoises
were different in their response. They circled me, their dark bluish gray backs and
fins rhythmically rolling in and out of the water. They seemed to be everywhere.
To my left, then my right. Behind. In front. Sometimes a quarter mile away,
sometimes thirty feet. Or twenty. Occasionally they snorted and splashed, in
preparation for deeper dives. But mostly they cut the water with no perceptible
sound, except their breathing. *Pffff.* . . . *Pffff.* . . . *Pffff.*

Smallest of the cetaceans (which include dolphins, porpoises, and whales),
Phocoena phocoena is widely distributed throughout the Pacific and one of only two
kinds of porpoise to frequent Alaska's coastal waters (the other being the Dall porpoise). The species' loud breaths have prompted some less-than-charming nicknames: "herring hog," "puffing pig," and "sea pig." But in my time with them, I
didn't see—or hear—the porcine connection.

The porpoises swam alone, or in small groups of two or three, often following each other in line. It was nearly impossible to get an accurate count of their
numbers because they constantly changed direction, diving, and reappearing where
I didn't expect them. Though at times I thought there must be fifteen or twenty of
them, my best guess was six to eight animals. That fits with what's known about
harbor porpoises; they usually travel in small, matriarchal-dominated pods of two
to ten animals. More rarely, they congregate in herds of one hundred or more, to
feed on schools of herring, cod, shrimp, or squid.

Once it was clear that they weren't intimidated, the question became
how close they would approach. Would they bump the kayak, somehow upset it,
knock it over, even in play? But harbor porpoises are small animals that only
rarely reach four feet long or weigh more than 130 pounds. And they're not

aggressive toward humans. Any initial anxieties dissipated, giving way to excitement and curiosity.

How did they perceive the kayak and me? As some sort of floating debris? Or did they connect me with other humans they'd met? Harbor porpoises are known to approach boats and sometimes follow them for hours, though unlike some other species they rarely jump clear of water or surface long enough for photographs. Marine mammal researchers aren't sure whether the boats provide shelter for fish that the porpoises feed on, or if they're simply curious. But all the evidence suggests that they like interacting with vessels.

The porpoises' leisurely rolling and diving also suggested that they were playing—having fun—rather than actively feeding. Perhaps I was a pleasant diversion.

The pleasure was mine, as well, on that August evening. It was an unexpected treat to be paddling among porpoises. None of them nudged the boat, or came close enough to touch, but there was one brief encounter that will stay with me always. After thirty minutes, two of the porpoises rolled directly in front of me. One surfaced thirty feet away. Then fifteen. "OMYGOSH," I whispered aloud. It was coming right at me. What was it going to do?

What it did was swim right under the kayak, a distinct though shadowy apparition five or six feet below. For the first time I saw the porpoise's entire form—the round head, squat body, triangular dorsal fin, dark flippers and tail—as it spurted past. My heart pounded and I smiled, feeling blessed.

The porpoises repeatedly came close and then left, sometimes disappearing for five or ten minutes. Their first prolonged departure was accompanied by a large splash, and my imagination again took flight. What if they'd been chased away by some larger ocean predator? Perhaps the black waters below me hid a killer whale, or shark, both of which prey on harbor porpoises. How would a shark perceive my black-bottomed kayak? But the fears subsided when the porpoises returned, backs rolling as before. I stayed in their company until almost 9:30 P.M., when fading light prompted my return to camp.

I would see porpoises twice more before I left Nuka Island; once a solitary animal, the other time a pair. But we were headed in opposite directions. And though I stopped, hoping for renewed play, the porpoises continued on their way.

WILDERNESS MUSIC: SHARING A VALLEY WITH HOWLING WOLVES

Camped alone deep in Alaska's Brooks Range wilderness, I found a comfortable spot along the North Fork of the Koyukuk. Then, placing my head beside the river's churning aqua waters, I listened closely to its fluid play of sounds.

I'd heard beautiful Celtic-like chanting, off and on, for the previous few days. The songs seemed to come from outside me, from the forest and tundra and especially the river, but I supposed they could all be in my head. I'd even put words to some of the music: *"Holy, ho-o-o-ly, holy . . ."*

As the melodies and words played through my mind, I wondered what combination of landscape and wind sounds mixed with my memories and thought processes—and several days of solitude—to produce these voices, this music.

My musings were interrupted by an unmistakably "real" voice that had nothing to do with my imagination: a howling came from the forest, behind my tent. A loud, clear, resonant wail of alto key that rolled across the valley, the howl triggered an immediate physical and emotional response: my heart raced, pulse quickened, spirit lifted. Instinctively I turned from the river, binoculars in hand, and faced the wooded hills above camp. With all the tracks and scat on this river bar and across the North Fork, I had anticipated—and sometimes imagined—wolf howls throughout my three-day campout here. Each morning and night I swept the hillsides with binoculars, hopeful of a miracle. Now one had come to me.

I peered at two tundra knobs a few hundred feet above camp, then scanned the spruce forest below. As I did, the howling resumed. The first baleful voice was joined by a second, higher pitched one, more of a soprano. The trembling howls blended and shifted key. Were there more than two singers? Hard to tell. Wolves are known to mix their voices in a way that produces a magnified sense of numbers.

The howls prompted me to consider whether the wolves had spotted me on the open gravel bar or noticed the tarp or tent. Were they protesting my intrusion into their territory? Announcing my presence, or theirs, to other wolves?

Rain that began as a fine mist earlier in the afternoon was falling harder, but I barely noticed. Or cared. The wolf songs lasted a minute or two, but resonated much longer. This is what I had long dreamt about, to share the wilderness with howling wolves.

I asked myself which was more desirable, to see wolves or hear them sing? No simple answer came to me, but there was this fact: over the years I had seen wolves a half-dozen times, yet heard them howling only once before. Those earlier songs had come from a distance in these very mountains, though in another valley miles to the west during my days as an exploration geologist. Decades have gone by since that rainy autumn afternoon in the mid-1970s, but a faint chill still passes through my body whenever I call up the memory, which is dreamlike yet remarkably vivid. On a gloomy and raw September day, with fresh snow powdering the higher mountaintops and the field season nearly ended, I left my tent to take a short walk. The still, fog-shrouded valley was absolutely silent, making it possible for the faraway conversation to reach my ears.

The first voice seemed a sort of moan, and it came from the forested lowlands north of camp. Turning toward it, I listened intently, expectantly. Minutes passed before the deep, bass howl sounded again, this time joined by another wail. The howls were so faint I had to concentrate to hear them.

That time, too, I could never quite say how many voices I heard. Neither could I explain why each time the howls reached me, I broke into a smile. Was it the beauty of their song? Or the realization of my good fortune, after a season of hoping? I have no idea how long I remained in that trance, just me and a distant wolf pack connected by the string of their notes as they moved across the John River Valley. The word "haunting" comes to mind as I recall those first howls; but it's the loveliest sort of haunting you can imagine.

I didn't think the wolves would disturb anything in camp; they're not notorious camp raiders like bears and squirrels and jays. But to ease any nagging doubts I walked across the gravel bar and checked my tent and then the tarp, where I'd placed my food cache for lunch. Then back to the water's edge for more searching. Even before I reached my lookout, I spotted a wolf, upstream from camp and halfway across the braided North Fork, not far from where I had crossed the river three days earlier. Maybe two hundred yards away. I couldn't be fully certain from this distance, but the wolf struck me as female and that's what the animal became.

If I had to name her color, I'd say white wolf. But that ignores the subtleties of her coat. Bringing her into focus with my glasses, I saw that she had a mostly white face, with some gray atop her head and on her neck. Her flanks were light gray, legs white, tail the color of gathering clouds, becoming darker, like storm clouds, at the tip. In her wettened coat, the wolf appeared lean but not skinny, and I assumed, for no sure reason, that she was in good health.

The wolf crouched low as she crossed the midriver sand and gravel bars, as if to avoid detection. She glanced now and then in my direction and I was sure she saw me. Moving slowly, she reached the final, deepest channel. She stepped gingerly at first, splashing through the milky green river. Then, for the final few feet, she plunged and swam across. The wolf stopped at the forest's edge and looked back intently—but this time not toward me. I swung the binoculars back and forth across the river, expecting another wolf to appear, but none followed.

The she-wolf moved into the forest and as she did, a large, brownish bird flew from a spruce tree: another predator, a northern goshawk. I assumed our encounter was over, but the wolf reappeared, walking slowly along the woods' margin. Once she stepped into the open and smelled something on the bar. Then back under the trees. She took one last look across the North Fork and turned away. Her walk became a trot and she was gone, melted into the forest's shadows.

Minutes later there was more howling, this time from my side of the river, though farther downstream. Perhaps the second wolf was unwilling to cross the stream within sight of me or the camp. The white wolf sang back, briefly. Then silence returned to the valley, except for the rushing, rattling, humming North Fork, and tapping of rain. In a growing downpour I remained still another thirty or forty-five minutes, maybe even an hour. I listened and looked, upstream and down, along the forest's edge and up higher, along tundra terraces. I wiped the lenses of my binoculars while pelted by what had become a cold, hard, Arctic rain. On this day, unlike many others, I didn't mind being out in it.

Finally I gave up my watch and grabbed shelter under the tarp. I noticed I was shivering; from the wet chill, yes, but also from the song of *Canis lupus.*

I love grizzly bears. They are one of my primary totem animals, maybe my most important. To share the landscape with grizzlies is always an honor and delight (and occasionally worrisome). But to be with howling wolves in the Arctic wilds; well, there is no greater magic. Beneath the tarp and later in the tent, I imagined distant, intermittent howling throughout the afternoon and evening. It's amazing how much a river or the wind can sound like wolves.

I had a feeling about this place since first seeing the many wolf tracks along the river. I was sure that the surrounding woods or tundra hills held an active wolf den and wished I might stumble upon it, or even see wolf pups from a distance while scanning the landscape. But I was satisfied now. I'd had my communion. Both body and soul had been stirred by songs that told, without words, of mountains and rivers, of mysteries as ancient as music itself.

Throughout this solo backpacking trip deep into Gates of the Arctic National Park and Preserve, my most memorable times had come as moments of surprise: sudden (even if anticipated) encounters with the Valley of Precipices, Mount Doonerak, grizzlies, a bear skull, and now wolves. Animals had been the best example of this. For all the looking and "hunting" I'd done, the wildlife I would remember most had come to me. It seemed I was being given new opportunities to let go of expectations and, at the same time, be open to possibilities. Both ideas, and the practice of them, had become important guideposts in my middle years.

After spending much of my life trying to keep things under control, I was learning to surrender to life's experiences, while also embracing the opportunities that come my way. It still wasn't easy, as demonstrated on this trip by my worrying, my off-and-on watch monitoring, and my efforts to stay dry and cozy in my overly large and weather-resistant tent. Yet I had remained flexible and taken some risks, both here and generally.

It still sometimes amazes me that a person so drawn to comfort, structure, and predictability would take the leaps of faith I've made from geology to journalism and then to freelance writing. And settling in Alaska, of all places! Not many of my childhood friends—or family members—back in Connecticut would ever have guessed that the small, shy, sensitive boy of long ago would become an author, wilderness lover, and activist, or that he'd someday ascend the continent's highest peak or trek alone across miles of untrailed Arctic wilderness.

The sun briefly returned in the evening and I hiked to a rocky knob above camp. From there I gained a better sense of how the landscape swept out and away from the Ernie Creek-North Fork confluence and the two streams' large gravel bars, first to lowland forest and then to upland tundra meadows and willow thickets, and even higher to encircling tundra-topped foothills and mountains with bare, jagged ridgetops. Beyond those hills and mountains were more waves of peaks and hidden valleys.

I felt so lucky, so happy, to be in the heart of this vast wilderness, where wild places still mostly free of human influence span dozens of miles in any direction. I realized again how much I need such trips, for so many reasons: to refresh my spirit, test my limits and stretch my horizons, embrace solitude, expand my sense of what's possible, encounter "the other," renew my bonds with wildness in its many forms, and see more clearly what's important, both here in the wild and back at home. Still, I couldn't imagine making a home here (if it were allowed), so far from other people and the conveniences of modern living. I didn't try to fool myself: this northern wilderness is a harsh, demanding place, and to live here year-round would require skills I hadn't acquired. And at age fifty, I likely never would.

Thinking about the trials and perils of Arctic homesteading, I again recalled Ernie Johnson, "the most famous trapper of the North Fork," for whom adventurer, author, and wilderness advocate Bob Marshall named Ernie Creek. According to Marshall, "Although [Johnson] had come north on a gold rush, he had also been drawn by his love of the woods in this greatest wilderness on the continent. Here he spent all but about two weeks in the year out in the hills, away from the 'cities' of Wiseman (population 103) and Bettles (population 24). . . . He trapped and hunted, averaging a yearly income of about twenty-five hundred dollars. 'I can make better money as a carpenter,' he said, 'but I am staying out here because I like it among these ruggedy mountains better than anywhere else in the world.'"

Here was someone who'd chosen the hermit's life I once talked about pursuing while fed up with people and relationships during my grad school days; someone who actually chose to spend most of his adult years in seclusion. What revelations and understandings did Ernie Johnson find here among the sheep and grizzlies? As much as I desire and seek out solitude, I can't imagine a life so empty of people.

From the perch above camp I traced much of the route I had followed along Ernie Creek, from the Precipices to the North Fork. Then I looked downstream, where I would be walking tomorrow. It appeared I was bound for "the dark forest." Thick stands of spruce pressed close against the meandering river. I would likely cut through the woods in places, either to shorten my route or where pushed into the trees by steep, river-eroded cutbanks. I hoped it wouldn't be too dense or brushy for easy path finding.

While plotting my route, I heard more howling, downriver. The wolf song was loud and clear, but brief. I wished for more, but instead heard only the rush of river. And gradually, more chanting voices. These were less pleasing, more eerie. My mind imagined a chorus of *"sorry . . . sorry"* sung in a mocking, almost malevolent tone. Was the darkness in this chant tied to my worries about tomorrow's route? The chant unnerved me and I was unable to get the words out of my head as I descended back to camp. Might such things come from too much solitude?

Again I wondered how much I was hearing and how much imagining. The presence of these landscape sounds and voices had been among the weirder aspects of this trek, sometimes unnerving and occasionally—like earlier today—exhilarating and fulfilling.

PART IV

ODDITIES, SURPRISES, AND DILEMMAS

A GIFT OF HALIBUT

The freshly cut herring bait had been sitting on Cook Inlet's sandy bottom for only a few minutes when I felt a sharp tug on my line. My first impulse was to set the hook, hard. Instead, I followed Mark Chihuly's instructions: I waited. "Don't be impatient," Mark had been telling us all afternoon. "Let the fish take the bait." It's the same advice my Uncle Peach gave me when we fished live minnows for bass and pickerel in Connecticut lakes more than thirty years earlier. Patience usually paid off then and it had worked so far today: already I'd landed a seventy-pound halibut, the largest fish I had ever caught and the biggest our party had taken on this splendid mid-July afternoon of blue skies, sixty-something temperatures, and calm seas.

Waiting for the right moment to strike, I considered what it would be like to catch a two- or three-hundred-pound fish. I'd read stories, even written stories, about people who caught such halibut, but it's not something I ever fantasized. Even today's seventy-pounder seemed huge; the idea of hauling in something three or four times larger seemed impossible to imagine. Yet this spot, we'd been assured, sometimes yielded giant halibut. How would I respond to such a monster fish?

Other, more disturbing, questions had earlier drifted through my consciousness, like fishing line through water. It wasn't the first time I'd thought about my decades-long desire to hook and "play" hard-fighting sport fish. But as usual, I refused to take that particular bait, while caught up in the excitement of the chase and catch. Instead of insight, action.

Guided by Mark, five of us had been saltwater fishing from his charter boat, the *Suzy Q*, since midmorning—first for king salmon, then for halibut, a member of the flatfish family. The king fishing had been slower than slow; no one in our boat got even a strike. "That's fishing," shrugged Mark, a stocky, muscular, good-natured outdoorsman and lifelong Alaskan who'd spent much of his adult life guiding anglers and hunters. A favorite phrase, he would repeat it a dozen times before day's end, as if to remind us—or himself—of the sport's vagaries.

Still, I was disappointed. Allen, my brother-in-law, was visiting from Florida and his best chance of catching an Alaskan king had passed. Like Mark, I believe that "going fishing" means more than simply catching fish, but on this day Allen and I had come to the inlet expecting to take home both sporting memories and meat. As we headed away from the Kenai Peninsula coastline toward deeper water, I could only hope that halibut would salvage our day, make it memorable.

We anchored up miles from land, at a fishing hole where halibut of 100 pounds or more were known to prowl the bottom. Back in the early 1980s, Mark told us, it was not uncommon to catch 100- to 200-pound halibut within a half mile of the beach. One year he pulled in a 325-pound fish and another weighing 250 pounds, "almost within stone-throwing distance of shore." But those days, he lamented, are gone forever, ended by a saltwater sport fishery and charter industry that had grown precipitously in the past two decades.

Trophy-size halibut were still being caught; but anglers and guides had to travel farther and expend more time and energy to catch them while facing greatly increased competition. By the late 1990s, hundreds of charter boats worked the central waters of Cook Inlet, a long, narrow, glacially fed estuary that stretches nearly three hundred miles from the Gulf of Alaska to the Mat-Su Valleys north of Anchorage. And every charter was seeking large fish: 100, 200, 300 pounds. Any halibut that big is bound to be a breeding female. And the bigger the fish, the more eggs it produces: a 50-pound female will on average release five hundred thousand eggs annually; a 250 pounder will produce four million.

Within minutes Mark had baited our hooks with herring and fish heads, and helped us to put our lines into the 160-foot-deep water. Joe, from Fairbanks, and I had fished for halibut several times before and knew the routine. But Allen, Floria, and Kim—the latter two also from Fairbanks—had little or no halibut experience, so Mark emphasized and reemphasized the two key elements to catching them: (1) keep your bait on the bottom, (2) "Don't set the hook too soon; let them really take it." Be patient, in other words.

Almost immediately, we got bites. Our first two fish were gray cod. Then a halibut grabbed my bait. I waited and waited and waited, then set the hook hard. And again. The fish took off, stripping one-hundred-pound line from my baitcasting reel. I tried to slow it by placing my thumb on the line, a foolish decision: it sliced an inch-long gash into my skin. After its initial run, the halibut came in slowly. Within fifteen minutes it was shot, gaffed, and pulled aboard. A good-sized fish, it weighed about seventy pounds, and someone offered to take a picture. Grunting, I lifted my catch off the deck. Excited by my own success, I hoped that Allen, too, would catch a nice-sized halibut.

For the next two hours, Mark kept busy untangling lines, baiting hooks, unhooking fish. By 3:00 P.M. our group had landed more than a dozen halibut and kept about half, most in the twenty- to fifty-pound range; Allen pulled in one of forty pounds, inspiring big grins and a high-five exchange. Not big fish, but large enough to satisfy clients who had spent $150 apiece for the charter—and good eating. Small halibut are juicier, tastier, and more tender than larger ones.

Mark, who clearly knew fish, told us he rarely brought home anything over twenty pounds to eat. He also knew how hard it is to shake the sport fishing truism that "bigger is better." Given a choice, it was unlikely any of Mark's clients would trade a hundred-pound halibut for a twenty pounder. I had come away from charters disappointed that I caught fish weighing "only" fifteen to twenty-five pounds. Partly it was ego I suppose. But the economics of guided fishing and a desire to fill freezers with halibut steaks also influenced whether I felt content or let down by my day's catch.

Still looking for my second halibut, I felt a tug, waited, then set the hook. At first I thought it was a cod, but it proved to be a small halibut, maybe fifteen pounds. With the seventy-pounder already boated, I would have been satisfied with this one to fill out my limit, but Mark tossed it back. Almost as an afterthought, he looked at me and said, "That was OK, I hope." It was as if he sensed the presence of a bigger fish in the waters below, ready to take the bait.

Again I let out my line. No more than five or ten minutes went by before I felt another tug. It was a solid take, a steady, strong pull. I let the rod tip go down, let the halibut swallow the herring deeply. Then, finally, I set the hook: once, twice, three times, to be sure.

This fish didn't run like my first halibut, but I could feel its heaviness. "I've got something," I said calmly, feigning nonchalance. Then I began a slow retrieve: lift, reel down; lift, reel down. This went on for several minutes, until the fish decided to sit. I couldn't budge it an inch.

"Keep lifting," Mark encouraged. "Stay with it."

Sweating and grimacing, I was surprised and a little chagrined that I couldn't move the fish. Where was that upper body strength? On the boat's opposite side, Floria's line had begun to do funny things and Mark guessed that he had somehow become tangled with my fish. He instructed Floria to give slack, then joined me. We worked together, with me lifting and reeling and Mark pulling the line, hand over hand, his heavily muscled arms and shoulders making my job easier. After five minutes of this, he looked at me and smiled: "You've got a big fish, maybe bigger than we've caught all year. We don't want to lose this one."

Everyone's attention had become focused on the fish at the end of my line. The others offered encouragement, told me to "keep at it." I continued lifting and grunting, working hard but also smiling, engaged by the growing drama. Slowly, reluctantly, the great fish was dragged upward until finally close enough to see through the murky water.

"It's huge!" someone shouted.

Guessing the halibut might weigh three hundred pounds, Mark exclaimed, "This is the kind of fish that will get you in the newspaper."

The flat, diamond-shaped fish hung from my line like a vertical slab of meat in the slack tide. Later, Mark would tell me that most sport-caught halibut come up from the depths with their bodies in a more-or-less horizontal position. Doing that, he said, they actually help the angler, make it easier to reel them in. But occasionally a fish would come up vertically. When they do that, it's like hauling dead weight through the water.

There was another problem: halibut are powerful fish. Once boated, they're capable of doing serious damage with their flopping tails. In August 1973, the *Juneau Empire* reported the story of an Alaskan commercial fisherman who'd been killed by a halibut he'd caught: "The body of Joseph T. Cash, 67, of Petersburg was found lashed to the winch of his troller after a 150-pound halibut had apparently broken his leg and severed an artery when he hoisted it aboard his boat while fishing alone . . ."

Because of this and other tail-thrashing incidents, sport fishing guides routinely shoot large halibut before bringing them aboard. Mark used a .22-caliber pistol. The best place to shoot, he said, is in the spine, at the base of the skull. But when a three-hundred-pound halibut is hanging vertically, it's almost impossible to put a bullet in the spine. How do you lift a fish that size out of the water for a clean shot?

Slowly working the halibut toward the boat, we noticed that another line, with forty-ounce weight, was tangled with mine. Complicating things even more was the fact that my line had begun to fray. Mark fired his pistol. But instead of the expected fury, the halibut just sat there in the water. Now it was time to spear the fish, using a small harpoon attached to a rope and buoy; that way, if my line broke, we would still have the fish. When Mark struck, the halibut thrashed wildly, then dived deep—without the harpoon, which somehow popped free.

"Oh no," Mark moaned. "Give it line."

That's what I was already doing, not that I had much choice. The fish disappeared into the inlet's grayish-brown depths and we began the process again.

The rod butt was bruising my inner thigh, so Mark dug out a harness. But we couldn't get it to fit properly and I kept the butt pinned against my upper leg and groin area, trying to leverage the rod as I worked it up and down. The next day I would have deep purplish bruises to remind me of this battle.

With the halibut wounded by the bullet, perhaps mortally, landing it became a more serious task. As Mark commented, "It would be a shame to lose it now."

Praying that the frayed line would hold, I hauled it up as gingerly as possible, inch by inch. Arms, shoulders, and thighs aching, I again brought the fish within harpooning distance and Mark jabbed it. Again the fish dived deep. And again the harpoon point somehow broke free, leaving a weakening line as my only link to the fish.

I sensed a frenzy around me. Mark's nerves, like the line, were fraying: he cursed our bad luck and scrambled around the deck, his clients in turn scrambling to stay out of the way. At one point Allen came over to pat me on the back, offer encouragement. I seemed a point of calm within the growing storm; hopeful, but without expectations or anxieties. I was exhausted, but focused on my role, which at this point meant simply holding onto the fish.

We hauled the halibut in a third time. Mark decided to shoot it again, before attempting to harpoon it. I winched the fish until its upper body was above the water, amazed that the shredded line continued to hold. Mark shot once, twice, three times, four times. I winced with each shot and my ears rang with exploding gunfire.

The wondrously large fish hung limply. Holding the line, Mark asked Allen to harpoon the halibut. A quick, hard jab. "OK, it's in," said Allen, who looked my way and smiled.

Finally, the fish was ours. Connected by the harpoon rope, it wouldn't get away or sink from us even if the fishing line snapped. Allen stuck a large hooked gaff into the halibut, then, with loud grunts, he and Mark hauled it aboard. We shouted our excitement, exchanged congratulatory handshakes. Only Mark had ever landed a halibut this big and everyone marveled at the fish. With the fight over, I was dumbstruck. Exhausted. Relieved. How long had it been? A half hour? An hour? I felt as though I'd been pulled outside ordinary time while connected to this giant fish by a thin thread.

I took some pictures then approached the halibut, lying on the boat's deck. The side that faced us was a brownish olive green, a predator's camouflage, while its underside, the side that faces the ocean bottom, was white. The skin was smooth and slippery—most would say slimy—when wet, but grew sticky with drying. I touched the skin of this great grandmother fish and something shifted in me: for a short while, at least, "it" became a "she." I watched her gills slowly expand, remain open for several seconds, then collapse. Was this a reflex or did some life force still flicker within? Except for the gills, she was still.

I felt drawn to her large, bulbous eyes, which protruded from the green, upper side of the head like golf-ball-sized knobs. Larger than a nickel, each black pupil was surrounded by a golden iris halo. Though unfocused, the eyes had an eerie depth to them. They pulled me in, enchanted me.

"It's a beautiful fish," said Allen, as though reading my mind.

"I'm glad you said that," Mark replied. "Most people think they're ugly, but I've always found them to be pretty fish."

Their comments prompted me to consider how we so often label these large fish "monsters." So and so landed a monster king or a monster halibut; I had used that phrase so many times when doing fishing reports as a newspaper writer. Later, a female friend would point out that such monster imagery seems a very masculine thing. Perhaps it adds drama to the hunt, accentuates the idea of doing battle with a large and powerful adversary. The paradox, with halibut, is that such monster fish are females. More than that, they're fecund mothers. I'm reminded that western men's traditional attitudes toward hunting have sometimes been linked with their passion for sexual conquest. Both beasts and women become objects of desire, something to chase and conquer. So which is it: beauty or the beast? A little bit of both, probably, in halibut as well as humans. And where do I fit in as fisher, as hunter? Surely while "fighting" the halibut, I felt something close to desire. Now other emotions began to intrude.

As the others resumed fishing, I fell into a cushioned seat, physically and emotionally drained. Earlier I'd been fully absorbed in the chase, the catch. But with the battle over, I began to question whether I should have given the rod and the experience to Allen, who in recent years had become an avid, if still largely inexperienced, fisherman.

Traveling north with his wife and three daughters, Allen enthusiastically spent most of his Alaska vacation on sightseeing and camping trips to Denali, Resurrection Bay, Kenai Fjords. We'd caught a few small fish along the way, but this was the one day he and I had devoted solely to angling. What an Alaskan memory this great halibut could have been for the forty-something businessman from Florida. But while I was hooked to the halibut, the thought of handing the rod to Allen hadn't even crossed my mind. Nothing in his actions or words suggested envy. On the contrary, he seemed as excited as anyone about my catch. Later, heading to land with two fish in the twenty- to forty-pound range, Allen would voice satisfaction in his own harvest. Still I asked myself: *Had I been selfish?*

I wondered too if killing this halibut was the right thing to do. Based on body measurements, a biologist would later estimate her to be twenty to twenty-five years old. Something about her age, her size, her eyes, combined with what Mark told me about the fishing pressure on female breeders, made me question my own desires and attitudes. Perhaps it was the knowledge that, during our struggle, I'd gotten caught up in the battle and given little thought to her life. Or death. She was something to be caught, a form of wild game—a slab of meat. I rolled the words around in my head: something to be caught, some *thing*. Before seeing her up close, the halibut had been an "it," a resource, not another being.

My thoughts drifted back to three days earlier, when Allen's young daughter, Emily, caught a fifteen-inch Dolly Varden char in the saltwater near Seward. Excited by the catch and charmed by the char's sleek beauty, Emily wanted to keep the fish. She would show it to her family, then we'd have it for dinner. I grabbed a rock and clubbed the Dolly, but not well enough to kill it immediately. The bloodied fish flopped on the beach. As I prepared to club it again, Emily had second thoughts: "Maybe we should let it go," she said softly.

"It's too late," I told her gently. It wouldn't survive.

Watching her stare quietly at the dying fish, I asked what she was thinking, feeling. She only shrugged, a half smile, half grimace on her face. Still silent, she bent and touched the fish, then slowly picked its limp body from the beach and carried it to her father. Later, Emily and I talked about the fish's death, and how it was natural, OK, to feel such contradictory emotions: the initial rush of excitement when catching and seeing the fish, then sadness, even regret, at the taking of another creature's life. Killing is not an act to be taken lightly, I reminded her. When necessary, as for eating, it should be done with respect for the animal's life.

Now I was having the same sort of second thoughts. It was only after I'd seen the old halibut's final breaths, looked into her eyes and felt her flesh, that I'd fully comprehended what I had done: taken a life. It's strange how the earlier, smaller fish we'd caught didn't affect me this way. No brooding with them, no self-analysis. Even after considerable reflection, I can't explain the difference. Maybe it's because the smaller fish were so quickly dumped into the holding tank, leaving no time for connection or remorse. Maybe it took something as huge, as miraculous, as that great mother halibut to shake things up inside.

Could I have seen, somehow perceived, her life flickering away? Did the halibut speak to me in some way? I wanted to honor this matriarch somehow, to show my respect for her being, her kind. Sitting in my chair, I looked again at the halibut's unblinking eyes, her huge and slightly opened mouth, with its rows of sharp teeth. In her world, she swam at the top of the food chain, an aggressive bottom-feeding predator who ate crabs, shrimp, schooling fish, cod, even other halibut. In taking my bait, she'd suddenly become the prey.

There was something else about the catch that bothered me: the "sport" aspect. We killed this halibut—all these halibut—for meat, but also for sport. For the thrill of the chase, the battle, the catch. Tutored by my Uncle Peach, a passionate angler who never showed guilt or second-guessed his motives, I'd been a sport fisherman since I was eleven or twelve. Sometimes gruff, often playful, Peach was a boisterous, bearded Hemingwayesque character with a passion for the outdoors. Under his guidance I learned to catch night crawlers and minnows for bait and place them on my hook. I learned patience and the proper way to present the bait, to set the hook, and play the fish.

We were fishing buddies for years, sometimes filling our limit, more often getting skunked. Almost always we kept what we caught in Connecticut lakes and streams, the fish becoming food for the table. But sport, not food, seemed to me our main motivation.

Later, when I'd moved to Alaska and took up fly fishing, I became an avid catch-and-release angler. In the world of fly fishers, catch-and-release is the highest, most ethical, and conservation-minded form of fishing possible. Anglers, biologists, and conservationists agree it has protected many fish populations that would otherwise be decimated by heavy fishing pressure.

There still were times when I enthusiastically embraced such "sport" fishing. But at other times—for instance on this halibut charter—I'd begun to have second thoughts. In the years since that fishing expedition, the idea of harming another creature for sport, as opposed to need, has troubled me even more. We have sport or game fish and we have big- and small-game animals. What it becomes is blood sport. A bloody game.

The questions go beyond simple killing. Nearly every sport fisherman and sport fish biologist I've ever met has accepted as truth the notion that fish feel no pain. At least not the way we humans do. Or even mammals and birds. That makes it easier to hook 'em, haul 'em in, and then either kill the fish or release them "unharmed." I thought about this even as a boy. But whenever I raised the question, Uncle Peach always assured me, "Fish don't feel pain." And that was that.

But is it true? Or are we humans torturing and sometimes killing these critters for fun? For play?

Because they are cold-blooded, live in water, have fins and scales instead of limbs and hair (or fur or feathers), we don't identify with fish the way we do with our warm-blooded relatives, mammals and birds. It becomes easy to rationalize that they don't have feelings, can't experience trauma—or if they do, it's "no big deal." As philosopher (and former angler) Jack Turner has commented, "Imagine using worms and flies to catch mountain bluebirds or pine grosbeaks or maybe eagles and ospreys, and hauling them around on fifty feet of line while they tried to get away. Then when you landed them, you'd release them. No one would tolerate that sort of thing with birds. But we will for fish because they're underwater and out of sight."

Yet for all of our rationalizing—and denial—there's increased scientific evidence that fish do in fact feel pain. One researcher, Michael Stoskopf, found convincing evidence that fish (and other nonmammals) have both biochemical and physical responses similar to those of mammals when subjected to pain. A growing number of other ethicists and scientists say it's unthinkable that fish don't suffer when hooked and pulled through water. Should this matter?

Tied to the pain of catch-and-release fishing is the question of respect for other life-forms. Back in the mid-1980s, while working at the *Anchorage Times*, I reported on fishing conflicts along the Kanektok River in Southwest Alaska. Native residents of Quinhagak, a Yup'ik village at the river's mouth, had been protesting the increased presence of sportfishing parties and their impacts on local subsistence uses of the Kanektok. I've forgotten many details of that conflict, but one thing has stayed with me. I remember that the villagers were especially offended and outraged by the visiting anglers' use of catch-and-release techniques. To locals, the practice was disrespectful to the fish. It was, in essence, "playing with the food," a taboo in their culture.

Initially I found it strange that catch-and-release might be offensive, even bad or unethical. But after listening to the Native perspective and reporting on this clash of cultural values, I began to reassess my own beliefs and biases. The more I thought about it, the more the Yup'ik attitude made sense. Even the terms "sport" fish and "game" fish imply the notion of play. It doesn't take much of a leap in logic to see that this western art form easily could be seen as playing with food, especially if the fish being "played" (as anglers like to say) is an important part of someone else's subsistence diet, a source of sustenance that's crucial for survival.

For all my increased resistance to the sport of fishing, I can accept the catching of fish for food. It certainly seems more honest to kill the fish and other animals we eat, rather than avoid or deny the loss of life by shopping in supermarkets for prepackaged products. So many in our culture—and I am certainly among them—have become distanced and disconnected from the food that gives us life. When done properly, fishing and hunting allow us humans to claim and perhaps even celebrate our role in the food web, our connection to the world that sustains us, instead of denying it.

If I'd shared my growing concerns with Mark that day on Cook Inlet, he likely would have responded, "That's fishing." At least for me such back-and-forth agonizing had apparently become a part of the ritual. A key to acceptance, I suspected then and firmly believe now, was to treat this halibut, or any animal, with respect; to have the humility to recognize the halibut as a gift, not a conquest. Many indigenous peoples believe that hunting success has less to do with any great skills than the fact that prey presents itself to the respectful hunter. Their traditions emphasize humility and restraint, a recognition of spirit and sacredness in all of nature, and a receptivity to mystery. More and more, such beliefs and customs make great sense to me.

Perhaps picking up on my somber mood or my questions about the halibut's size and age, Mark said he'd like to see a limit placed on the number of hundred pounders that a sport fisher could keep. After one lunker, what's the need for more? He then recalled a story from the previous summer, about a fishing charter that brought in ten or twelve halibut weighing one hundred to three hundred pounds. Mark viewed that not as some special triumph, but a waste. The big females are the ones that need protection, he again emphasized. Why not have a system in which it's possible to arrange some sort of halibut trophy mount, without killing the fish? It was already being done with certain species, like rainbow trout.

Fishery biologists who monitor Cook Inlet insisted the increased sport harvest of breeders wasn't threatening the inlet's population. But their assurances didn't ease Mark's worries. The inlet was home, it's where he had fished since childhood, and he saw a local problem developing if guides and anglers didn't ease up on large female halibut. "Somewhere down the line, it's going to catch up with us," he fretted. "We need to show some restraint."

But restraint is a difficult thing when you own a charter operation. Trophy fish make for good advertising. The walls, doors, and windows of charter offices are plastered with pictures of "barn-door" size halibut. And at day's end, crowds naturally gather around the largest fish.

"He who can get the biggest fish is he who will get the business," Mark shrugged. "You'd be cutting your own throat if you didn't go after the big ones. But what's going to happen when they're gone?"

Mark then told me about a halibut sport-fish tagging program run by the International Pacific Halibut Commission. Even as we were catching our limits, on another Chihuly charter boat customers were catching and releasing large halibut: by day's end, several in the 80- to 150-pound range would be tagged and let go.

The tagging program gave people another option. Guides bought tags from the halibut commission and, if clients were interested, they tagged their fish, got an estimated size, and turned them loose. In return, tagging participants received a pin and certificate; and if a tagged fish was eventually recaught, that information would be passed on to the original halibut catcher. Tagged-and-recovered fish, in turn, gave the commission helpful data on halibut movements and growth.

Recognizing that his tagging clients might wish to preserve some record of their released fish, Mark had constructed a half-dozen plywood replicas of halibut. Each a different size, the plywood pieces were cut and painted to look just like the fish; they even had blood running out their gills. I wasn't sure I wanted my picture taken with a plywood halibut, but I liked the tagging idea. I couldn't imagine myself ever again keeping a trophy-sized halibut; the idea of returning grandmother fish to their saltwater homes pleased me.

On our return to shore, Mark suggested I get a "tail mount" of my halibut. On my catch the fish's tail fin measured twenty-one inches from tip to tip. At first I was repulsed by the idea: for years I had opposed the act of collecting animal trophies, whether fish or bears. Big-game trophy hunting especially bothered me. Killing for meat I could understand; but killing for heads or hide alone? Killing to place a prize upon a wall or floor? This deadly game reeks of self-aggrandizing pride and ego, at the expense of another's life. I found it offensive, unacceptable.

Was a halibut tail mount any different from a grizzly bear mount? I eventually decided it was, at least partly because of intent: I didn't come here looking for trophies, I came to harvest meat. And yes, engage in sport. But there was something else: A tail mount would preserve the memory of all that had happened that July day, including the inner debate that had raged since I peered into the halibut's eyes, touched her skin. In a sense it could be my memorial to the great fish, a way of honoring her spirit. Placed on my wall beside a picture of the halibut, it would be a reminder of the day's ambiguities and revelations, and my own contradictory nature. This was not one in a series, but once in a lifetime.

After still more agonizing—was I being hypocritical?—I decided to do it. For $125, a local taxidermy shop would prepare the halibut's tail fin, to be hung upon my dining room wall.

Back on land, we weighed the halibut at Chihuly Charters. The scale read only 220 pounds, which surprised us all. Mark explained it was uncertified and only gave approximate weights. Next we measured the fish: she was eighty-two inches long. The International Pacific Halibut Commission has put together a table that correlates halibut length and weight; by its measure, an average halibut of eighty-two inches would weigh 299½ pounds. So I split the difference and figured my halibut went about 298.

Chihuly's, like most charters, had a "hang 'em and shoot" ritual for its customers. Halibut were hung, white side out, on a fish rack and their catchers then posed with the fish. As we brought our catch in, mine naturally got everyone's attention. It was both exhilarating and embarrassing to be at the center of such commotion. Soon our images would join others on Chihuly Charters' office door and the big halibut in our Polaroid would grab people's attention. Mark might not like it, but that's part of charter fishing too. My trophy catch symbolized the growing pressures on Cook Inlet halibut, but it was also good for business.

After the photo session, Mark and his guides filleted the halibut. We catchers of the fish stood aside, oddly detached from this part of the harvesting process. Even after the head, guts, and bones were removed, Allen and I took home more than 250 pounds of fish from our four halibut. I got caught up in the picture-taking frenzy, the meat packing, the preparation for our drive back to

Anchorage, and the halibut, for a while at least, again became an object—something for the freezer.

On Sunday, the day after our fishing expedition, Allen and I cut the halibut fillets into smaller, meal-sized pieces and bagged them for refrigeration, a three-hour process that became part of our shared ritual. He took fifty pounds back to Florida; I kept the rest here in Anchorage, giving some to friends. It was satisfying, to have a fresh supply of halibut for the winter. The year before I hadn't put any fish in the freezer.

I barbecued several pounds of the fish for Sunday dinner and seven of us held hands as Allen thanked God for the halibut. Silently, I added my thanks to the halibut for giving herself to us. Then we ate.

LEONARD PEYTON'S REDPOLL PROJECT

As flocks of redpolls cross Interior Alaska during annual winter flights, large numbers invariably head up Pearl Creek Bowl, where they are funneled by the landscape toward neighborhoods in the foothills north of Fairbanks. Most years, these small northern songbirds begin to visit bird feeders by early December, in groups of ten to fifteen. As the weeks pass, more and more stop over from their seasonal journeys, until by March hundreds of redpolls may swarm yards in the aspen-birch forest. In daily feeding frenzies they fatten up on seeds, which will help them make it through the exceedingly long and often bitterly cold nights. Tiny "chipped" sunflower seeds are especially irresistible to these amazingly hardy birds, among the tiniest to endure the subarctic's severe, extended winters.

For more than three decades, exceptionally large redpoll flocks descended upon the many feeders maintained by Leonard Peyton. He figured his yard must have been located smack-dab in the middle of a major redpoll flight corridor, because "at times there wouldn't be another redpoll in all of Fairbanks, but I'd have some in my yard." But what really distinguished Peyton from his neighbors were his many speculations and theories about the birds, based on thirty-six years of serious study. Between 1968 and 2004 Peyton captured, banded, and released more than twenty thousand redpolls. Once he banded four thousand in a single year.

Those impressive numbers become more remarkable when you learn that Peyton's long-running project was essentially an amateur study. He did it as a hobby, simply because he was "interested in birds."

Still, it was an amateur study done professionally, because Peyton the hobbyist was keenly influenced by Peyton the scientist. An Alaskan since the mid-1950s, he assisted in large mammal physiology studies at the Arctic Health Research Center in Anchorage, then joined UAF's newly formed Institute of Arctic Biology in 1962. Initially the institute's executive officer, Leonard moved back into wildlife research in 1968 and then studied northern birds and mammals until his retirement in 1990.

Inspired by his affinity for birds, Peyton's pet project during those IAB years focused on fox sparrows, whose songs vary greatly from one region to another. From 1968 to 1985, he carried thirty-five pounds of recording gear eight to ten hours a day for three or four weeks a summer. By project's end, he had taped the songs of 720 individual fox sparrows, from Prince William Sound to the Arctic's Colville River.

Fox sparrows probably remained his favorite birds, admitted Peyton, who fondly remembered them as "pugnacious little characters." But redpolls were the birds that passed through his yard in large numbers. They were easy to trap and band. And they didn't require lengthy travels or the daily grind of field work—an important consideration for an ornithologist whose aging body, by the late 1990s, had been surgically enhanced by the replacement of both hips, one shoulder, and one knee with artificial parts. Doctors told him he likely wore the joints out while lugging heavy equipment around all those years.

While Peyton's long-term relationship with redpolls might have been a marriage of convenience, he did, over those three and a half decades, come to appreciate the mysteries the birds enfold. And though he likely would have rejected the notion, the evidence suggests that redpolls added passion to his life, while inspiring a desire to learn more about their nature. Or perhaps my own fascination with redpolls colors my interpretation of the facts.

I learned about Peyton's redpoll studies in serendipitous fashion, while contacting other researchers about the species' northern adaptations. Put in touch with Leonard, I arranged a visit to the home he shared with his wife, Irene, in mid-March 2000, to find out more about his investigations and the redpolls themselves.

Having ignored songbirds for most of my life, I didn't even know such a creature as a redpoll existed until a few of them visited my feeders on New Year's Eve, 1993 (shortly before I turned forty-four). As I soon discovered, redpolls are among the smallest and hardiest of Alaska's birds. Five to five and a half inches long, they are sparrow-like members of the finch family, with distinctive red splotches or caps on their heads, small black bibs, and heavily streaked brown-and-white wings and back. Adult males also sport pinkish to bright red breasts that intensify during the mating season.

Like Leonard, I began to track the redpolls that annually visited my Anchorage feeders, though not in such a scientific manner. Here too they usually arrive in December, then stick around till April. Occasionally I counted more than one hundred at my Hillside home, an impressive number but substantially less than Peyton sometimes attracted. Redpolls zoomed in from neighboring spruce trees while others zoomed out, as though at some avian fast-food diner. Gradually their numbers built as they settled in to feast. Squeezed wing to wing in food line, they chirped and screeched and fluttered about in frenzied pandemonium. For such little creatures, they make a mighty racket.

Watching redpolls on subzero days or during snowstorms, I marvel that they survive Alaska's winters. Anchorage is tough enough. In Fairbanks, temperatures fall far below zero degrees (Fahrenheit) for weeks at a time and midwinter nights last twenty hours or more.

To endure the subarctic's extreme conditions, redpolls have evolved a way to store the seeds they take from willows, alders, or people's feeders. While eating, they (like other finches) stockpile seeds in a pocket-like esophageal pouch, or crop. Once settled in a sheltered perch for the night, the redpolls then gradually digest their surplus seeds through the long hours of darkness.

Exactly where redpolls spend their nights remains uncertain. Some may seek out cavities, while others perch on spruce tree boughs. There have also been reports of redpolls burrowing into the snow to escape the cold. Though many scientists remain unconvinced, it's known that certain songbirds in Europe and Asia regularly roost in holes within the snowpack.

Another survival device: redpolls have dense winter plumage that they fluff up for added insulation, giving them the appearance of little feathered balls. The performance of these winter coats is extraordinary. Redpolls maintain their core body temperatures at 105° even when the air temperature drops to minus 60°F. That's a temperature difference of 165°, over a distance of a quarter to half inch.

As former UAF physiologist Pierre DeViche once commented, "Think if you could make a coat with that sort of insulative ability. It's incredible, really."

In my own quest to learn more about redpolls, I heard bits and pieces about Leonard Peyton's work. When contacted, he played down his research, describing himself as an "amateur ornithologist" and emphasizing the hobby aspect of his study (which he had a government permit to do). Other scientists were more enthusiastic. Anchorage biologist and former redpoll researcher Declan Troy summed it up: "You've got to talk to Leonard. There's no Alaskan more deeply involved with redpolls."

Leonard came north in 1955 on the advice of his parents, who fell in love with Alaska while visiting a relative stationed at Elmendorf Air Force Base. Knowing their son's interests, they imagined he might, too. Leonard expected his stay to be a short one. But while vacationing here, he learned his California employer was "closing its doors." Free to explore possibilities, he got a job in Anchorage, working as a biologist.

A life-long New Englander, Irene crossed the continent in 1958 on something of a whim, simply because she was curious about "this place called Alaska." Hired as a data processor by the Arctic Health Research Center, she met Leonard. They dated some, but didn't get seriously involved. Feeling a pull back home, Irene left Alaska after a year, briefly visited Hawaii, then returned to Massachusetts. She and Leonard stayed in touch by mail, and in 1960 he invited her to a family wedding in Fillmore, California. There, on his parent's citrus farm, he proposed.

Married in November 1960, the newlyweds resettled briefly in Anchorage, then migrated north to Fairbanks, where Leonard rejoined his old boss, Dr. Laurence Irving, at the brand-new Institute for Arctic Biology. At first the Peytons lived along College Road, near the university. But after Fairbanks' disastrous flood of 1967 inundated their basement with water and muck, the Peytons headed for the hills and found a four-and-a-half-acre forested plot only a few miles from town. Though they had no construction experience, the couple built their dream home in the woods, spurred on by a shared love for adventure and Leonard's problem-solving acumen. Depending mostly on "book learning," with occasional advice from professional builders, he did all the carpentry, electrical work, and plumbing. Irene helped out where needed.

"Leonard did the fun stuff," she joked when recalling those years. "I did the sanding and painting."

Whatever the division of duties, the two agreed it was a collaboration from beginning to end: planning, design, construction. The end product, as Irene described it, was "a good, old-fashioned two-story Alaska house that's energy efficient."

A "Peyton Place" welcome mat greeted visitors to their home. I found it to be a practical, down-to-earth place filled with good cheer and a passionate embrace of life.

Both Irene and Leonard were in their midseventies when they welcomed me into their home, but the two maintained an active lifestyle, busy with travel and hobbies. "Leonard's hobby is birds, mine is volunteering," said Irene, a slender grandmom with an easy smile, short-cropped silvery hair, and a slight accent that betrayed her New England roots. A fidgety sort, she couldn't sit still for long. Leonard, on the other hand, moved slowly in deference to his artificial joints and degenerative arthritis. Mostly bald, with a rim of white hair and a ruddy complexion, he wore wide-brimmed glasses over pale blue eyes and hearing aids in his ears. Leonard's speech, like his movement, was deliberate, as he talked in a deep but soft voice. And his stance was slightly hunched from the wearing down of his body.

"I used to be five feet eight and a half," he chuckled. "Now I'm down to five feet eight."

Irene spent a lot of time in the kitchen during my visit; it was clearly her domain. But beneath a north-facing window, sharing counter space with her catalogs and fruit bowls, was a pair of binoculars. That window, it turned out, was an excellent spot to watch the birds at Leonard's ten feeders. Seven hung from a rope tied off to aspens, all but one topped by umbrella-shaped plastic domes to keep squirrels away and protect against snow or rain. Three hanging feeders contained suet or peanut butter for jays, chickadees, and woodpeckers. The others were filled with shelled and chipped sunflower seeds: redpoll food. Always the inventive tinkerer, Leonard had built a rope-and-pulley system to raise and lower the feeders, another defense against squirrels. And neighborhood cats.

The three remaining feeders sat atop piles of worn tires stacked waist high. All were baited with seeds. I say "baited" for good reason. Those platform feeders were metal cages divided into four compartments, each with its own trap door. When Leonard wasn't banding, he propped the doors open so redpolls could freely come and go. When it was time to catch some birds, he set the doors to fall shut when tripped by hungry redpolls. Three of Leonard's hanging feeders also did double duty as traps. Each could be set so that redpolls easily entered, but not so easily escape.

The system worked admirably. Working alone for a few hours in the afternoon, Leonard might capture and band twenty to eighty redpolls on a given day. Not wishing to harm them, he wouldn't trap when temperatures fell below 10°F. Any colder, and redpolls might freeze their eyes against a trap's metal mesh as they struggled to escape. "I've seen it happen," he admitted. "Tissue will pull right off the eye."

Given the temperature constraints and Fairbanks' frigid winter weather, Leonard wouldn't normally start banding until late February or early March. He then stopped in April or May, when the redpolls dispersed to breed. Though slowed by arthritis and artificial parts, he still aimed to band a thousand birds every winter and most years he succeeded. When I arrived on March 9, he had already caught, banded, and released five hundred birds.

My first full day at the Peyton homestead, I followed Leonard out to the feeders, along a path he had shoveled through three feet of snow. The thermometer registered 18° on a beautifully clear afternoon, the sun blazing across a cobalt-blue sky like a slow-moving welder's arc. A stiff breeze quickly numbed fingers and hands when removed from gloves.

Plenty of seed remained in the cages, so all that Leonard had to do was set the trap doors. Finished within fifteen minutes, we returned to the house to wait and warm up. Soon enough we were back outside, transferring redpolls from cages to a plywood box. An avian jailhouse, it was divided into six holding cells, each with an inward-swinging front door and wire-mesh window at the opposite end.

We went from cage to cage, Leonard repeating a routine he'd done thousands of times: reaching in, he cornered a desperately flapping redpoll, gently grasped the bird in his hand, and transferred it from cage to box. Though they fluttered wildly and chirped noisily while trying to escape Leonard's grip, most redpolls went limp once in his hand. Only pounding hearts and shining black eyes hinted of the distress they must feel.

"Would you like to try?" Leonard asked.

Of course. He cautioned me to hold them firmly but gently. Weighing less than an ounce, redpolls and other small songbirds can easily be squashed or suffocated.

Earlier in my visit, I had asked Irene if she too was interested in birds. Her blunt "Nope" was followed by a long pause. Then she added, "I had a bad experience once, when netting birds. That was enough for me." Working with Leonard, I learned the rest of the story. Long ago, when banding migrating songbirds in their yard, he invited Irene to help. Grabbing hold of a robin, Irene squeezed the bird tightly, afraid it might escape. The robin died. Since then she had stayed apart from Leonard's studies.

Before I attempted to grab a bird, Leonard showed me another of his tricks. Redpolls seem to especially calm down when their heads are gently grasped between two fingers. Holding one this way, he inspected the left leg, to see if it already wore an aluminum band. If so, he would check the numbers imprinted on it; if part of the series being used that particular winter, the redpoll gained its freedom. If from a previous year, the bird would go inside for further study. Such recaptures were exceedingly rare. Of the twenty thousand-plus redpolls Leonard would eventually band, surprisingly few were caught again, by Leonard or anyone else. The average, he figured, was two or three per thousand.

Leonard believed that the low recapture rate reflected redpolls' short lifespan—few live beyond three years, he said—in combination with their erratic, gypsy-like lifestyles and occasional long-distance travels. Redpolls, like other northern seed-eating songbirds, sometimes go on southbound "irruptions," when local seed crops are poor. Those flights may take them from the Interior into Southcentral Alaska or even into Canada and the Lower 48. One of Leonard's banded birds was found two years later near Montreal, four thousand miles to the southeast. Another bird, banded at Quebec City, ended up in his trap. Other banded redpolls were found in Nome, where a cat killed the bird, and in Wasilla, near Anchorage. "What this tells me," he said, "is that they're spread all across Alaska and Canada. That's a helluva big area without a lot of people looking at birds."

Besides watching birds, someone would have to be looking for bands and somehow catch the bird (or find one that had died, such as that one in Nome) to report the recapture. Though hundreds, perhaps thousands, of different redpolls visited my Hillside feeders over the years, I rarely checked to see whether or not a metal ring encircled any of their legs (and then only after learning about Leonard's project). The chance of a banded redpoll visiting a feeder and being noticed were slim; the odds of one being caught were miniscule.

Though admittedly frustrated by the low return on his investment, Leonard was a persistent man who embraced a challenge. "I think most people would get discouraged," said Irene. "Not Leonard. He just keeps doing what he loves."

Finally, I got my chance to hold a redpoll. I cornered one of the caged birds and carefully cradled it in my hand. A mature male with a trace of pink on his breast, he felt incredibly light. I noticed the softness of the feathers and the rapid beating of the heart, and I saw alertness in those dark, shining eyes. *What do birds make of us?* I asked myself yet again. *Do they feel fear or resignation while in our grasp? Or something similar to relief, when released?*

Leonard never worried about such fanciful possibilities. While I may ponder the emotional lives of birds or how they perceive the world, he was concerned with the nuts and bolts of redpoll behavior and coloration, the nature of their seasonal travels, and whether redpolls should be classified as one species or two.

Ornithologists for many years have divided redpolls into two species: common (*Carduelis flammea*) and hoary (*Carduelis hornemanni*). Hoary redpolls are pale birds, with white, unstreaked rumps and undertail feathers; commons are darker, with heavier streaking. This sounds good in theory and looks even better in guidebook illustrations; but in the wild, even birding experts often have trouble telling them apart.

Influenced by field guides and knowledgeable birders, I had always imagined hoaries to be very light birds, almost white on their rumps and undersides—descriptions that fit only two or three of the many redpolls I've seen. But during my visit, Leonard showed me birds that I would unequivocally identify as common redpolls and told me with great certainty that they were hoaries. And he showed me why. Number 92201, for instance, had a relatively short bill, weak rump streaking and only partial streaking of its undertail feathers. All were characteristic of hoary redpolls. Yet overall the bird appeared dark, with dark brown streaking of wings and back.

Leonard wasn't surprised a bit by my confusion. "I've probably handled more redpolls than anyone, and even I can't be sure until I've got one in hand." Even with his standardized codes, the distinction sometimes would become an arbitrary one, because there's so much apparent overlap between the two types.

After closely observing thousands of redpolls, Leonard was convinced that common and hoary redpolls are variations of a single species. "From what I've seen," he told me, "there's a complete gradation from almost white to dark brown redpolls and everything in between." Once he found a mating pair in which "the female was almost dead white and the male was very dark."

Though he held a minority opinion, Peyton wasn't alone in his lumping. In 1985, after years of studying redpoll plumage and skeletal characteristics, Declan Troy recommended in a professional paper that hoary and common redpolls be considered extreme forms of a single species. Still, the consensus has been that the two are separate. After visiting the Peytons, I contacted Dan Gibson, manager of the University of Alaska Fairbanks bird collection. And he admitted, "It's a complicated thing and not completely resolved. I'm not sure it will ever be."

As Leonard shared more of his findings and ideas, it became clear he was something of a maverick who relished taking on the conventional wisdom. And speaking his mind. Another example: his theory on hoary redpoll migrations. Over time, he had noticed that large numbers of pale redpolls invade the Fairbanks area every four to six years. They stick around briefly, then disappear. Because no one had found an Alaskan locale where hoary redpolls are consistently abundant from year to year, Leonard speculated they're Siberian residents that "get blown over here when the winds are just right." Once in Alaska, they disperse. "Redpolls are very strong flyers," he added as an afterthought. "And it really isn't that far [from Siberia to northwest Alaska]. It could happen."

Gibson called Peyton's theory "interesting," but emphasized, "like Leonard says, it's speculation. There's no data that I know of to support his idea."

In contrast with Gibson's polite response, was Leonard's blunt comment: "Other ornithologists think I'm crazy. They say there's no evidence. But no one is studying redpolls in Siberia. How can anyone know?"

The winter of 1999–2000 happened to be one of those hoary-abundant winters. Of the first five hundred redpolls he banded, Leonard identified 71 percent as the pale variety. I imagined what he might thinking. *Where do they come from? Where do they go?*

●⟩

With fifteen birds in the holding box, Leonard entered the cellar workshop that doubled as his laboratory. About ten feet square, its walls held dozens of carpentry tools, while paint cans, cords, and jars overflowing with nails and screws filled wooden shelves. A board placed beneath a south-facing window became his lab bench. On it were the tools of his banding trade: pliers, rulers, a notebook.

Irene greeted us and, smiling sweetly, she warmly wrapped her hands around Leonard's, still numbed from handling traps and birds. Then he shuffled over to the bench and, one by one, began taking redpolls from the box.

First he squeezed an aluminum ring onto the bird's left leg. Next he measured the length of wings and beak. Then, using a standardized code that he'd adapted from another researcher, Leonard determined the color of the redpoll's cap (yellow to wine red), breast (no red to much pink or red) and cheeks (no red to large red patch), and the extent of streaking on its rump and undertail feathers (none to very strong). In all, he collected data in ten categories including age and sex. In many cases, he could only write a *U*—unknown—for sex. He couldn't get very specific about their age, either.

Leonard believed that the color of adult male redpoll breasts intensify with age, from light pink to dark red. But he admitted it was difficult to prove, given his low recapture rate: "I've just about given up trying to correlate breast-color intensity with age; I just don't get enough returning [banded] birds to be sure."

While Leonard worked, the still-boxed birds raised a ruckus. From their cells came a cacophony of fluttering wings, high-pitched whining trills, and a loud scraping from the pecking of beaks on metal screen. Once in hand, most birds again fell quiet. An occasional redpoll would open its beak, a defensive posture that offered little menace.

The entire process lasted two to three minutes. Then, the indignities ended, Leonard released each bird through the workshop window. The freed redpolls streaked for nearby trees, where they perched for up to fifteen minutes or more, as if regaining their bearings or composure. Again the question rose: *What must it be like, to be handled so and then turned loose?* I was reminded of the TV show, *The*

X-Files, and other stories of alien abductions. No harm was intended here. Leonard was gentle as he stroked, probed, and measured the birds. Yet even he admitted, "it's got to be a traumatic thing for them."

That trauma is an inherent part of the scientific process, so it wasn't something Leonard dwelled on. I, by contrast, instinctively reflected upon it. I habitually weigh the pros and cons whenever watching scientists capture and study wildlife, whether bears, moose, or songbirds. Scientists are taught to think in terms of populations. I see individuals being handled. How much of the darting, drugging, trapping, poking, measuring, collaring, or banding is necessary? I recognize the value of wildlife studies, yet I also see how they feed on the western notion of other creatures as "things" instead of beings.

Leonard assured me, "Any animal that's wild, I treat with respect." But how respectful is the science?

Long ago, while growing up in California, Leonard would take walks with his father. A self-taught naturalist, Sidney Peyton knew the landscape around his home as well as anyone. He was especially good at identifying birds and knowing where to find them. "If anyone wanted to see California condors in those days, they'd go with Dad," Leonard recalled. "I remember seeing twenty or thirty in the sky at once."

Among his other interests, Sidney collected bird eggs. It's something "the environmentalists would have a conniption fit over" nowadays, Leonard reflected, "but back then it wasn't as big a deal." Over time, his dad brought home hundreds of eggs, and sometimes the nests in which they lay (Leonard noted that birds often lay a second clutch in response to predation). Later donated to the Western Foundation for Vertebrate Zoology in Camarillo, California, the collection has been used by scientists studying DDT and its effects, because many of the eggs were taken before the age of DDT.

As a researcher, Leonard had also done his share of collecting: birds, small mammals, plants. Most occurred decades ago. When collecting birds he would shoot the desired specimen, gut it, fill the skin with cotton, and give it to the university or museum for study and display. In retirement the only specimens he collected were the occasional window-strike kills. "It's a job when you're doing it," he said matter-of-factly. "You're trying to gain as much information as possible. You need to have specimens if you're searching for evidence, for proof of something."

In the two days I spent with him, Leonard banded 54 redpolls, nearly two-thirds of them hoaries. That brought him to 559 for the year. He also trapped a northern shrike. Nicknamed "butcher birds" because they sometimes impale prey on sharp objects, shrikes are predatory songbirds with sharp, hooked bills. About the size of gray jays, they are mostly gray and white, with a black mask, wings, and tail. Handsome.

Leonard had suspected one might be in the neighborhood, because the redpolls—a favorite shrike prey—seemed so spooky. Any doubt was erased when we found a decapitated redpoll inside one of the traps. Leonard disliked having shrikes around, because they're disruptive and feed on "his" birds. So after finishing the day's redpoll banding, he baited a trap with the dead bird. A half hour later, watching from the kitchen, I saw the shrike fly in and try to grab the redpoll without going into the cage. Failing, it entered and triggered the trapdoor. Fluttering wildly and banging its head against the metal bars, the shrike bloodied its face in its aggressive attempts to escape.

"Oh, that's normal," said the unflappable Leonard.

Back out in the yard, he inserted his hand into the cage and deftly grabbed the shrike without being bitten—a much riskier task than corralling docile redpolls. The shrike was one he'd caught previously, in April 1999. After a few measurements, Leonard released the bird back into the wild, hoping the episode had been traumatic enough to keep the bird away from his feeders, for a few days at least.

Squirrels too were a problem, not only because they steal seeds, but will, when given the chance, prey on redpolls. Leonard admitted he had killed his share, but in recent years he'd found a less lethal solution: hot pepper sprinkled with the sunflower seeds. "It discourages them for a while," he explained. "And it's better than killing them, I guess." It proved to be an ideal solution, because birds are unaffected by the pepper.

No bears had been attracted to the feeders, but a moose calf once developed a taste for Leonard's seeds. In the process of feeding, the calf knocked over his tire platforms and generally raised havoc. An especially heavy dose of pepper prompted that moose to change its diet.

While he specialized in redpolls during his retirement, Leonard had banded more than fifty species of Alaska birds since the mid-1960s. Notebooks piled in his lab were filled with notes on everything from juncos to phalaropes. Once he did a sharp-shinned hawk. Yet for all the effort he'd put into banding, Leonard was best known locally for his recordings of bird songs.

During the eighteen years he chased fox sparrows across the north, Leonard also recorded other birds, taping seventy-two species in all. Years ago, he sent 270 reels of Alaska bird calls and songs to Cornell University's Library of Natural Sounds. Cornell's Lab of Ornithology later teamed with the Alaska Bird Observatory in Fairbanks to produce a tape of Alaskan bird songs, presumably recorded by Leonard. To his dismay, several songs didn't sound right. Upon checking, he learned that many had been recorded outside Alaska, sometimes thousands of miles away.

"I called the lab and told the guy in charge of sound that they'd screwed up," Leonard remembered. "Here they have all my Alaska recordings, and they're using ones from somewhere else. They'd been lazy about it."

The autumn before my visit, the Lab of Ornithology issued a brand-new double CD of Alaska bird songs and calls, with performances by 260 Alaska species, including several corrected renditions. Though more than fifty people helped out, Leonard was the major contributor. Both he and the CD had been praised by other Alaska ornithologists and the CD's release made news in both Fairbanks and Anchorage.

Leonard's fling with fame pleased Irene, a more public figure in Fairbanks because of her volunteer efforts with groups like the American Association of Retired Persons and League of Women Voters. "Usually it's been 'This is Leonard, Irene's husband.' Now he's better known around town for his own work," she cheerfully exclaimed.

Already well known among Alaska ornithologists for both his banding and recording work, Leonard would undoubtedly have gained greater acclaim—or notoriety—within scientific circles if he had published professional reports about his work, whether with fox sparrows or redpolls. "I'd like to write something up, some day. But the fact is, I have a lot more fun banding than writing a paper," he explained my last night at Peyton Place.

Our final conversation covered lots of territory: banding, CDs, volunteering, overseas travel, retirement, and memories of California. As we talked, Leonard's hearing aid occasionally squealed and Irene asked him to turn it down; it was set too high. Making an adjustment, Leonard sighed. Even with the aid, he could no longer hear high-pitched tones. "You can imagine how frustrating it is," he said, "for a birder to be unable to hear bird songs."

We talked a while longer, then Leonard slowly lifted himself from a chair. Stooped body supported by aching ankles, he shuffled to the computer room. For the next hour or two, he would transfer banding data into a program developed by the U.S. Geological Survey's Biological Service's Division. Eventually, the information would go to the agency's Maryland headquarters via the Internet.

In the morning, Leonard would again check the temperature and feeders. If the day warmed enough, he would set his traps, catch more redpolls, band, and release them. He would continue to do this, day after day, until the redpolls dispersed, while trying to figure out more details of their lives. It's what a determined, problem-solving scientist does, retired or not. Call it a hobby if you like. I call it passion.

Nine years after my visit and five years since his last redpoll banding season, I caught up with Leonard, who had moved with Irene to Seattle to be closer to their children and grandkids. He was more convinced than ever that common and hoary redpolls belong to a single species. In scientific lingo, they represent a cline, or physical variation found within a species or even population. "When you've checked and banded as many redpolls as I have and seen every shade from light to dark, you just know they have to be the same species." Furthermore, he added, "I think the light ones tend to occur along the coast and high in the mountains, though it's hard to say why."

Besides the substantial physical evidence he had gathered, Peyton pointed to genetic proof. Some years ago he had taken the lightest and darkest redpolls he could find and brought them to a geneticist at the University of Alaska Fairbanks. The outcome: "No difference."

Though Peyton's opinion had remained a minority view, there did seem to be movement toward his stance. He cited well-known artist and birding expert David Sibley as one prominent example.

Even stranger, perhaps, was this observation: during his backyard studies, Peyton banded a redpoll that returned, six years later, to nest in his yard and raise a brood. For a redpoll to live six or seven years is unusual in itself. But what really shocked him was the bird's coloration: the female had a reddish breast and flanks, normally considered characteristic of male redpolls.

"That shook me up for a while," he admitted. "But since then I've found a few other females that also had reddish breasts. My theory is that some females develop pink or reddish breasts as they age. If you look very closely, there are subtle differences with males. But it's further evidence that our assumptions [about redpolls and other life-forms] aren't always true."

During his years of banding, Peyton also distinguished males from females by measuring the length of their wings, known to ornithologists as "wing chords." By and large, female birds have shorter chords, from sixty-seven to seventy-three millimeters long. Male wing chords mostly ranged from seventy-four to eighty millimeters. Even with wing chords, then, there is room for ambiguity. Still, Peyton believed the male-female sexing data was significant enough to send to the USGS's banding lab at the Patuxent Wildlife Research Center in Maryland.

"That's the only data I've ever submitted," he said. "I've thought about publishing some of my findings, but never got around to it. The banding itself was the thing, not publication. And right now my data is a big mess. Maybe someday I'll try to put it all together, but I don't know. It would be a lot of work."

Leonard told me he continued to feed and watch birds, though he hadn't yet spotted any redpolls at his Washington feeders. "They just don't get down here very often." And though happy to live closer to family in a place with shorter, milder winters, he admitted he missed Alaska, his home for half a century. He missed the redpoll banding, too.

"It was such an interesting project," he recalled, "and so much happening. Sometimes there were so many redpolls that if I stood still, I could reach over and just pick one up. It was something, to be surrounded by so many birds."

Note: Leonard Peyton died in December 2010. This essay is dedicated to him and his work, his passion.

OTTER CATASTROPHE

We had been on Augustine Island less than half an hour when William reached into the seawater, pulled out a whitish, rounded object, and carried it back to shore.

"What do you think this was?" he asked, holding out a well-preserved skull.

Ellen and I took turns inspecting the skull, which was about the size—and roughly the shape—of a large pear. The big canine teeth told us the animal was some sort of meat eater, but the overall form was more rounded than any dog or bear skull I'd ever seen. So I was pretty darn sure its owner was neither ursine nor canine. Beyond that, we really couldn't say, since neither my friends nor I were well schooled in vertebrate anatomy.

Our best guess, given the skull's size and our location—a small Alaska island nearly seven miles from the nearest mainland shore—was a sea otter or a seal. We had already seen members of both species swimming through the lagoon.

William and Ellen were soon distracted by rising waters that threatened to soak our gear, piled on the sandy beach. Finally I set the skull aside, envious that William had discovered it and hopeful we would solve the species riddle.

A few hours later the riddle became a larger puzzle. On our evening beach walk, Ellen found another skull. Though slightly larger than the first, it had the same shape, bone structure, and tooth arrangement. Very strange. Back at camp, I felt my interest in the island shift ever so slightly.

What had drawn me here was the 4,500-foot rocky cone that formed, and continues to reshape, this seven-mile-wide piece of land in lower Cook Inlet.

Augustine Volcano has been popping its top on a regular basis since the first recorded eruption in 1812. Scientists have documented fourteen major "eruptive episodes" since then, which makes Augustine a hyperactive member of that exclusive club called the "Pacific Ring of Fire."

Some 180 miles southwest of Anchorage and only 75 miles from the Kenai Peninsula town of Homer (where we caught our plane ride here), Augustine had most recently vented a bunch of ash and larger debris in January 2006. Following the patterns of earlier eruptions, Augustine spewed ash several times, up to eight miles high, and the island rumbled with earthquakes for weeks. The volcano also vomited lava and pyroclastic flows, sometimes called *nuées ardentes*: explosive, superheated masses of gas-charged ash and debris that can roar down a volcano's flanks at speeds of up to one hundred miles per hour. The heated gases and liquids melted snow on Augustine's upper flanks, which resulted in several snow- and mudslides.

What better time to explore the island, I reasoned, than soon after its face had received an extreme makeover? As long as the volcano had reentered a dormant phase.

I scheduled my trip to coincide with a visit by volcano researchers. I figured that if a geology crew was on the island, it must be safe. Then I recruited friends to join me. Ellen and William rose to the bait of an unusual summer adventure and so here we were, camped along the edge of an explosively active volcano, but one that had recently been downgraded to "green." To scientists, that meant a "noneruptive background state." To us it meant safe to visit.

Our third day on the island, we amateur explorers headed out on an extended beach walk. We were determined to find a break in the thick walls of alder that bordered the recently benign side of Augustine, and investigate its newest lava flows.

Within a quarter mile of camp, we were surprised to find the body of a sea otter, floated by tides up on the boulder beach. The animal must have died recently, because the body remained intact. There was no sign of scavenging or decay, no stench, no sign even of the flies and other insects that lay eggs and feed upon dead flesh. No sign of trauma, either, as we turned the animal with our feet.

I'd never been this close to a sea otter before, and its size surprised me: four feet long and hefty; fifty to sixty pounds, I guessed. I couldn't imagine its death was tied in any way to malnutrition. A close inspection of the animal's head and teeth confirmed that the skulls we'd found earlier also belonged to sea otters. What was going on?

A hundred yards farther up the beach, we were shocked to find another dead otter on the beach, also an adult. This one had begun to decay, but just barely. The body emitted a faint stench and the densely furred back feet had begun to decompose. Again, there was no evidence the otter had been physically harmed.

Our discoveries seemed bizarre, especially given our short time on the island, and the fact that the skulls and carcasses had been scattered along a mile-long stretch of beach. We questioned whether the deaths were somehow tied to Augustine's eruption. Could toxic chemicals have accumulated in the lagoon? Yet this part of the island had been barely touched, if at all, by the 2006 eruption. I made a mental note to contact the U.S. Fish and Wildlife Service (FWS) upon my return to Anchorage and see if its marine mammal researchers had some answers.

Near the end of our nine- to ten-mile walkabout, William noticed several sea otters scattered through the lagoon. A quick count identified at least a dozen, including some youngsters calmly back paddling, diving for food, or playing among themselves.

"I guess here they don't have to worry about getting eaten by orcas," William observed.

"But little do they know that something more insidious may lurk in the lagoon," I added, only half joking.

Not long after my return to Anchorage, I sent an email to the local FWS office, describing our discoveries and seeking answers. My query got passed along to Angela Doroff, a marine mammal biologist, and she quickly responded with a request for the dates and locations of our finds.

Doroff wasn't surprised. Augustine's dead and dying otters were likely part of a larger die-off that was tied to a bacterial infection. Researchers had connected the bacterium *Streptococcus infantarius ss coli* to scores of sea otter deaths since 2002. The bacteria spread through the blood and, it appeared, lead to an inflammation of tissues lining heart valves. The result was paralysis and, from what the scientists had learned so far, almost certain death. But they still didn't fully understand the relationship of the bacteria to the heart problems.

Though the *coli* bacteria had infected otters from the Aleutians to Cook Inlet, the great majority of reported deaths were in and around Kachemak Bay, fifty miles west of Augustine Island. The die-off there had prompted the FWS to declare an "Unusual Mortality Event," or UME. Researchers studying that event were especially troubled by the fact that nearly half of the otters they'd studied were in the prime of sea otter life, between four and ten years of age. As Doroff noted, it was worrisome to see prime-age animals dying.

When most people think about sea otters, they likely picture cute, cuddly animals swimming placidly on ocean waters, perhaps cracking mussel shells or nibbling on crabmeat. Or bobbing in ocean swells, looking with wide-eyed curiosity at a passing boat filled with camera-toting humans.

For all their brown-eyed, furry cuteness, sea otters are ferocious predators, kept healthy by a seafood diet that includes clams, crabs, mussels, sea urchins, and fish. The otters help keep near-shore ecosystems healthy. Their role is important enough, Doroff said, that scientists consider sea otters a "keystone species." Their presence ensures a richer and more diverse community of life-forms.

From a big-picture perspective, the otters' most important prey may be sea urchins. Without otters to hold their numbers in check, urchins in some coastal areas have laid waste to the kelp beds that provide shelter and food for all manner of sea creatures, from fish and crabs to seabirds and marine mammals. That loss, Doroff remarked, is nothing short of alarming.

Nearly six months after my visit to Augustine and five months after the FWS issued its "unexplained sea otter die-off" news release, the agency put out an international call for help to experts in marine mammal diseases, but a scheduled meeting in Homer was canceled for lack of funding. Plans were being made to study otters in Lower Cook Inlet and Kamishak Bay the following summer, and the researchers hoped to visit Augustine, assuming they had enough money. In the meantime, the UME team continued to receive dead otters found by locals and also arranged for a volunteer to monitor beaches in the Homer area.

Up north in Anchorage, I pulled the two sea otter skulls from a plastic bag for closer study (both had been properly registered with the FWS as required by federal regulations), then added them to other mammal remains I had collected over the years: a grizzly bear skull, a moose jaw, horns from a young Dall sheep, vertebrae from a caribou.

The naturalist in me wondered about the sea otter die-off: how it started, how the bacterium was passed around, how it all would end. But another part of me was haunted by our disturbing discoveries and images I'd carried home from Augustine.

On our last day on the island, a sea otter had swum near camp, about one hundred feet offshore. Now and then the otter would turn toward shore and appear to watch us intently, seemingly curious about our doings. But mostly it swam back and forth, back and forth, as if it didn't have a care in the world.

"NICE" WEATHER GETS SEALS HOT

We had come to the Pribilof Islands during a most unusual summer in the Bering Sea. Notorious for its rain, fog, wind, and 45°F summer days, this group of remote volcanic islands off Alaska's southwest coast had by late June already experienced a year's worth of blue skies. During our weeklong visit, the Pribilofs were blessed by six straight days of bright sunshine, with occasional fog and clouds mixed in to keep things from getting too boring. A sublime stretch of weather, my companions and I agreed as we luxuriated in near-sixty-degree temperatures, the Bering Sea's version of a heat wave.

Of course "blessed" and "sublime" offer a narrowly human perspective on the weather. Or to be more specific, a tourist's point of view. We visitors to Alaska's outer reaches have a great appreciation for sun, blue skies, and warmth, especially when the stay is short and there's an abundance of wildlife to be seen and photographed. But it's unlikely that St. Paul's fur seals welcomed this extended spell of unusually warm and sunny weather.

Located some three hundred miles from the mainland, St. Paul is the largest and best known of the Pribilof's five islands. It's also the one that's a tourism magnet: people come here from around the world each summer to see wildlife. Among the primary draws are the island's many species of birds. And its seals.

At the time of our visit, the Pribilof archipelago was summer home to nearly a million northern fur seals, two-thirds of the world's population (though the islands' population would later drop dramatically, to less than seven hundred thousand animals, for unclear reasons). The great majority of those Pribilof seals congregate on St. Paul's boulder and sand beaches. Black to brownish-black in color, these fish- and squid-eating predators spend most of their time at sea, but they return here each summer to mate and produce young; or, in the case of nonbreeders, to simply hang out and rest.

Being built for watery environments, fur seals don't mind the Pribilof's usual mix of fog, drizzle, and occasional downpours. In fact they rather appreciate moisture and cloud cover when hauled up on land. Long periods of direct sunlight, on the other hand, tend to overheat the seals with their high fat content and thick fur—three hundred thousand hairs per square inch. (Dense enough to be waterproof, the species' impressively warm underfur is what made *Callorhinus ursinus* so popular with fur traders in the eighteenth, nineteenth, and early twentieth centuries.)

Sunshine is especially hard on mature male seals, which arrive at St. Paul in May to stake out their breeding grounds; females don't show up until weeks later. Once they've established a territory—in which they build harems that may number up to one hundred females—breeding bulls usually don't leave their turf for several weeks. They may lose up to 25 percent of their 450- to 600-pound body weight during this period, while neither eating nor drinking.

Such fasting combined with an intense competition for females can make a fella irritable. So fur seal males don't show much patience with each other—or in some instances the females with which they breed. In fact they become violent while competing for prime harem-collection sites, the best being those nearest the ocean.

The baking effect of sunny weather only serves to aggravate an already tense situation. My theory is that it makes ornery fur seal males even grumpier.

While it's hot and sunny, bulls are hesitant to fight, because of overheating. So, in human terms, they stuff their anger. (This is only a theory, remember.) Eventually, all the pent-up frustration has to be released. And I believe that's what happened one evening during our St. Paul sojourn.

It began at 10:00 P.M. with a strong, cool wind blowing and a thick, newly arrived blanket of clouds overhead, thus ending a long spell of mostly sunny weather. Apparently, conditions were right for the pressure valve to be released. For the next half hour, two to three dozen bulls directly in front of the viewing blind (built for fur seal watchers and photographers) raged out of control. Mostly they snarled, roared, and threatened each other. But there was fighting, too. Intense, vicious battles.

Heads bobbing and weaving like two heavyweight boxers, the seals feinted, ducked, jabbed. But instead of throwing punches, they came at each other with wide-open mouths filled with sharp, flesh-tearing teeth. Showing incredibly quick reflexes, they snapped and counter-snapped, pulling out clumps of hair, tearing gashes in each other's flesh, and giving new clarity to the phrase "the fur is flying." Occasionally a bull would grab its rival's fur, usually around the head or neck, and keep its mouth clamped there for several seconds.

As a fight progressed, other males moved closer as though drawn by the energy of combat. The interlopers often ganged up on any bulls that showed weakness in battle. And in a couple instances, defeated combatants were forced to run a gauntlet of slashing teeth, assaulted from all sides as they retreated down the beach and escaped into the water. Nasty business, being a beaten bull. No mercy was shown, none at all.

At about 10:30 P.M., the charged atmosphere seemed to dissipate as suddenly as it had erupted. With territories for the most part unchanged, bulls settled back in. Some napped, others attended to their harems. And a few licked their wounds. One old fighter lay slumped on the beach, his head and body laced with jagged, bleeding cuts.

Locals told us the fighting would worsen as the breeding season progressed, as unimaginable as that seemed. Even females are sometimes ripped apart when caught between bulls who are fighting to increase their harem size. But I'm guessing the fights we witnessed had a lot to do with weather as well as sexual drive and frustration. Being a fur seal is tough enough without having to endure long spells of sublimely sunny weather. One of the reasons they spend their summers at St. Paul is the island's cool, moist climate.

The seals finally caught a break in the weather our final day at St. Paul, when blue heavens gave way to thick gray clouds and heavy downpours. Drenched by chilling, wind-driven rain, we visitors watched the seals one last time. Lifting their heads toward the storm-darkened skies, they barked loudly, uproariously. I like to think it was their way of saying thanks for the long-delayed arrival of beautiful weather, a reminder that what's best for us tourists is not necessarily what's best for the locals, fur seals or otherwise.

MYSTERY OF ALASKA'S
DEFORMED-BILL CHICKADEES

It took me decades to really notice birds, to give them my full attention. When I did finally invite them into my life at age forty-four, I fell deeply—and, some friends might say, madly—in love with our winged and feathered neighbors, especially the little ones that swarm backyard feeders throughout Alaska's long and harsh winters.

In the beginning, while caught up in the pure delight of feeding wild birds, I believed the activity to be an absolutely benign and good thing, offering rewards to both the birds and me. Over time, however, I experienced what might be called the "shadow side" of backyard bird feeding: the loss of feeder birds to window strikes, predation by raptors and cats, and the spread of avian diseases, for instance the salmonella outbreak that devastated Anchorage's redpoll population in the late 1990s.

Then in the early 2000s I learned that we Alaskan bird-feeding enthusiasts might inadvertently be contributing to a new epidemic of sorts, one that has harmed thousands of resident songbirds, particularly my beloved black-capped chickadees.

Researchers emphasized that any connection between backyard bird feeding and Alaska's unprecedented outbreak of deformed-bill songbirds was mere speculation, an unproven, working hypothesis. A long shot, at best. Even if bird feeding was ultimately implicated, they explained, it was only part of the problem, a secondary factor. And in the bigger picture, feeding seeds to local wild birds still likely did more good than harm.

And yet I agonized over the possibility, haunted that in some complicated and roundabout way, I might be harming the critters I love. But it wasn't just me, of course. Thousands of Alaskans annually feed chickadees and other songbirds. Should I keep my worries to myself? Or should I at least alert people to something insidious that *might* be going on? What were my obligations to chickadees and other bird-feeding enthusiasts?

As with most of life, there are no easy answers. But there is a story to share about the strange and disheartening phenomenon of Alaska's deformed-bill chickadees and its broader implications.

The story, as it involves me, begins in the mid-1990s, when Southcentral Alaska was hit by a devastating outbreak of spruce bark beetles. By the time the beetles reached Anchorage, they'd already swept through millions of forested acres, killing innumerable spruce. To protect their trees, many local residents sprayed pesticides or hired companies to do so.

The weapon of choice was carbaryl, a supposedly "gentle" toxin—a notion that has always seemed oxymoronic to me—that entomologists and forestry experts insisted would do little, if any, harm to forest wildlife. I've always questioned that.

Despite lingering doubts, I too chose to protect "my" trees on Anchorage's Hillside by spraying them with carbaryl. And I prayed my choice wouldn't do more harm than good.

Two years after starting the carbaryl treatments I began to hear and read stories of strange-looking chickadees with malformed beaks. By fall 1999, scores of sightings had been reported throughout Southcentral Alaska.

The stories stirred my interest and disheartened me in an abstract sort of way. Could the disfigured birds somehow be connected to the widespread carbaryl spraying? But the truly awful nature of the deformities didn't jolt me until a black-capped chickadee with a grotesque, hook-shaped bill showed up at my feeders.

Could I have contributed to this chickadee's plight by spraying chemicals in my yard? Anxious that I was somehow complicit in the bird's disfigurement, I contacted the researchers studying the outbreak. They assured me they'd found no evidence linking carbaryl to the beak deformities. Still, they hadn't ruled out contaminants. In fact human-produced toxins seemed a likely causative agent.

I knew I had to learn more.

Black-capped chickadees first gained my attention a half century ago, when I lived along the edge of rural Connecticut. Like other common New England birds, they quickly faded into the background of my world, for as a boy I was drawn to more exotic creatures: snakes and salamanders, frogs and turtles and trout.

My general disinterest in birds lasted nearly four decades, until I settled in the foothills along Anchorage's eastern edge. On a Saturday morning in 1993, shortly before the winter solstice, I was lolling in bed, when I happened to glance outside. In the wooded backyard, several black-capped chickadees flitted about a backyard spruce.

Wonderful, I thought. *Here's a chance to meet some of my new neighbors.*

Inspired by their presence, and on something of a whim, I put an old, slightly bent baking pan on the back deck railing and piled on sunflower seeds. Nothing happened that first day. But on Sunday, while seated at the dining room table, I watched a chickadee land on the tray, grab a seed, and zoom off to a nearby tree. Then in flashed another. And a third. For each, the routine was similar: dart in, look around, peck at the tray, grab a seed, look around some more, and dart back out. Nervous little creatures, full of bright energy, they soon had me laughing at their antics. By the time they moved on, I sensed an all-too-rare upwelling of fascination and joy.

Within days, a whole new world opened up as woodland neighbors I'd never known, or even imagined, joined the black-caps at my feeders: red-breasted nuthatches, common redpolls, pine grosbeaks, and pine siskins.

My newfound interest in birds grew quickly, surprising even me. What started as mere curiosity quickly bloomed into a consuming passion. I roamed bookstores in search of birding guidebooks; spontaneously exchanged bird descriptions with a stranger; and purchased fifty-pound bags of sunflower seeds. All of this seemed very strange to a middle-aged guy who had previously judged bird-watchers to be rather odd sorts. I didn't know what it meant, except that a door had opened. And I passed through.

My interest soon expanded outward from my feeders to the local landscape's forests, coastal flats, and tundra, and even farther beyond, to Alaska's far reaches. Helped along by local experts, I gradually learned to recognize the songs, calls, and markings of dozens of species. But my favorites have remained the songbirds that stay here year-round, adding bright voices and lively energy to our largely dormant winter landscape.

Several years after black-capped chickadees flew back into my life, our evolving relationship took an unexpected and alarming turn. A photograph in the March 1, 1998, edition of the *Anchorage Daily News* foreshadowed that disheartening twist. The image grabbed my attention because it featured two black-caps, perched on a spruce tree hung with Christmas lights. Only on close inspection did it become clear that one of the chickadees had an unusually curved beak. Though it struck me as weird, I didn't dwell on the deformity. Freakish things sometimes happen in nature.

The photo also grabbed Colleen Handel's attention. For her, it presented a disturbing sense of déjà vu.

A biologist with the U.S. Geological Survey's Alaska Science Center, Handel had seen similarly deformed chickadees only weeks earlier. Sandy Talbot, a friend and colleague, had invited Handel over to see some odd-looking black-caps that were visiting Talbot's south Anchorage feeders. The women captured one, trimmed its beak to normal size, and then released it back into the wild.

"I didn't really think much about it afterward," Handel later told me. "I just considered it an anomaly, one of those things that happen now and then."

Then Handel came across the picture of a deformed-bill chickadee. Though just like the birds she'd seen at Talbot's home, this one inhabited the Big Lake area, some thirty miles away as a raven flies. A chickadee would rarely, if ever, travel so far.

"That's when the alarm bell rang," Handel recalled. "It seemed more than a coincidence."

Wanting to know how many more curved-bill chickadees might inhabit Southcentral Alaska's woodlands, Handel "put out the word" through local birding and conservation groups and the media. Almost immediately, she was inundated by phone calls, e-mails, and letters: "It was crazy. The phone was just ringing off the hook."

It turned out that many residents had sighted chickadees with strange-looking beaks. All had assumed they were simply seeing oddities of nature. Yet those oddities quickly added up to some four hundred curved-bill birds. Nearly all inhabited Alaska's heavily populated Southcentral region. And the great majority were black-caps.

Handel learned that the earliest deformed chickadee sightings had been recorded in 1991, some three hundred miles apart. The great distance between those two initial sightings and the fact that chickadees are strongly faithful to their home territories suggested to her that "the causative agent was widely spread across the region" when the outbreak began, rather than starting at a point source and widening outward.

Startled by the huge response, Handel followed up with residents who reported deformed-bill songbirds at their feeders. None could recall seeing deformed birds before 1990, including several "old-timers" who'd been feeding birds for many years. And few people noticed them before the middle of the decade. She was therefore confident that the deformed-bill epidemic began in the early nineties and began to pick up steam in the following years.

Though she'd previously worked mostly with shorebirds and water-fowl, Handel found this puzzle too intriguing to ignore. In 1999 she got approval to study Alaska's deformed-bill songbirds. Among her team's priorities: put together a list of things that might produce deformed beaks. Some, like blunt trauma and exposure to extreme heat, were easy to eliminate. When finished, the researchers had a list of five possible causes that had to be considered: disease, parasites, genetic abnormalities, nutritional deficiencies, and exposure to contaminants.

Handel and her colleagues also extended their citizen outreach effort through press releases, media interviews, newsletters of local Audubon Society chapters, and personal appearances at local schools and meetings hosted by conservation and birding groups. The public response was overwhelming and greatly impressed Handel: "People have been wonderful in keeping track of deformed-bill birds. We've had many incredible observers, people meticulous in their notes."

Media reports of Handel's work grabbed my attention. I mentally filed it away as possible story material, but didn't think much more about either her study or the deformed-bill birds until months later. While glancing outside at twilight in November 1999, I noticed a small bird on the peanut butter feeder that hung above my upper deck.

A closer look revealed the bird to be a black-capped chickadee, perched motionless on the feeder; most peculiar behavior for a bird that is normally among the most frenetic of creatures. A minute or more passed and still the bird remained stationary, feet clutching the spruce-bough feeder, head tucked against its breast.

Something had to be wrong.

Through binoculars, I focused in for a closer look. As the bird's image sharpened, it became clear that this chickadee was indeed unusual: its upper bill was the shape of a hook. Instantly, my stomach and mind began to churn.

Not here, not in my yard, I silently moaned. Just like that, the outbreak of deformed-bill chickadees became a personal concern. *What the hell is going on? Why is this happening?*

The chickadee finally began poking at the peanut butter, but the elongated bill clearly hampered its efforts to get a good mouthful. Bits of peanut butter stuck to the outer bill and the bird would stop occasionally to wipe the excess off.

This lone, sad black-cap continued to cling tenaciously to the feeder long after the other chickadees had left to find shelter for the night. Then, with twilight easing into darkness, it fluttered off into the gloom.

The hook-billed chickadee continued to visit deep into December, often alone. It had adapted well to peanut butter feeding. Head turned to the side, the bird scraped its curved beak across the cold-stiffened goo and then maneuvered the food from bill to mouth. In more than a month of observation I didn't once see the black-cap grab a sunflower seed, its species' preferred winter food.

Once settled on the hanging feeder, the hook-billed bird was hard to dislodge. It largely ignored the other chickadees that came zooming in, intimidated into giving up its spot only by the more-aggressive nuthatches and larger woodpeckers. I tried to determine if the beak was growing longer, but couldn't really say. My desire to call Handel was tempered by the fear that she'd want to "collect" the chickadee as a specimen. I figured I could simply say no to that, but decided to hold off contacting her. I also worried anew about my spraying of carbaryl to protect the yard's spruce.

As the weeks passed, the hooked-bill chickadee's plumage grew ever more disheveled and dirty, as its deformed beak made grooming more difficult. Consequently its feathers provided less insulation from the cold. That, plus the challenges of eating, seemed to rob the chickadee of its vitality and tenacity. Finally, after weeks of daily visits, the black-cap failed to show. And it never came again.

Another leap forward, this time to May 2001. The staff at Anchorage's Campbell Creek Science Center had invited Handel to discuss her chickadee study at its monthly "Fireside Chat." Now deeply immersed in the deformed-bird phenomenon, I joined dozens of other locals in the center's meeting room.

After a few introductory comments, Handel directed her attention toward the younger audience members. "Who knows Sherlock Holmes?"

Several wiggling hands shot up and a young voice rose from the seats up front. "He's a detective."

"Right," Handel smiled. "Well my colleagues and I are sort of like detectives, too. This is kind of like a murder mystery. A lot of birds are dying, but we don't know why. We don't know the ending.

"What we do," she added, "is sometimes called scientific sleuthing."

Over the next hour or so, Handel described how she got involved in this particular case, the team she put together, what they'd learned so far, the possible causes of the deformities and "next steps." By spring 2001, the number of deformed-bill chickadees sighted in Alaska had jumped to more than seven hundred; by contrast, only nine had *ever* been reported elsewhere in the United States and Canada. Deformities had also been found in twenty other Alaskan species, but in much smaller numbers.

A couple of Handel's comments were especially startling. First, "whatever is happening, is happening right here in Alaska." More specifically, the data suggested a concentration of deformed birds in Alaska's most populous region, Anchorage and the neighboring Matanuska-Susitna Valleys.

Second, the number of disfigured chickadees in those areas had increased exponentially since the winter of 1991–92, with "a big jump" since the winter of 1995–96. In 1999, the prevalence of deformed chickadees was 2 percent of the population; by 2001, it has skyrocketed to 10 percent. To make those results perfectly clear to her audience, Handel noted, "Those numbers are high and quite alarming."

Almost nine years later, the numbers remained alarming. And though they had eliminated some possible "suspects" in their nearly decade-long investigation,

Handel and her fellow sleuths were still a ways from solving this deadly riddle.

By late 2009, Handel and her research team had documented more than twenty-five hundred deformed-bill birds in Alaska, spread across thirty species. Their numbers included both migrants and year-round inhabitants, but the vast majority were resident passerines. The one constant: most had been observed since the late 1990s, primarily within Southcentral Alaska.

In recent years, a growing number of corvids—jays, magpies, crows, and ravens—had turned up with deformed bills. But no single species, or even group of birds, was as hard-hit as black-capped chickadees. Between 1991 and 2009, Alaskans reported some three thousand sightings of deformed-bill black-caps, which researchers were confident represented at least twenty-one hundred individual birds. That was nearly fifteen times higher than the second-most affected species, northwestern crows, and more than eighty percent of the total count.

From citizen reports and their own studies, the researchers were able to identify several different types of deformities. In most birds the upper bill was overgrown, often with a conspicuous downward curve. In some, the lower bill was also overgrown and curved upward, producing a distinctly crossed beak. A few had overgrown upper and lower bills that didn't cross; that typically caused a noticeable gap between them. More rarely, only the lower bill was elongated. And rarest of all were bills that curved to the side.

In every case but one, beak deformities were limited to the beak's outer, keratin sheath, known as the "rhamphotheca." Like human fingernails, the rhamphotheca grows continuously throughout a bird's life and—in normal circumstances—is simultaneously worn down through pecking and feeding. The net effect is a bill that retains its "normal" length and shape.

Anything that affects the alignment of a bird's mandibles, bone growth, or rate of bill growth and abrasion could cause a beak deformity, whether genetic or developmental. Possibilities include mutagens that affect the proteins tied to beak growth, liver disease, avian viruses, certain parasites, nutritional deficiencies, or an imbalance of calcium and phosphorous.

More than a tenth of the deformed-bill chickadees displayed other physical abnormalities. Those included missing patches of feathers and dry, reddened skin, especially in the head area. Some also had dry, flaky legs. All could be symptomatic of vitamin or calcium deficiencies. Handel noted that seed-based diets were usually lacking in vitamin A and calcium; and the high fat content of seeds could also interfere with calcium absorption. If chickadees became overly reliant on, say, sunflower seeds put out by bird feeders, they might develop nutritional shortages that could in turn affect beak growth.

❧

To put this epidemic of chickadee deformities in perspective, consider that over the same eighteen-year period, less than two dozen deformed-bill black-capped chickadees were reported from the rest of the United States *and* Canada, despite a national call for sightings of such disfigured birds.

Another measure of the outbreak's severity was the prevalence of beak deformities in black-capped chickadee populations, as determined by catch, tag, and release studies in the Anchorage area and Matanuska-Susitna Valleys. Handel and her colleagues had found beak deformities in more than 8 percent of the chickadees captured since 2000—one in twelve birds. In other words, deformed-bill black-caps were shockingly common in parts of Alaska. Strangely, the prevalence of beak deformities remained low for boreal chickadees and red-breasted nuthatches, two species that share similar habitat and have similar foraging behaviors to black-caps.

Nothing like this had ever been recorded among wild songbird populations in North America or even worldwide.

Besides the obvious question of what could cause such deformities, several others came to mind. What about black-capped chickadees made them especially susceptible to malformed beaks? Why were the deformities concentrated in Alaska, of all places? Why had the deformities occurred—or been documented—only since the early 1990s? Why had the number of deformities risen so dramatically over the past decade?

❧

As part of their studies, the researchers conducted a nest-box-monitoring program from 2000 through 2004. To their surprise, they found negligible deformities in young birds. They also "collected" several nestlings and adults and sent those bodies, along with unhatched eggs and blood samples, to labs for analysis. No results suggested disease, parasites, or nutritional deficiencies alone as the culprits.

Contaminant analyses, however, yielded some promising—and disturbing—results. While eliminating several suspect toxins, lab findings suggested two groups that might be causing the deformities. One of those is PCBs, a group of synthetic organic chemicals. Here, according to a report by Handel's team, was the crux of the PCB angle: "Chickadees in Alaska may be deficient in vitamin D3 during the shortest days of winter, and *relying on calcium-deficient sunflower seeds may further exacerbate this condition. Thus, there could be a synergistic condition involving low levels of PCBs and deficiency of calcium and D3.* [My emphasis.]"

In other words, contaminants and vitamin deficiencies, combined with winter's low daylight and a sunflower seed diet, might have worked together to produce these bizarre bills.

Many of the deformed-bill chickadees also exhibited chromosomal damage, which Handel noted "is consistent with contaminants. We also know that DNA is tied to beak growth. What we *don't* have is a direct link between the DNA breakage and what controls beak growth."

Organochlorine compounds known as PCDDs and PCDFs also remained suspects, though concentrations in chickadee tissue samples were below laboratory detection limits. That made any meaningful comparison between normal and deformed birds impossible.

Finally, it should be noted that eighteen samples of locally sold black-oil sunflower seeds—the number one choice of black-caps at feeder stations—were tested for contaminants. No toxins were widespread enough, or in high enough concentrations, to raise any red flags.

After more than a decade of studying the deformed-bill phenomenon, Handel's outlook could be described as frustrated but hopeful. The key questions—What's the cause? Why black-capped chickadees? Why Alaska? Why now?—remained unresolved. But at least some answers seemed to be taking shape.

Contaminants appeared to be the most likely "causative agent," though there was insufficient evidence to show with certainty which one(s) were responsible. Or how. There's also the matter of where the contaminants originate. One likely source is toxic clouds transported by prevailing winds from Asia to Alaska, where they precipitate out and drop to Earth. Changes in either (or both) the makeup or abundance of semi-volatile chemicals discharged by Asian industrial plants could explain the increased deformities observed since the early 1990s. And atmospheric currents might explain the geography of the outbreak.

Because they had reached an impasse in their chickadee studies, the researchers widened their reach and began a comparative study of northwestern crows, which have suffered a smaller but substantial outbreak. Nearly two hundred disfigured crows had been reported by 2009, from southern Alaska to the Lower 48, and teams started collecting deformed birds for analysis. Crows would give lab technicians more material as they searched for traces of toxins. And the similarity of chickadee and crow disfigurements, combined with their different ecologies, might help to clarify the roots of the problem. "Crows eat different things, they live in different habitats, but they have the same kind of problem. Why is that?" Handel asked.

Researchers also would continue to explore how contaminants, Alaska's wintertime paucity of daylight, and chickadees' feeding habits might be working in tandem to produce deformed bills. "The answers are out there," Handel sighed. "But for all we've learned so far, it's still a mystery."

Even bigger mysteries were how contaminants entered the bodies of chickadees and other birds, what their deformed bills might tell us about the presence of unnoticed toxins in Alaska's landscape, and the implications for human health.

After years of closely following the researchers' effort, I too had become frustrated by the continued uncertainty. But more than that, I was troubled and anxious. Though the scientists wouldn't dare say it until they had proof positive, there seemed little doubt that toxic stews are somehow involved. Alaskans might be absolved for their spraying of carbaryl to stop the beetle infestation. But we humans, whether here or abroad, were nonetheless brewing up trouble in ways we couldn't fully know. And the birds that changed my life were paying the price for my species' reckless, life-damaging behaviors.

Even more disturbing was the possibility that we Alaskan bird feeders might unwittingly be involved in this tragedy. Our supposedly benign activity could be enticing toxin-bearing chickadees away from normal foods and increasing the chances that their beaks would grow disfigured.

That possibility seemed excruciatingly real when, in 2006—the same winter Colleen Handel shared her contaminant hypothesis with me—*two* curved-bill chickadees began visiting my Hillside feeders. The beak of one was especially deformed; its upper mandible curved sharply downward and crossed the lower mandible, which in turn was bent sharply upward. I didn't see how the bird could eat enough to survive, yet it continued to show up at my house from New Year's Day until late March, subsisting on peanut butter and the fine-chipped sunflower seeds I spread on the deck for redpolls. Turning its head sideways, the chickadee would somehow maneuver the seed bits into its mouth.

In late winter, the chickadees were joined by a third disfigured bird, a red-breasted nuthatch with an abnormally long and stout beak, slightly crossed at the tip. It was almost too much to handle, especially given Handel's hypothetical contaminant scenario. That's when the inner debate began: should I stop putting out sunflower seeds? Are they doing more harm than good? Because the feeding season was nearly over, I set the questions aside.

Not long after, I moved off the Hillside to Anchorage's Turnagain area. The following winter, no deformed-billed birds appeared at the feeders. My guilt eased, though the questions remained.

But in both 2008 and 2009, a curved-bill black-cap appeared in my west Anchorage yard. I watched each one turn its head to scrape peanut butter from the hanging feeder. I saw their feathers get dirty, their reflexes become slowed. The uncertainties surfaced again, including this one: shouldn't Alaska's bird-feeding community be told about all this?

Because the data was inconclusive, and because researchers tend to be cautious sorts, Handel saw no reason to warn people about the possible role of sunflower seeds in the deformity epidemic: "Right now it's a stretch to say the seeds are causing deformities or that they're even a factor. At most they're a secondary cause, not the real problem. It would be irresponsible to tell people to stop feeding chickadees sunflower seeds, based on what we know."

But shouldn't we bird lovers err on the side of caution? How much certainty must researchers have before telling the public that feeding sunflower seeds to Alaska's chickadees may be doing unexpected harm?

Was I being an alarmist to even suggest it?

Handel remained sure that the benefits to birds outweighed the costs. "Feeding birds," she explained, "helps their survival. There are so many benefits to bird feeding, that even if there is a nutritional deficiency [in a sunflower-seed diet] it might overall still be a positive."

For the worriers among us, Handel suggested putting out a variety of foods: "Some suet blocks have insects and fruits, so they more closely mimic what birds eat in the wild. It's also better to put out whole seeds rather than chips, because opening the shells produces some wear and tear on the beaks."

While adding variety seemed a great idea, in my experience black-caps still inevitably go for the sunflower seeds. It's what they love.

What to do? Despite what I'd learned and suspected, I continued to put out sunflower seeds each winter, supplemented by peanut butter. I did this largely because chickadees and nuthatches flock to my yard, looking for the handouts they've come to expect. It is so damn hard to refuse them food, to lose their good company.

I rationalized that I had moved off the Hillside, where the percentage of deformed chickadees was exceptionally high, to a part of Anchorage where beak deformities hadn't been such a problem—although, yes, I'd seen a couple of disfigured birds. And, using Handel's reasoning, I convinced myself I was doing more good than harm, by supplementing the winter diets of chickadees and other songbirds.

Yet I winced when my girlfriend, Helene, asked, "How can you put out seeds when you know they may be causing harm?"

I told Helene—and myself—that I would stop putting out black-oil sunflower seeds if and when there was clear proof they are linked to deformed bills. But why wait? How much proof did I need? How much evidence would the researchers need before they cautioned the public against a favorite wintertime activity? And how many bird feeders would stop, even then? Anchorage residents are warned over and over not to leave out garbage or dog food—or keep their bird feeders filled—in spring and summer, because all of those attract bears. Yet many residents stubbornly ignore the warnings and several bears are annually killed here as a consequence.

Handel offered one final thought to assuage the guilt: "If so many people weren't feeding birds, I never would have known about the extent of the deformities; or it would have taken a lot longer to figure it out. That's been a huge benefit."

It was, I suppose, a reason for solace amid all my bird-feeding angst. And still the questions remained. The biggest, of course, have nothing directly to do with sunflower seeds. The larger worry is the way we're messing up our planet, whether through toxins or greenhouse gas emissions or war. When will we recognize the importance, the necessity, of being better neighbors, better cohabitants on this blue-green planet? What can we do—must we do—to turn things around?

Maybe chickadees, along with polar bears and other species under duress, can help us see the absolute necessity of living more lightly, more respectfully, more responsibly on the Earth. That may be the best argument of all for feeding birds and encouraging others to do the same, even if there are some tradeoffs, some losses and discouragements, along the way. In an age of increasing disconnection from the wild Earth, feeding birds links us intimately to the "natural world."

For many people, the feeding of wild birds is the primary, perhaps only, link to larger nature. And isn't that a critically important thing? I'm among those who believe that only when we welcome wild critters (or any life-form) into our lives and hearts do we truly care about their well-being, their place in this world. It's something the chickadees remind me, every time I hear their voices or see their feathered forms alight in my yard.

In early 2014 I checked in with the deformed-bill study team to get an update, and talked with Handel's colleague, Caroline Van Hemert.

She informed me that researchers have now documented more than three thousand observations of deformed-bill birds, spread across more than thirty species. Most of those have been sighted in Alaska and the Pacific Northwest, but others were scattered across the United States and Canada. While most of the deformity reports in Alaska are from black-capped chickadees (and to a lesser degree crows), disfigured chickadees haven't been as prevalent outside the state. Most deformed-bill birds in the Puget Sound area, for instance, have been crows and red-tailed hawks, while malformed woodpeckers and nuthatches have been seen in many areas.

Curiously, a new cluster of deformed birds has been reported in the United Kingdom, most of them taxonomically similar to chickadees (several species of tits) and crows (rooks), but also including starlings. Van Hemert says the occurrence of "two totally discrete epicenters—one in Alaska and one in the United Kingdom—is very strange." She adds that the growing information—and expanding geographic range of the deformities—"complicates the picture. It's become more and more complex." Van Hemert also notes that within Alaska, "over the past five to seven years there's been a large increase of deformed birds [mostly black-capped chickadees] in Fairbanks and other parts of the Interior." Again, it's difficult to explain such a "time lag" within the state.

The quest for causes is ongoing. Though researchers have ruled out infections, "viruses are harder to track down and are still a possibility," Van Hemert says. So are toxins. Of the environmental contaminants they've studied, none have been confirmed as a likely source of the deformities. But Van Hemert adds, "there are emerging contaminants that we know less about. And it's possible that multiple contaminants are somehow acting in concert." Contaminants may also be interacting with other factors in a synergistic way.

As for the role of bird feeding, Van Hemert says researchers have become more certain that black-capped chickadees' (and other songbirds') use of feeder foods is a consequence of their deformities, not part of the cause. The evidence suggests that birds "shift their diet from natural foods to feeder foods once they have the deformity." So there's apparently no reason, after all, for bird feeders to feel guilty or wary about putting out sunflower seeds and other foods to supplement their winter diets. Though the overall situation remains puzzling and discouraging, this small bit of good news brings me great relief.

AN OVERLOOKED MARVEL: IN SEARCH OF ANCHORAGE'S WOOD FROGS

Eager to hear some of springtime's earliest and most marvelous love songs, I left my Turnagain neighborhood on a late April afternoon and drove west along Northern Lights Boulevard to the Point Woronzof overlook. Pulling into the large, paved lot, I counted a half dozen or so cars and trucks. All were parked on the lot's western side, facing Cook Inlet. I found a spot that faced east, less than twenty feet from a small, unnamed pond.

Anchorage residents come to this northwest tip of town for all sorts of reasons: to watch jets coming and going from our city's international airport; to gaze across the inlet toward Sleeping Lady or Denali and other high, snow-covered peaks; to access the Coastal Trail or hike down to the rocky beach below these coastal bluffs; to watch the setting sun or search the inlet for beluga whales (or in winter, search the night sky for northern lights); to cuddle with a sweetheart; or simply to hang out with family, friends, or visiting relatives.

I'd come to listen for frogs.

One of the things that most delights me about Anchorage is that my adopted hometown—like much of Alaska—is also home to *Rana sylvatica*, the wood frog. One of the north's true wonders, this smallish frog has carved out an ecological niche that reaches well beyond the Arctic Circle, the only amphibian to do so.

Not only do wood frogs share the Anchorage landscape with moose, bears, ravens, gulls, and us humans, they are here in surprisingly large numbers. It's likely that thousands of them hop and swim among us, mostly unnoticed, in places that most people wouldn't suspect.

Though we normally associate frogs with water, wood frogs (as the name suggests) actually spend most of their lives on land, showing a preference for wooded areas. Only during their brief mating season—which in most of Anchorage ranges from late April through late May—do adults congregate in lakes and ponds and sometimes even temporary pools.

Soon after settling into the water, male wood frogs join in grand singing competitions. Actually their voices are more call than song. While most researchers and literature liken those calls to a "duck-like quack," to my ears they more closely resemble a hiccupy gulp. (Still, I can understand why someone not aware of the frogs' presence might imagine a pond or lake to be teeming with mallards and pay little attention to the calls.)

During my own informal quest to learn their aquatic haunts, I've found frogs in several local lakes, plus vernal pools in Bicentennial, Kincaid, and Earthquake Parks; airport wetlands; the back side of Potter Marsh; and a subalpine pond in the Chugach Mountains. One favorite spot was a small, manmade pond sandwiched between Point Woronzof Road and the airport's fenced boundary, a mile or so past the overlook. Sadly, that was plowed over, a victim of airport expansion.

Not long afterward, I first heard frogs in Point Woronzof's pond.

As strange as it seems, several years ago I discovered this small and ordinary pond beside a parking lot to be among the best places in Anchorage to listen to the calls of impassioned, lovesick frogs. On a day in early May, the frogs were making a riotous racket. Even from the car, I could tell that something special was happening.

I should mention here that wood frog monitors have developed a "calling intensity" index to qualitatively measure the number of singing frogs. The scale goes from zero (no frogs calling) up to three, a full chorus in which calls are "constant, continuous, and overlapping."

On all my previous trips to Point Woronzof, I hadn't heard more than a few frogs, calling sporadically. Once or twice their voices might have overlapped slightly. Barely a two on the calling scale.

But on that particular May day in 2008, the frogs were sounding off in a way I'd never heard in my decade of listening to amphibian love songs throughout Anchorage. Simply put, their frenzied chorus was off the charts, though it was early afternoon on a sun-drenched day, with temperatures already in the sixties.

This too seemed extraordinary, for according to those who know them best, wood frogs normally call most aggressively after twilight. In fact standard North

American protocol requires those who monitor wood frog calls to do so a half hour after sunset.

Given the length of Alaska's spring and early summer days, the protocol is relaxed here. Still, evening is generally recognized as the best time to hear frogs sing. Yet here they were, going bonkers in bright sunshine and midday heat. The hiccupped calls were so loud, so constant and overlapping, that there was no way I could estimate their numbers, except to say "a bunch."

Leaving my car, I walked to the water's edge, closed my eyes, and breathed in the love songs. Then, stepping quietly, I headed to the pond's southern end, where the calling seemed most intense.

Until that moment, I had always found wood frogs to be secretive, elusive, and easily spooked critters. They would stop calling, and usually dive for cover, at the slightest approaching noise. But on this bright afternoon, the frogs must have been totally absorbed in their mating rituals, because they seemed oblivious to my presence. Of course amphibians are hardly the only creatures to be driven to distraction by sex.

A few feet from shore was what I can only describe as a riot of frogs. Or an explosion. I'd read that wood frogs are "explosive breeders" and now I better understood the term. They were everywhere, it seemed: singly, in pairs, and in small groups. And none made a dive for cover. Some frogs crouched in the shallows, while others floated in deeper water, front and back legs splayed in what appeared to be a relaxed pose. I saw no actual mating, but a few individuals appeared to have a strong interest in others and engaged in a hop and frog-stroke sort of watery pursuit.

Because they moved about, I couldn't get a specific count, but I guessed at least fifteen to twenty frogs squatted and swam before me.

To see even one frog in an Anchorage pond has often struck me as something of a miracle. But this orgy of frogs seemed so out of place, it strained the imagination. It would have been an amazing sight even in the tropics.

Four years later, on that April afternoon in 2012, loud, hiccupy calls again filled my ears as I lowered my car's window. Once more, Point Woronzof's frogs were in a frenzy.

How many frogs make their way back here each spring—and how they manage to do so—remains unknown. But based on my admittedly unscientific observations, I'd guess at least two to three dozen successfully complete the annual vernal trek. That seems a surprisingly high number, since the pond is not only small, but also mostly surrounded by a grassy meadow and an asphalt parking lot. And not far away are a paved trail and street. So it's not exactly a short or easy hop from forested overwintering grounds to pond.

I headed for a section of shoreline where the calling was grandest. Though I walked softly, the frogs nevertheless heard or otherwise sensed my approach and went quiet. Standing within a few feet of the water, I saw ripples where the frogs had dived for cover.

Knowing I would be rewarded if I was patient, I stayed in place and waited. Gradually the calling resumed, first on the pond's far side, then ever closer. Five minutes after my appearance alarmed the frogs into silence, the ones nearest to me began to resurface.

More time passed and some of the frogs started to move about. Others crouched among the long brown blades of last year's sedges, or simply floated in the water, legs extended. Then, within three or four feet of where I stood, a frog called. And another. *Gulp . . . gulp. Gulp, gulp, gulp . . .*

For only the second time in my years of listening to Anchorage's wood frogs, I watched males in their act of calling. Their sides bulged out and then deflated. Bulge, deflate, bulge, deflate, over and over and over.

In my stillness, I admired their small, handsome bodies. Measuring two to three inches with legs extended (females are slightly larger than males), the frogs ranged from brown or bronze to a bright, coppery orange, speckled with dark spots. Each wore a dark band across its face, the species' so-called eye mask. Beneath that mask, a thin, whitish "lip line" ran across their mouths.

While some frogs remained in relaxed poses, others engaged in chases. It was hard for me to distinguish territorial disputes from romantic pursuits, until I spotted one frog climb atop another. In successful pairings, the female releases eggs, which are then fertilized by the male's sperm. These two were joined only briefly, then parted and swam their separate ways. Within days, gobs of black, rounded, gelatinous egg clusters would hang in these waters, eventually producing hundreds, if not thousands, of tiny tadpoles. Those that survived would, like their parents, abandon the pond sometime during the summer, to spend most of their year on land.

This seemed another sort of miracle: that these frogs would scatter into a surrounding landscape that has more asphalt and open fields than trees and somehow make their way into the safety of birch-spruce-cottonwood stands. And enough would survive to renew the ritual next year.

Finally ending my frog watch, I returned to the car. The frogs again went silent. But even before I'd closed the door, they began to sing once more. *Gulp, gulp, gulp* . . .

I can appreciate the fact that many—and likely most—Anchorage residents have no idea that frogs live among us. An Alaskan outdoors and nature writer since the mid-1980s and a life-long frog lover, I didn't know a thing about their local presence until 1998, when I joined twenty other citizen scientists in our city's first-ever frog-watch program. I spent much of that spring and summer listening and looking for frogs and searching for tadpoles in our city's waters, a delightful urban adventure.

Sixteen years later, I am still amazed by wood frogs' mostly quiet—and overlooked—presence among us. Who, after all, associates frogs with far northern landscapes? While six species of amphibians reside in wet and (relatively) warm Southeast Alaska, only wood frogs inhabit most of our state, their range extending deep into the Arctic. During a trip into the Brooks Range one year, a friend of mine stumbled across a wood frog while squishing his way through wet tundra, only a couple of miles from the Arctic Divide and many miles from anything resembling a forest. He was startled. I was ecstatic—and then disappointed that the frog disappeared before I could see it.

You want miracles? Imagine creatures that survive northern winters by having their bodies freeze solid.

Wood frogs' preparations for Alaska's longest, harshest season begin in autumn, when cooling air, shortening daylight hours, and diminished food prompts the frogs to find a convenient hiding place close to water (though whether they return to their breeding pond or the nearest available pool remains uncertain). There they burrow beneath moss or decaying leaves or dig their way into sandier soils.

And this is how they'll spend their winters: huddled alone in shallow, earth- and snow-covered shelters, somehow surviving even when the ground around them drops to subzero temperatures. Which brings us to another curious fact about Alaska's wood frogs: they not only survive colder conditions than their Lower 48 counterparts, but do so for much longer periods—up to seven or eight months in some locales.

As air and ground temperatures drop toward freezing and below, the frogs' still and slowly hardening bodies internally remain hard at work for a while, with one organ kicking into overdrive.

While their eyes freeze into a whitened stare and ice crystals form in their abdominal cavity, the liver of hibernating wood frogs produces unusual amounts of glucose, a syrupy, sugar-rich solution. Entering the bloodstream, the glucose is flushed into all of the body's cells, which keeps them from icing up and also prevents dehydration or other damage. So freezing occurs only in spaces outside the cells.

Put another way, wood frogs "effectively become super sweet" as they freeze, says Brian Barnes, a researcher who has long studied the hibernating strategies and mechanisms of Alaska's animals. And that ultra sweetness is what keeps them alive. But neither kicking nor breathing.

Director of the University of Alaska Fairbanks Institute of Arctic Biology, Barnes adds that Alaska's frogs appear to become sweeter than those farther south. The increased glucose production helps to explain their greater tolerance to extreme cold—the more sugary a solution, the lower its freezing point—but it raises other questions. For instance: how the heck do they do that?

By the time their winter preparations are complete, wood frogs from the Panhandle to the Brooks Range will have frozen eyes, frozen limbs, frozen lungs, frozen liver, and a frozen brain. In the end, even the heart freezes up.

In all, about two-thirds of a wood frog's body will turn to ice. In essence, it has become something of a frogcicle. Barnes says that if you were to drop a frozen frog onto a table, it would sound much like an ice cube. And if bent too far, its limbs will simply snap. And yet the animal is alive, in what is truly a state of sus- pended animation.

Barnes emphasizes that this process is a gradual one. For all of their amaz- ing adaptations, not even wood frogs are able to survive being put into a freezer and left overnight.

Besides learning more about wood frogs themselves, Barnes and other researchers believe that a better understanding of the amphibians' cold-weather strategies could benefit humans. For instance, we might learn how transplanted organs might be frozen and thawed without being damaged. Or perhaps scientists will come to better understand, and manage, diabetes in humans.

Just as remarkable as their winter freeze-up is the wood frogs' springtime meltdown. The frogs thaw from inside out. First the heart begins to beat (though scientists don't know exactly how it's "jump started"), then the brain and other organs kick into gear, and glucose levels return to normal.

Once completely thawed, the frogs dig their way out of the ground and hop to the nearest pond or lake, as if nothing astonishing had just occurred. Back in the water, they will briefly but heartily engage in explosive amphibian orgies and produce a new generation of frogs.

And for my first sixteen years in Anchorage, I had no idea.

Though Anchorage's initial frog-watch venture petered out after only a few years, a second one began in 2004, this time as part of a much broader citizen-science effort. Headed by state biologist David Tessler, with help from his Department of Fish and Game colleague (and project coordinator), Marian Snively, the Alaska Wood Frog Monitoring Program is still going strong. In fact Tessler and Snively have expanded their reach to more than seventy communities, spread from Cordova to Coldfoot.

Most participants reside along Alaska's limited road system, but others live in such remote locales as Shageluk, Shungnak, and Upper Kalskag. Through 2012 (the most recent year for which complete statistics were available), more than 200 volunteers (which include individuals, families, and groups) had completed 953 surveys at 426 locations. Using data forms provided by the state, those volunteers collect basic information about the wood frog's distribution, abundance, habitat use, and breeding phenology, or timing.

Wood frogs have been found in about three-quarters of those four hundred-plus locales, though Tessler admits, "the survey results are heavily biased toward sites where frogs are present because negative results are presumed to be under-reported." In other words someone checking out a pond that doesn't have frogs is less likely to continue monitoring it or send in the necessary data to have it included in the study.

The ongoing program has three main goals: figure out (in a more precise way) where wood frogs live in Alaska; determine baseline populations; and document the habitats they prefer. Without baseline data, there's been no way to know whether Alaska's wood frog population is increasing, decreasing, or holding steady, but across much of the continent frog and other amphibian numbers have dropped, for a variety of reasons: disease, contaminants, habitat destruction, fish introduction, and a deadly fungus. In some areas, the decline has been alarming.

There's no evidence to suggest that Alaska's wood frogs are decreasing, but U.S. Fish and Wildlife Service biologist Mari Reeves and other federal researchers *have* found more than twenty kinds of deformities in wood frog populations that inhabit five of Alaska's national wildlife refuges. Deformities were especially high in Kenai Peninsula waters, with up to 20 percent of frogs showing abnormalities at one site.

No formal studies have been done locally, but Reeves (whose work isn't part of the state's monitoring program) says it's likely Anchorage frogs have similar deformities to those in Kenai waters. Whether or not the frequency is similar remains unknown. Of the hundreds of surveys and reports that Tessler and Snively have received from Anchorage area residents, only "a very few reports" noted deformities. However it's worth noting that Reeves studied "metamorphic frogs"—those changing from tadpoles to frogs—and frog-call monitors aren't focused on those stages.

Because wood frogs aren't especially mobile, biologists naturally assume their distribution is closely tied to breeding habitat. But Tessler notes there's still a lot to learn about the places where wood frogs prefer to reproduce.

Using the data they'd gathered up to that point, he and Snively in 2006 did a preliminary habitat analysis. Though they eventually decided their data set was both too small and biased for a rigorous analysis (they hope to eventually do a "more robust" one), the two feel comfortable in saying that Alaska's wood frogs "prefer permanent, nonflowing water bodies (lakes or small ponds) three to thirty meters in diameter . . . characterized by herbaceous emergent vegetation primarily with organic or silty substrates where no fish are present." In other words, fishless lakes and ponds with nonwoody plants like grasses or sedges and silty, organic bottoms. Meanwhile the terrestrial habitat surrounding frog-bearing waters is "overwhelmingly birch-spruce forests," which they prefer to all other habitats by a two-to-one margin.

Despite that preference, "Woods aren't a habitat prerequisite for the species—they don't live in trees—and we find them above timberline," Tessler notes, "where trees are absent and the climate, the growing season, and exposure to avian predators conspire to make their life quite difficult.

"I am always amazed and surprised at the places we find these little guys surviving and thriving. The ability to persist across a wide variety of circumstances—provided the water is clean and the environment relatively healthy—is the main trait that has enabled this species to be the most widely distributed amphibian in North America."

I hadn't yet participated in this newer frog-monitoring venture when I stood enraptured by point Woronzof's frogs in 2012, but given my ongoing fascination with *Rana sylvatica*, I figured it was time to learn more about what's been happening locally. Tessler and Snively told me that since their monitoring program started, Anchorage-area residents have monitored wood frogs at some two hundred sites, "scattered quite literally all over the city." Many are ponds and lakes on public lands, others are ponds and "squishy areas" (wetlands) on private property. A few are on school campuses.

Some volunteers do road surveys, which require that they pick a route that includes from three to ten sites, ranging from lakes to bogs to roadside ditches. Those with lakes or natural pools nearby their homes may instead prefer to do backyard surveys. But the most common, Tessler said, "is the incidental observation, when someone comes across a calling frog and realizes for the first time there are frogs in Alaska. That's when they call us, full of amazement and wanting to share their story."

On their survey forms, the citizen scientists are asked to describe the site (type of water body and vegetation, distance from the road, presence of fish, etc.) and weather conditions, and estimate both the calling intensity and number of frogs. Though not scientifically rigorous, the data will eventually yield a detailed picture of Anchorage's wood frog distribution and a better sense of both their local numbers and habitat preferences.

It turns out that no one has kept official watch on Point Woronzof's pond and its wood frogs for several years, so I've considered going the extra step and becoming its official citizen monitor. Tessler and Snively have welcomed that possibility and I already know the frog-monitoring drill, which hasn't changed much since 2000.

◆

After witnessing the wood frogs' frenzy in late April 2012, I returned to Point Woronzof Pond on May 3, shortly after 5:00 P.M. Once more the frogs called loudly and abundantly. Quietly patrolling the pond's edges, I counted eighteen frogs and I'm sure I missed others. In the background, jets whined and roared, and a steady stream of vehicles rumbled in and out of the parking lot.

By the afternoon of May 7 what had been a full chorus dropped to intensity level one, with intermittent soloists breaking the pond's silence. To see if the calling might pick up in the evening, I returned at 9:30 P.M. Point Woronzof was again noisy with jets, cars, and trucks. In a light breeze, I heard sporadic calls, some of them overlapping. The sinking sun cast a golden light upon the landscape and the parking lot was nearly full of people, but I was the only one listening to frogs.

No frogs called when I visited the evening of May 13. I returned the following night at about 9:30 P.M. and again the pond was quiet. Stranger still, I could find no trace of frogs. It was as if they had vanished. And perhaps they had, once again abandoning the pond for land, where they would spend the next eleven and a half months.

Squirming tadpoles might have already begun to hatch from gooey egg masses and in several weeks they would begin to change shape. Yet another marvel: metamorphosis.

Sometime in July or August, tiny "metamorphs" would follow their parents out of the pond, searching for cover, for a new home. After leading solitary lives, the survivors would return here in another year or two, ready to breed. And males would again raise their voices to join earlier generations in a frenzy of hiccupy love songs.

OF WAXWINGS AND GOSHAWKS
AND STANDING UP TO POWER

Walking through my Turnagain neighborhood on an early winter day, I kept my head down and hunched my body against a ferocious north wind. That bent head of mine was busy with thoughts, after attending a Sunday morning book discussion hosted by Anchorage's Unitarians.

Despite my preoccupied mind and lowered gaze, I somehow managed to glimpse movement in the air around me. A small flock of birds swooped across the gray sky, wings beating rapidly in a telltale way.

My mind immediately shouted, *Waxwings!* Among my favorite winter neighbors, these handsome gray-suited songbirds with russet-tinted heads, black eye masks, waxy red-tipped wing feathers, and tails edged in yellow brighten our city during Alaska's darkest days, drawn here by the promise of abundant and easy pickin' food.

In recent decades, local residents have planted hundreds, if not thousands, of fruit-bearing trees in yards and along Anchorage streets. Over time, Southcentral Alaska's bohemian waxwings learned that when food becomes scarce in their normal habitats—the forested lands beyond the city—there is still plenty to eat here.

Singly, in pairs, and small groups, these wide-ranging "gypsy birds" head into town for an amazing feast. As the days and weeks pass, they coalesce into ever-larger flocks, until by December multitudes of the birds swirl through the sky. In synchronized flight they circle and dive, while roaming from neighborhood to neighborhood and street to street, descending on yards and greenbelts to strip ornamental trees of their fruits: mountain ash berries, elderberries, chokecherries, and crab apples.

Most years since the early 1980s, thousands of waxwings have settled into Anchorage. During a recent Christmas Bird Count, participants spotted more than twenty-two thousand of them spread through the city, a phenomenal number. Even more amazing to imagine, local birder Dave DeLap once told me he'd seen flocks of three thousand waxwings and knew others who'd watched five thousand or more spiral through the sky.

To see such enormous swarms of songbirds in the depths of Alaska's winter always seems cause for celebration.

Though I had seen a few scattered waxwings in recent weeks, that November Sunday marked my first seasonal sighting of a flock. The handful of birds that initially caught my attention soon grew into a dozen, then two dozen, and more.

The waxwings circled in tight formation, some breaking ranks to form their own spinning groups. Chill forgotten, my full attention was now on the birds, and I watched them converge on a tall cottonwood tree, limbs bare in the early winter grayness.

In the cottonwood's upper limbs was a much larger bird, a raptor, huddled as if in response to the cold, stinging wind. But in fact that bird—whose size, shape, and coloring suggested a northern goshawk—was hunkered down against the ranks of songbirds that had come to harass it.

It is always an amazing thing to watch, the way that groups of songbirds will fearlessly "mob" a much larger bird of prey, one that given the opportunity (often through the element of surprise) would attack, kill, and eat the much smaller creatures that are pestering it.

Scientists tell us that such mobbing behavior is a cooperative anti-predator strategy, most commonly used by birds during their breeding season. Yet much remains to be learned about mobbing and why—or when—it occurs. In winter, the waxwings have no young to protect, but clearly the goshawk's presence riled them up.

What I observed might simply have been an instinctive group response to a natural enemy at a time when waxwings were emboldened by a strength of numbers and the goshawk couldn't benefit from its usual hunting strategy, a stealth attack. Still, that waxwings would choose to take on a raptor famous for its great ferocity struck me as especially impressive. And I found it odd that the goshawk made no attempt to attack the much smaller and less powerful songbirds, even when a few of them perched on branches just a few feet away.

The number of waxwings circling the cottonwood tree grew until several dozen were joined in synchronized flight. Where did they all come from, and so quickly? Had their trilling voices somehow changed in tenor and volume, to alert others of their kind who happened to be in the area? The goshawk refused to budge, patiently enduring the magnified insults of the much smaller birds.

It's likely that this confrontation between waxwings and goshawk would have stopped me in my tracks and held me spellbound on any day that I happened to be out walking and notice such a rarely observed encounter of predator and prey. (To witness it while on foot is a key; speeding past in a car, the chances that I'd stop to watch things play out would be greatly diminished.) What I was witnessing would inevitably engage my senses, mind, and spirit, while prompting me to consider, once more, how little we know about the world we inhabit and the lives of our wild neighbors.

But on that Sunday morning, the event took on greater meaning, because of the meeting I had just attended.

In the latter half of my life, I've come to embrace the notion that things happen for a reason. (Though to be honest, a part of me remains a skeptic, not fully convinced.) It therefore strikes me as no coincidence that I was witness to this impressive show of community strength and purpose after participating in a spirited discussion inspired by a provocative book, *The Wealth of Nature: Economics as if Survival Mattered*, and a good friend, Gary Holthaus, who had recently been installed as the minister of the Anchorage Unitarian Universalist Fellowship (AUUF for short).

It's not my intent here to dive deeply into the book's many challenging ideas, which are far from mainstream economic thinking. But a few points are worth repeating. One is that our culture's most widely accepted economic theories have it wrong (in large part because they're based on faulty assumptions and unexamined world views). Even worse, these theories are helping to lead us down a path to disaster. Another point is that modern Western culture—and the United States in particular—has come to confuse money with wealth. Author John Michael Greer makes a strong (and to me, convincing) case that money and wealth are two very different things and, furthermore, our society's confusion about the two is one reason we're in such dire economic and cultural straits. There's a lot more to chew on, including Greer's discussion of the U.S. as a world empire in decline, but that will have to suffice for now.

The picture that Greer paints is dreadfully gloomy, but to his credit he does offer some ways out of our mess and reasons for hope. While I found the book's message unsettling, I was in a way encouraged by Greer's unflinching critique of our capitalist, consumer culture and the grim future we face. This book (among others), plus Bill Moyer's weekly show on PBS, a number of recent documentaries (*Inside Job, Bag It, Vanishing of the Bees*, and *Food, Inc.* come immediately to mind), and efforts by groups like The Orion Society and 350.org, make it clear that some of our nation's more intelligent and thoughtful people are challenging what's become an exceedingly harmful status quo.

Just as encouraging to me, and certainly inspiring, was the conversation that occurred at the AUUF's 9:00 A.M. Forum, which offered clear evidence that growing numbers of other thoughtful and engaged citizens are also paying attention, and wish to change, what's become (in more ways than one) a bankrupt system.

Though not a Unitarian, I find myself increasingly pulled to the fellowship's principles, ideals, and community of people (and in fact I've become a regular enough participant that some AUUF members recognize me as "a friend of the fellowship"). From what I can tell, most Unitarians are situated toward the far left of the political and religious spectrum, yet there is no shortage of diversity in their opinions. In the discussion led by Holthaus, several participants expressed their discouragement and, in some instances, their despair. And anger. But people also shared their hopes and ideas. And, more importantly, their actions. They discussed ways that members of their congregation can make a difference. And in some cases, are already making a difference.

Nowadays I am often struck by the discontent and disillusionment expressed by Americans across the political spectrum, from the Tea Party to the Occupy Wall Street movement. The focus of our unhappiness—and anger—differs, but in every case our corrupted political system is at the center.

Whether Democrat or Republican, too many of the people in power don't *really* seem to care about the needs of what might be called "common folk," the vast majority of citizens: the 99 percent. While many on the right seem to believe that "big government" is *the* problem, I and many others on the left see the problem as collusion between our elected and appointed officials and big business. This is leading—or has led—to the formation of what many are now calling a corporatocracy, which favors corporations and moneyed interests over the great majority of people, and with increasingly harmful consequences for both humans and the larger world of which we're part.

Most people would likely say it's pure coincidence that I would see a large and riled-up flock of songbirds mobbing—or, put another way, brazenly confronting—a much more powerful and dangerous bird, on the same day that my own thoughts have been roiled by emotional, yet clearheaded, talk about the need for change in America's political and economic system. (Of course the two are intimately connected.) Heck, most days I might call such an occurrence pure coincidence. And I'd say that trying to make anything more out of it is pure silliness.

On the other hand. . . .

Maybe the waxwings were—or could be—a metaphor for what's possible in our own dreary human nation, if we liberals and conservatives and centrists could set aside our differences and join in a collective movement that stands up to the powers that be, the powers—both Democrat and Republican—that have put us on such a wrong track and which pose such a great and growing threat to us and the larger world we inhabit.

Maybe in these birds I witnessed additional reason for hope. Or inspiration. And maybe there was a reason I happened to notice the waxwings and goshawk while walking home from the AUUF Forum.

Ah, but what do I know? It's just foolish thinking. Crazy.

I'm not sure how long I watched the birds. Ten minutes? Fifteen? Longer? However long it was, after awhile the bulk of the waxwing mob began flying off to the west and it appeared that the confrontation was approaching an end. Still, a few of the waxwings continued to stake out the goshawk, some circling and others perched.

Perhaps figuring it wise to depart while its tormentors were few—and with no assurance that the larger flock wouldn't return with even more waxwings—the raptor suddenly dived from the branch and dipped low to the ground. Then, with strong beats of its large wings (those flapping appendages being plenty strong enough to strike down a waxwing, should one get too close), the goshawk flew east through the neighborhood, past house after house of people who had no idea of the drama being played outside their homes.

Because my sympathies were with the songbirds, I couldn't help but smile when the waxwings still hovering around the cottonwood tree give chase. And then, apparently circling back, the larger flock joined in the pursuit.

A TALE OF TWO WOLVERINES
AND ONE BELOVED DOG

On a crisp and clear fall afternoon, I stood on a ridge high above Anchorage, right hand clutching a plastic bag and mind filled with vivid, bittersweet memories.

Named Rusty Point, the rocky ledge on which I was perched lies at the western end of a mountain spine that drops from the summit of Wolverine Peak, in the Chugach Mountains' Front Range just east of the city.

My thoughts were pulled to a summer three years earlier, when I walked this untrailed and rubbly ridgeline with my eight-and-a-half-year-old collie mix, Coya. Though I've been a "dog person" all my life, Coya was the first I had made my own. Not long after our lives intersected, it became clear that she loved to roam the hills as much as I. And in the years since then, the dog I affectionately called my "pound mutt" had proven to be as companionable and enthusiastic a hiking partner as any mountain rambler could ever want.

I vividly recalled sitting side by side with Coya while taking a snack break and our surprise when a wolverine, on its own alpine wanderings, stepped onto the ridge. Apparently as shocked as Coya and me, the wolverine had briefly frozen in place then slowly circled, no more than ten yards away. While I sat in quiet amazement, Coya had begun to squirm and pull away. Holding her against me, I could feel her strong desire to give chase. That, I knew, could have ended badly, given wolverines' fierce demeanor. So I gripped my sweet but excitable collie mix even tighter. And with Coya safely in my arms, she and I had stayed in the wolverine's remarkably calm company for a quarter hour or more, until the animal finally loped away. Over the years I'd shared many other memorable wildlife encounters with Coya, but nothing could match our meeting with wolverine, so rarely seen even where the species' population is healthy.

Memories of that summer day still evoke wonder and delight. But now they were tempered by sadness and longing. In May my zestful, mountain-loving dog had become seriously ill with what her doctor described as a rare—and, it turned out, virulent—cancer. With Coya no longer able to venture into the hills or even go on extended walks in town, she and I had to settle for short neighborhood strolls and time spent lolling in front-yard sunshine. Less than three weeks after she first showed symptoms of the disease, I gently and sorrowfully held Coya in my arms one last time while she was injected with a euthanizing potion.

Now in September I had come to Rusty Point to leave a handful of Coya's ashes. Other hikers rarely visited this location, so I had all the time I needed to be alone and quietly reminisce, at a place rich with memories of our rambles together.

I'd brought my Chugach journal to record some notes. Browsing through it I saw that Coya and I last journeyed here the previous fall. As usual, we'd had the spot all to ourselves. My jottings reminded me that the day had been sunny and crisp, the autumn air made colder by a brisk northeast wind. A pair of ravens circled around us and I'd found some late-blooming wildflowers up high, including an alpine forget-me-not with its petals still a deep and vibrant blue. Four Dall sheep grazed far below on a south-facing hillside, while atop the ridge we'd come across a pile of wolfish scat, containing crowberries and light brown hair.

I set the journal aside. Whispering something like a prayer, I spread Coya's dusty gray remains and tiny bone fragments among alpine plants and beneath a couple of lichen-crusted rocks, in places where I know we once sat side by side. Then, in peaceful solitude, I lay on the tundra beneath brilliantly blue heavens.

With the sun warm on my face, I closed my eyes and both mourned my loss and recalled the joy that Coya had brought me. I imagined her handsome body nestled affectionately against mine, mostly white with a few large brown patches along the side and back. Her head and smiling face were mostly brown, becoming black along the snout. She had a small, white, irregular splotch, freckled with black, just behind her nose, sniffing the air for alpine smells.

I lingered up high for more than an hour, thoughts of wolverine inevitably mixed with those of Coya. Our meeting along this ridge still struck me as an amazing thing. After one last look around, I began an unhurried descent across untrailed tundra and twenty minutes later rejoined the heavily used path that hikers follow to Wolverine Peak's summit.

As usual, I carried binoculars. Noticing them, a middle-aged couple ascending the trail asked, "Seen any wildlife?"

"Not much today," I replied. "A couple of distant moose, a soaring bald eagle. That's about it."

A few minutes after that brief exchange, I happened to glance off to my left, toward a slope Coya once routinely explored on our return to the Prospect Heights trailhead. I could still clearly picture her weaving back and forth, head bent and nose searching the tundra.

Movement high on the same hillside Coya had loved to roam grabbed my attention. Crossing it at an unhurried pace was a slender, dark, long-tailed animal built low to the ground. Waves of recognition once more exploded through my body while my mind shouted, *wolverine.*

Bursting to alert other hikers to the animal's presence, I glanced up and down the trail, but no one was in sight. So I returned my gaze to the wolverine and stood absolutely still. This was a different animal than the ear-tagged female that Coya and I had met three years earlier. For reasons I can't fully explain, it struck me as a young adult male.

Whether following a scent or otherwise preoccupied, the wolverine appeared unaware of my presence while zigzagging downhill in the sort of hop-stepping way that weasels move. Though coming steadily closer, he didn't once look my way that I could tell. Only upon reaching the trail, no more than a dozen feet from where I stood, did the wolverine seem to notice me. He reared up on his back feet and peered at me a few moments, then turned and retreated back uphill. But instead of racing away, he moved at a casual pace, even stopping now and then to gaze back in my direction.

Reaching the top of the rise, the wolverine loped out of sight. But a few seconds later he reappeared and again looked my way, still inquisitive. He then repeated this behavior a couple of more times. Not until the voices of approaching hikers broke the silence—and the spell—did he vanish.

No more than a mile from where Coya and I had encountered the other wolverine three years earlier, I remained still, mind and emotions churning.

It's easy enough, in our modern Western culture, to consider this second wolverine's appearance pure chance. But the details of the day and the circumstances of our encounter suggest to me that something more, something not easily explained or understood by the rational mind, may have been at play here.

The famed psychiatrist Carl Jung might have said I experienced synchronicity: a "meaningful coincidence" in which two events are linked by something other than cause and effect. Often an association is made between some aspect of a person's inner life and an occurrence in the outer world. There's no question that I feel a deep connection between this wolverine's appearance and my earlier remembrance of Coya and the spreading of her ashes, the reason that I returned to this mountain. The more intuitive part of me somehow understands that what happened here was no simple coincidence, no accident.

While the notion of synchronicity seems to fit, the word, the idea that flashed through my mind in those moments was visitation. I can't say for sure that the wolverine carried some message or that Coya's spirit was somehow present, but there's no question I was visited by something mysterious, something marvelous in nature.

Taking a deep breath, I glanced uphill one more time, toward the place I spotted this second wolverine. Then I resumed my own retreat to the trailhead, both shaken and exuberant.

ABOUT THE AUTHOR

 Born in Bridgeport, Connecticut, nature writer Bill Sherwonit has called Alaska home since 1982. He has contributed essays and articles to a wide variety of newspapers, magazines, journals, and anthologies and is the author of more than a dozen books, including *To the Top of Denali: Climbing Adventures on North America's Highest Peak*; *Living with Wildness: An Alaskan Odyssey*; and *Changing Paths: Travels and Meditations in Alaska's Arctic Wilderness*. Most of Sherwonit's work focuses on Alaskan subjects, with an emphasis on wilderness adventure, wildlands preservation, environmental issues, natural history, our species' complex relationship with place and wildlife, and notions of wildness, including the wild nature to be found in and around his adopted home, Anchorage. Sherwonit also teaches nature and travel/adventure writing and is a contributor to the blog site, "The Nature of Cities." His website is www.billsherwonit.alaskawriters.com.

CPSIA information can be obtained at www.ICGtesting.com
Printed in the USA
BVOW05s1607150914

366581BV00003B/4/P